"IT CRACKLES! The richness of McGinniss's reporting accumulates powerfully . . . his writing glows invitingly— just as a warm fire does when the temperature outside in Fairbanks is 49 below."—*Newsweek*

"ENTHRALLING . . . McGINNISS WRITES WITH THE UNCENSORED, SENSUOUS PERCEPTIONS OF A NATURALISTIC NOVELIST."
—*Los Angeles Times Book Review*

"What a pleasure this book is! It's funny, acute, tender— overflowing with marvelous stories set down by a brilliant and sympathetic observer."—Mordecai Richler,
Book-of-the-Month Club News

"HIS IMPRESSIONS ARE SCATTERED ON THE PAGE LIKE DIAMONDS IN A CREEKBED. Some of these gems are the damnedest characters and events ever seen on either side of the Arctic Circle."—*Chicago Sun-Times*

"WONDERFULLY IRONIC AND PERCEPTIVE!"
—*San Francisco Chronicle*

"THIS BOOK SOARS! It is one book to buy if for no other reason than to marvel at the writing, the craft of non-fiction prose as art." —*LA Weekly*

JOE McGINNISS is also the author of four nonfiction works—*Blind Faith, Fatal Vision, Heroes,* and *The Selling of the President, 1968*—and the novel *The Dream Team.*

Also by Joe McGinniss

HEROES
THE DREAM TEAM
THE SELLING OF THE PRESIDENT, 1968

JOE McGINNISS

Going to

Extremes

A PLUME BOOK

PLUME
Published by the Penguin Group
Penguin Books USA Inc., 375 Hudson Street, New York, New York
10014, U.S.A.
Penguin Books Ltd, 27 Wrights Lane, London W8 5TZ, England
Penguin Books Australia Ltd, Ringwood, Victoria, Australia
Penguin Books Canada Ltd, 10 Alcorn Avenue, Toronto, Ontario,
Canada M4V 3B2
Penguin Books (N.Z.) Ltd, 182–190 Wairau Road, Auckland 10,
New Zealand

Penguin Books Ltd, Registered Offices: Harmondsworth,
Middlesex, England

Published by Plume, an imprint of Dutton Signet,
a division of Penguin Books USA Inc.

First Plume Printing, September, 1981

19

A hardcover edition of *Going to Extremes* was published by Alfred
A. Knopf, Inc., 201 East 50th Street, New York, New York 10022. The
hardcover edition was published simultaneously in Canada by
Random House of Canada Limited, Toronto.

 REGISTERED TRADEMARK—MARCA REGISTRADA

LIBRARY OF CONGRESS CATALOGING-IN-PUBLICATION DATA
McGinniss, Joe.
    Going to extremes/by Joe McGinniss.
      p.   cm.
    ISBN 0-452-26301-8
     1. Alaska—Description and travel—1951–1980. 2. McGinniss, Joe-
Journeys—Alaska. I. Title.
F910.M24 1989   89-8291
979.8'05—dc20   CIP

PRINTED IN THE UNITED STATES OF AMERICA

BOOKS ARE AVAILABLE AT QUANTITY DISCOUNTS WHEN USED
TO PROMOTE PRODUCTS OR SERVICES. FOR INFORMATION PLEASE
WRITE TO PREMIUM MARKETING DIVISION, PENGUIN BOOKS USA INC.,
375 HUDSON STREET, NEW YORK, NEW YORK 10014.

TO CHRISSIE
AND SUZI
AND JOE

Actually, only a small minority of the
human race will ever consider primeval
nature a basic source of happiness. . . .
Mankind as a whole is too numerous for
its problem of happiness to be solved
by the simple expedient of paradise.
> —Robert Marshall, an early
> explorer of the Brooks Range
> in Alaska

Acknowledgments

Among the many dozens of Alaskans without whose warmth and openness and generosity it would not have been possible to write this book, I would like to express special gratitude to a few of those who became not just (in some cases) characters in a book, but also (in many cases) lasting friends.

These would include Howard and Barbara Weaver, Ray and Barbara Bane, Paul Nussbaum and Suzan Nightingale, Jim Kendall, Sukey Forsman, Ron and Marian Hendrie, Cheryl Barsness, Dale Rushton, Stan and Jeanne Abbott, Kay Fanning, Gary Williams, Duncan Pryde, Mike Kennedy, John Anttonen, Mike Anastay, the whole crew in Bethel, and, most of all, Tom and Marnie Brennan, who not only provided shelter from the storm for so many weeks, but who did so with such grace and good humor as to leave me with the feeling that they had just been sitting by the phone for their first ten years in Alaska, waiting for my call.

In the time that has passed since I have returned from Alaska, it is hard to say which I have come to miss more—the land or its people. Suffice it that both made an indelible impression.

Though no one I encountered ever requested anonymity, or even asked that any aspects of his or her life remain unpublicized, I have chosen, in a few instances, to change names and to alter or omit certain identifying details in order to avoid any possibility of embarrassment to people who so freely shared with me major or minor portions of their lives.

This is a work based largely on personal experience and it has not, therefore, involved massive amounts of library research. I would be remiss, however, if I neglected to mention several books which proved both enjoyable and educational and upon which I have drawn for certain brief passages of history and background.

Where the Sea Breaks Its Back (Little, Brown, 1966), by Corey Ford, offers a vivid portrayal of the final voyage of Vitus Bering, which resulted in the discovery of Alaska by the white man.

Both *North of 53°* (Macmillan, 1974), by William R. Hunt, and *The Klondike Fever* (Knopf, 1958), by Pierre Berton, are splendidly detailed works about the gold rush. Duncan Pryde's *Nunaga* (Walker, 1971), from which I have quoted in my chapter on Barrow, is a memorable account of a lavishly adventurous portion of a highly original life. The Federal Writers Project book *A Guide to Alaska: Last American Frontier* (Macmillan, 1939), edited by Merle Colby, from which the diary at the start of chapter 10 has been excerpted, is, in its entirety, a remarkably comprehensive achievement. Robert Marshall's *Alaska Wilderness* (University of California Press, 1970) is a vivid introduction to the Central Brooks Range.

I would like to thank Ray Bane for sharing with me the notes he made during the hike we took together in the Brooks Range. His impressions influenced my own writing, even beyond those sentences of his which I have quoted. For anyone interested in seeing how some of that Brooks Range country looked to us, I would highly recommend *Alaska: Wilderness Frontier* (Reader's Digest Press, 1977), by Boyd Norton, who was there.

Finally, I would like to thank Elaine Koster of The New American Library for her enthusiasm, patience, and faith, and, most of all, my wife Nancy who shared with me not only the excitement of life in Alaska, but the many bleak and tedious months which followed as I attempted to portray the experience through words.

Map of Alaska

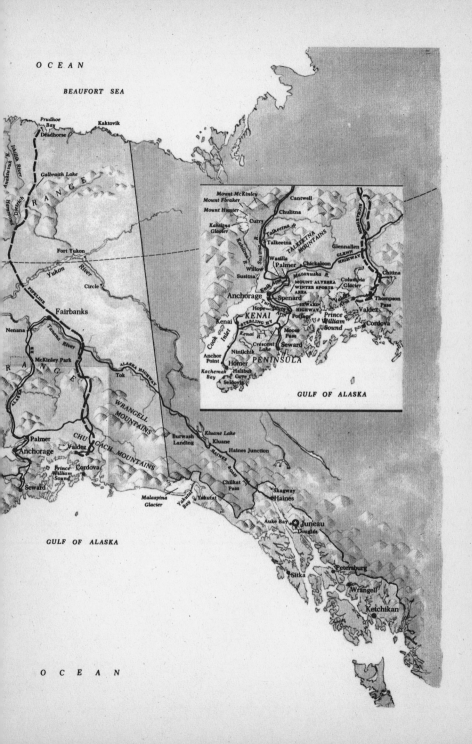

1 Winter

1 The Ferry

November. A Friday night in late November; the week before Thanksgiving. A soft mist was drifting down upon the pier. This, apparently, was not unusual for Seattle. Through the mist, the lights of the Space Needle glowed; and the lights of glass-and-steel office buildings and of traffic on the multi-leveled freeways.

The ferry was supposed to leave at 9 p.m. But it had been announced that there would be a delay. The ferry was going to Alaska. To Ketchikan and Wrangell and Petersburg and Juneau and Haines and Skagway, which were towns in southeastern Alaska. Haines was the only one that had a road leading out of it that went anywhere. From Haines you could drive to Anchorage or to Fairbanks or to anywhere you liked. Haines was three days, by ferry, from Seattle.

Because it was November, there were not many people waiting for the ferry. There was room for 750 on board, but only 250 would travel. In summer, the ferries ran twice a week and carried tourists. There was light for more than twenty hours of the twenty-four, and retired couples and backpackers and schoolteachers on vacation could sit up most of the night in the big observation lounges, or could stand outside on the deck and look at the glaciers and the forests and at the mountains that jutted up from the sea.

But in November—late November—there was rain and wet snow and darkness came early.

The ferry ran only one day a week.

There were few tourists.

The people who rode the ferry in November were people who were going to Alaska for a reason.

On my way to Seattle, I had stopped in Washington, D.C., to talk to the congressman from Alaska, the only congressman Alaska had. He had come from California in the 1950s and had settled in Fort Yukon, an Indian village located directly on the Arctic Circle. Fort Yukon was a hundred fifty miles northeast of Fairbanks, and sixty miles north of Circle, where the nearest road, the road from Fairbanks, stopped. The congressman had been a schoolteacher in Fort Yukon.

"I believe," the congressman said, "that Fort Yukon holds the record for the lowest temperature ever recorded in the state. Seventy-nine below. Went down there and stayed for four days. The next summer we set a record for heat—a hundred and one.

"Now I'll tell you a little story about the cold. One winter I'm up there and I'm out doing a little drinking with this friend of mine, another teacher. Well, you know how it is, dark all the time and real cold outside and you're never in a hurry to leave the bar. So it gets to be pretty late, finally, and I say, 'Hey, school tomorrow, we better get going.' Now I'm feeling pretty good but I guess he's feeling even better, because we go outside to his car—there's only a couple hundred yards you can drive around there, you know; no roads that go anywhere; but when it's that cold you keep a car just to drive the couple hundred yards. Anyway, he's got the keys in his mitten there—he got that all arranged while we were still inside—but then we get out by the car and damn if he don't drop the keys. Snow all over the ground, you know, and he drops the keys right in the snow. So, 'Goddamnit,' he says, and he takes off his mittens and squats down there and starts trying to dig the

4

keys out of the snow. Well, like I say, I'm feeling pretty good, I guess, because I just stood there and watched him do it. Took me about twenty or thirty seconds to realize what the hell is going on. Soon as I did, of course, I yelled right at him: 'Hey, get your goddamn mittens on!' But it wasn't quite in time. He lost about three or four fingers altogether, as I remember. I guess that night it must have been sixty, sixty-five below."

The congressman inserted a cigar into his mouth and lit it. He blew a cloud of smoke across his desk. Maybe, I said to him, sometime over the winter, I would make a trip to Fort Yukon.

He grinned. "Well, now, I'll tell you. You're planning to go up there, you'd better let me know ahead of time. These little Indian villages aren't too crazy about people just droppin' in unexpected. Especially Fort Yukon. Especially if you happen to be a writer.

"See, we had a problem up there with a writer a few years back. Least this fellow said he was a writer. Plane comes in one day and he gets off and says he's from the *Reader's Digest*, and they're going to do a big story on Fort Yukon. Life on the Arctic Circle, you know; stuff like that. He says he wants to stay a while and really get to know us. And he says the *Reader's Digest* is sending his money up in a week or two. So, no problem, we find him a place to live and we feed him and all that, and he's got his tape recorder that he takes with him everywhere he goes, interviewing people. He must have interviewed half the town. Funny thing, though. I notice one day that even though he's always punching the buttons on this tape recorder and adjusting the microphone and all that, there isn't any tape in the machine. None of those—what do you call them?—cassettes.

"Well, this seems a little peculiar, but we just watch him a few days longer—nice, friendly fellow, you know—and then one day these two planes come in together and out jump these three or four guys in business suits, and then what must have been half a dozen state troopers. All of them with guns drawn. Turns out this fellow didn't work for the *Reader's Digest* after all. Turns out he had just killed three people in Chicago."

In Seattle, I visited a man who had been blinded by a bear. He lived alone, in a small white house at the edge of the city. The bear had attacked him fifteen years earlier, when he was seventeen, while he was walking in the woods, a mile and a half outside of Juneau, the capital of Alaska, his home town.

He was a small man, neatly dressed. He wore dark glasses. There were many scars on his face—scar tissue behind the edges of his glasses, and scars running from temple to jaw on either side of his face. There also was a heavy scar that curved from the right side of his nose across his cheek and back to the corner of his mouth. He spoke in a flat, toneless voice from which significant emotion seemed to have been drained long ago.

The bear had blinded him with one swipe of a paw. Then, he said, the bear had circled, had charged again, and, the second time, had bitten through his skull. Later, during surgery, the bear's toothmarks had been observed on the brain. The attack not only had left him blind, and in need of plastic surgery which would require years to complete, but also had deprived him of his sense of smell.

He had lived in Seattle for years. He said he could never live in Alaska again. Not because of bitterness, and not because of fear, but because his memory of the beauty was so strong. It was not so bad, he said, being blind in Seattle. Seattle was only a city. It was not so bad when what you could not see was the Space Needle and the glass-and-steel office buildings and the traffic on the multi-leveled freeways. But in Alaska it would be different. He knew. He could remember. And to live amid such beauty—while no longer able to experience it—would, he said, be asking too much of himself.

The next morning I went shopping in an Army-Navy store and bought long underwear and flannel shirts and blue jeans and a duffel bag and woolen socks and a woolen face mask. Then I went to Eddie Bauer and bought a down parka and down overalls and down mittens and two woolen shirts. I also bought two pairs of boots. One pair was made of caribou hide and had thick rubber soles and removable felt liners. They were said to keep the feet warm at temperatures down to 20 below. The other pair was made of white rubber and had valves that, when properly adjusted, would trap a layer of warm air next to the foot. These boots had been developed by the United States armed forces in Korea. They were extremely heavy and clumsy, and cost almost a hundred dollars per pair, but they were said to keep the feet warm at 80 below.

At lunchtime, I walked down to the waterfront. There was hazy sunshine and, for November, the day was unusually warm. I sat outdoors and ate some clams and drank some beer. Then I went back to my hotel and took a nap. In the evening, I went back to the waterfront. This time by taxi, with all my bags, ready to board the ferry for Alaska.

An instrumental version of "Leavin' on a Jet Plane" was playing through the loudspeaker system inside the terminal. Word circulated that the delay was due to a Coast Guard inspection. Since midsummer, when one of the boats had slipped into gear while still tied to the Ketchikan dock—taking half the dock with it out to sea—the Coast Guard had been paying closer attention to the ferries that went to Alaska.

There was a long line of vehicles waiting to board. Campers and vans and pickup trucks, and bigger trucks, loaded with produce and construction materials and machines. There were very few ordinary cars. Ordinary cars, it seemed, were considered not big enough, or tough enough, for Alaska.

Many of the vehicles carried the new Alaska license plate, which showed a bear on its hind legs amid the numbers and the letters. There also were many license plates from Texas. And plates from Oklahoma, and from Oregon, and from California, and from the state of Washington, and from Idaho (Famous Potatoes) and Montana (Big Sky Country), and even a couple from North Dakota (The Peace Garden State). I did not see any license plates from eastern states.

Eventually, the Coast Guard completed its inspection. The line of vehicles began to move, slowly, through the mist, down a ramp and onto the ferry. Those passengers without vehicles—such as myself—boarded from a separate ramp. There were no porters. Some people—such as myself—had to make five and six trips back and forth, from the pier to the ferry, carrying bags.

The ferry was named the *Malaspina*, after a glacier in southern Alaska that is larger than some European countries. There had been a period of Spanish exploration of the waters along the Alaskan coast, and a number of Spanish place names—Cordova, Valdez, Malaspina—survived. During the Klondike gold rush, some people believed that the easiest route to the gold fields lay across the Malaspina Glacier. They were wrong. Many of them died on the glacier, and others were crippled by frostbite or permanently blinded by the glare of snow and ice. The gold had not been easy to get to no matter which way you went, but across the Malaspina Glacier had been the worst.

The ferry pulled out at midnight, three hours late.

The first stop—Ketchikan—lay a day and a half to the north.

It was not as if Alaska had always been there, lurking, in my mind. I had scarcely given a thought to the place until the spring. Then, one night, a friend named Peter Herford came to dinner and we got to talking about mountains, and he said the best mountains he had ever been in—the finest mountains he had ever seen—were in Alaska. He had lived in Anchorage for a year; his first wife, in fact, had been weather lady for an Anchorage television station. He said the mountains—and the glaciers and lakes and miles and miles and miles of open tundra—started about half an hour from downtown Anchorage and just kept going, in all directions—north beyond the Arctic Circle; west to the International Date Line; further than the mind of an urban Northeasterner could comprehend.

I was by no means a mountain climber; nor, in fact, an outdoorsman of any sort. But I had hiked briefly, a few years earlier, in a small section of the Canadian Rockies, and had once walked, for a month, through the Alps. Those experiences had made a lasting impression. Now I was told, by a man who also had seen the mountains of Canada and Switzerland, that, by comparison, Alaska was a different dimension. It was, he said, a wild and raw and stimulating land; like no place else he'd ever seen. It would, he suggested, change, in some way, anyone who ventured there.

About a month later, a copy of the *National Geographic* magazine came in the mail—an issue devoted almost entirely to Alaska. The magazine was accompanied with a map which was almost wall-poster size. I am a person who likes maps. I read maps for pleasure. Sometimes, on a rainy evening, I will pick up a road map instead of a detective story. Once, after browsing through a map of Pennsylvania, I drove for hours to a town called Oil City, a place I had discovered on the map. I just wanted to see what a town called Oil City, Pennsylvania, would be like. The map of Alaska, however, was like no other map I'd ever seen.

It could not really be called a road map, because, in Alaska, there seemed to be hardly any roads. The state was more than twice as big as Texas—it was, in fact, one-fifth the size of the whole rest of the country—yet contained fewer miles of road than did Vermont. There was not even a road into Juneau, the state capital, which was accessible only by sea or air.

Juneau was also two time zones removed from Anchorage and Fairbanks, the two largest cities in the state. Alaska was so big that it contained four time zones; yet its population was smaller than that of Columbus, Ohio. There were fewer than 400,000 people living in the state, and half of them were in Anchorage. The rest were scattered like dots in a connect-the-dots picture in which no one had connected the dots. Alaska was so vast that if a map of it were superimposed upon an identical-scale map of the Lower Forty-eight, Alaska would extend from Canada to Mexico, north to south; and, east to west, from Savannah, Georgia, to Santa Barbara, California. If Alaska's population density, even with Anchorage included, were applied to New York City, the population of the borough of Manhattan would be fourteen.

I spent a long time looking at the map. At the place names: Dime Landing, Farewell, and Ruby. King Salmon, Talkeetna, Yakutat. And at the mountains: the Brooks Range, located entirely above the Arctic Circle, the northernmost mountain range in the world; the Wrangells, parts of which were so inaccessible that they contained peaks of 10,000 feet and more which not only had never been climbed but had not yet even been named. And at the Alaska Range itself, with Mount McKinley as its centerpiece. The highest mountain on the continent; with a vertical rise, from base to summit, that was the greatest of any mountain in the world.

And as I looked I tried to imagine all the empty space; all the darkness; all the cold. And tried to imagine the people who would choose to live in such a place. Alaska was, clearly, a land which one would have to choose. Not a place one just happened to stumble across. In this generation, except for the Natives—the Eskimos, Indians, and Aleuts, who made up 20 percent of the state's population—the adult population of Alaska was comprised almost entirely of people who had decided to leave wherever it was they had been, and whatever it was they had been doing (and, in many cases, whomever it was they had been doing it with), and start over again in a place about which, if they knew anything at all, they knew only that it would be cold and dark and lonely much of the time, and—all of the time—radically different from the place they were leaving behind.

Who were these people? What were they looking for? Or: What were they running from? And what had they found, once they arrived in a land that remained, to a degree unimaginable in any other part of the United States, unchanged by the presence of man?

I knew only two people who had moved to Alaska. I had worked with them on a newspaper in Massachusetts ten years before. One summer they had just upped and went, and I had heard nothing from them, or of them, since.

Eventually I put the map away, but the notion of Alaska lingered on. It began to grow, in fact, and spread: through the spring and into early summer. What was it like up there? What would it be like to be there? I had spent most of the previous couple of years cooped up inside a stuffy little workroom in New Jersey, writing a book that had turned out to be mostly about the inside of my head. I was hungry for something different: something big, something fresh, something new. Like Alaska.

I imagined it as a vast and primal wilderness: an immovable object of sorts; frozen in time. But under attack now—under sudden and vicious assault—by the irresistible forces of big business, modern technology, and greed.

The pipeline, it seemed, was changing the state in ways that would never be undone. Not just physical changes, though they, in places, were severe; but changes in the psychological climate; deep scars cut not just across the tundra, but across Alaska's very soul. The pipeline's advocates had claimed it would be merely a piece of string across a football field; its detractors feared it would be a knife slash across the "Mona Lisa." Whatever it was, it was there now; would soon be complete. The Americanization of Alaska had begun.

It had become a cliché, perhaps, to say that Alaska was America's last frontier; but, if so, it was a cliché that contained a certain irreducible level of truth. For always, in America, there had been an edge; a furthest reach; a place to which one could travel in order to live a different and a simpler sort of life. To escape pressure and progress and crowds. To start anew, perhaps; building on inner resources.

After Alaska, there would no longer be any such place. It began to seem important to me to go there while at least some of its original qualities remained intact. Before it became just another place you went to get rich quick.

I decided that I would travel to Alaska in the fall. That I would remain there through the winter, and through the summer that would follow. That I would wander, as freely as possible, across the land. In order to experience, and, perhaps, to some degree record, what I suspected might indeed be the last days of the last frontier America would ever have.

I was in an inside cabin, over the engines. There were two bunk beds, but with the ferry two-thirds empty, I expected to have the cabin to myself. Then I heard a clattering and banging outside the door.

"*Shit.*" A sound of grunting. "*Son of a bitch.*" The door opened and I saw a short, curly-haired man of about thirty-five, with a belly that protruded over his pants. He was trying to drag a pair of toolboxes through the doorway. "Goddamnit. Oh, 'scuse me, buddy. Want to give me a hand with one of these?"

This was Eddie the Basque. My roommate as far as Ketchikan. Wearing highly polished cowboy boots, a spangled shirt, and a large brass belt buckle which, when his stomach permitted a view of it, showed a cowboy atop a bucking bronco.

He had been living most recently in Pocatello, Idaho, tending bar. His real training, however, was as a pipefitter. Fitting together large pieces of pipe. As in the Trans-Alaska Pipeline. He did not have a pipeline job yet—those were going only to people who had resided in Alaska for at least a year—but he had lined up work in Ketchikan. He planned to stay there for a year, fulfilling his residency requirement, and then move up to the pipeline. Two years on the line, he figured, and he would be able to retire for life. Like myself, Eddie had not been to Alaska before.

He wiped some sweat from his brow. He was not himself a Basque, but was of Basque descent.

"Jesus Christ, I got to change my fucking shirt. You sweat like

11

a pig on a night like this, carrying them fucking tools around. Say, you ever been to this Ketchikan? That what it's called? What kind of a fucked-up name is that? You know anything about this outfit I'll be working for? Ketchikan Pulp? I hear it's run by a bunch of Japs. I hear the Japs are buying up all of the wood in Alaska."

Eddie pulled off his shirt, revealing large arm muscles and a soft stomach that had, running in a jagged line diagonally across its center, a deep and livid scar—a scar that was, quite obviously, the result of circumstances less controlled than hospital surgery.

"Hey, what's the cunt situation on this boat? You checked it out yet? Just let me comb my hair a little and then we can go get a beer."

The bar was in a room with no windows. Duane Archer and a high state official were drinking there. Duane Archer was a skinny man with a moustache. He was wearing a leisure suit and a loud Hawaiian shirt with the shirt collar out over the jacket, and he wore rings on at least half of his fingers. He ran a restaurant and bar supply business in Anchorage, and was into five or six other deals on the side. Meat-packing, real estate, things like that.

He had gone to Seattle to accompany his wife, who had been in need of major surgery. While there, he had bought himself a pickup truck. There were two things, Duane Archer said, for which it was always worth going to Seattle: major surgery and motor vehicles of any kind. His wife was still in the hospital, re-cuperating, but Duane Archer was heading back. He had too many deals going; he could not afford to stay away for very long.

Eddie the Basque moved quickly to a corner table, where he had spotted two heavy young women with teased hair. I sat at the bar and ordered an Olympia beer. Duane Archer was telling the high state official about his new truck, a Ford, and about the way he had bought it. He had two cigarettes going at once.

"So I said to that son of a bitch, 'Listen, you son of a bitch, I want that heavy-duty bumper on there and I want them studded snow tires on there and I want that extra layer of undercoating on there and I want that auxiliary heater hooked up, and I want this all taken care of by four o'clock tomorrow when I come back here to pick this baby up and I don't want any more shit about it.'"

The high state official was nodding. Duane Archer took a swal-low of his drink. V.O. and water was what he drank.

"Well, let me tell you, that turkey was getting nervous. So then

I said, 'One more thing: If it's not done when I come back here at four o'clock tomorrow, I'm gonna step in behind the wheel of that baby and I'm gonna drive her right out through your big beautiful plate-glass window and I'll run over any son of a bitch that tries to stop me.' Well, let me tell you, by now that turkey was *worried*."

The high state official continued to nod.

"When I got back there at four o'clock yesterday, that heavy-duty bumper was on there and those studded snow tires were on there and that extra layer of undercoating was on there and that auxiliary heater was hooked up and purring like a cat. And they had that baby so polished up and shiny that the goddamned President would have been proud to ride in it. If I'd 've let him, which I don't think I would, the dumb son of a bitch."

Then Duane Archer turned to me. "Say, buddy, I don't drink with strangers. Duane Archer is my name, what's yours? Where you from? How come you're drinking that shit? Let me get you a decent drink. Hey, Lil, another round over here. Why don't you have a V.O. or something? That goddamned Oly don't have enough alcohol in it to disinfect a mosquito bite. At least not a bite from an Alaskan mosquito. Hah-hah!"

The high state official was a short man, rather heavy, and almost totally bald. He was on his way back to Juneau after having just attended a conference in Seattle. He was taking the ferry because he too was transporting a new car. He spoke in a soft voice that you had to lean very far forward to hear. His lips scarcely moved. It was as if he were keeping them poised for the next sip of alcohol, which, it seemed, was never more than a few seconds away.

He had come to Alaska, he said, on Memorial Day of 1949, after getting drunk with two friends at the midget-auto races in Portland, Oregon. It had been one of those deals where nothing would do but to drive to the airport and get on the first plane for anywhere. Which happened, in this case, to be Fairbanks. It was a twelve-hour flight in those days, and by the time the plane landed they were sober. The two friends turned around and went home, but the high state official, with only $1.70 in his pocket, knew at once that Fairbanks, Alaska, was where he wanted to live for the rest of his life. There *was* still an American frontier and he had happened to stumble across it. He found a room in a boarding-house where they said he would not have to pay until he got work, and then he got work the next day. Construction work. There was a lot of that in Fairbanks in the summer, even then. When winter came and there was no more construction, he joined the city police. Ten years later, when Alaska became a state, he switched to the state police; eventually, he obtained a position in another area of state government. The trouble with that was that eventually he had to move to Juneau. The high state official hated Juneau: he considered it to be a sodden, sordid suburb of Seattle. Not the real Alaska, in his opinion; not at all.

"Goddamn right," Duane Archer said. "The real Alaska is Anchorage, where a man can make a buck if he hustles, and where nobody gets in his way."

No, said the high state official; Anchorage wasn't it either. The real Alaska was Fairbanks—the way it had been in 1949 when he had first seen it, and the way it had remained for the next twenty-five years. Until the pipeline.

"Now," said the high state official, sad and pale, "Fairbanks isn't even a city any more; it's an open wound." He stared through cigarette smoke at his drink. "Hell," he said, "these days I don't think there is a real Alaska."

I finished my beer and went back to the cabin, and slept until about four, when Eddie the Basque came in and woke me up, asking me what the hell was wrong with me, why hadn't I joined him at his table, didn't I even want to get laid?

I got up early and went for a walk on the deck. It was slick and cold. There was no one else out. The Seattle drizzle was still there, but ten degrees colder. And no longer drifting down: blown now by a thirty-knot wind.

I zipped up my new rubber poncho. My nose started running, my cheeks began to sting, and, even inside the poncho pockets, my fingers grew stiff from the chill. Vancouver Island was off to the left; the mainland of British Columbia to the right. And the ferry moving north; steadily north.

It was that afternoon that Eddie the Basque got the bad news about the pipeline. He was at the bar with Duane Archer and the high state official, and with Sandy, a slender young woman with light brown hair. Sandy was from Hastings, Nebraska.

Duane Archer was chuckling and shaking his head slowly from side to side. "First of all, buddy, you're not gonna be able to get off the boat at Ketchikan. They haven't fixed the dock yet. You can get off, but not your truck. Your truck's gonna have to go on to Wrangell."

"So how long's it take to drive from Wrangell?"

"To drive where from Wrangell?"

"To Ketchikan."

"Well, that depends." And here Duane Archer winked, first at the high state official, and then at Sandy, who had lived in Juneau for a year.

"Depends on what?"

"Depends on how long it takes to build the road."

At this, Duane Archer dissolved so totally into laughter that it was the high state official who had to explain to Eddie the Basque that there was no road between Wrangell and Ketchikan, or, for that matter, because of the mountains coming right down to the water, between Wrangell and anywhere. Or between Ketchikan and anywhere. Eddie would have to stay aboard the ferry until Wrangell and spend the night there. Then take a smaller ferry south the next day. A ferry that could unload vehicles at the Ketchikan dock. A ferry that would not reach Ketchikan until Monday night, or maybe even early Tuesday morning.

"Son of a bitch," said Eddie the Basque. He was supposed to start work at Ketchikan Pulp with the 4 p.m. shift on Sunday.

"And second of all . . ." Duane Archer was trying to speak again, but already he was beginning to laugh; to laugh so hard that little drops of moisture came to his eyes. "Second of all, by the time you put in your year at that Jap pulp company, the pipeline . . . the goddamn pipeline . . . will be finished! You ain't even gonna *see* that pipeline, turkey, much less help build it, unless you charter yourself an airplane and fly over it."

Laughter made Duane Archer's face red and caused him to gasp for breath. Eddie the Basque blinked rapidly, his lips tight. He was beginning to turn a little pale.

"And one more thing," Duane Archer said through his cough, when he was able. "You know how much rain they get in Ketchikan? Three hundred inches a year."

More laughter. And Eddie turning paler. And clenching his fists. Until the high state official put a hand on his shoulder and said softly, "Don't worry, buddy. Things'll work out. Compared to the way I came up here, you've already got one foot inside the governor's mansion."

The bar was dark; no clock on the wall; no windows; no way to look out and see the sky. Sandy, from Nebraska, did not care. She knew what was out there because she had seen it before, and once she hit Juneau she would be looking at it all the time. She combed her brown hair frequently, and she kept a toothpick in the corner of her mouth. For someone from a plains state—with a family history of temperance—she could drink an awful lot of rum and Cokes. She was reading an August edition of *Rolling Stone*, trying to catch up on what was happening. With nothing else to do, she decided to tell the story of her life.

Hastings, Nebraska, flat and lonely, and she was eighteen years old at the end of the sixties, and felt that she had missed out on it all. That she had missed all the action there ever had been. So, out to California, where, she had read in *Rolling Stone*, the action was. But no luck. The action was not in California any more. As far as Sandy could tell, it was not anywhere. Gone. Poof. Just like that. So, gradually, aimlessly, almost imperceptibly, she drifted up the coast. Carried along on some sort of psychological ebb tide of the early seventies. San Francisco, Portland, Eugene, Seattle, and, eventually, Juneau, Alaska. The end of the line. Such a haunted, beautiful, somber, mysterious, deadening town. Where all the driftwood finally came to rest. And then slowly rotted in the rain.

The San Francisco flower children, a decade later, a thousand miles north; dazed and weary, at the foot of the mountain, at the edge of the sea. Gone now as far as they could go. Wearing pea coats and wool hats and rubber boots. Keeping their drugs dry, and huddling together for warmth against the rain.

Oh, such rain. It fell day after day, week after week, month after month. Sometimes sleet, sometimes snow, but, in the end, rain again. Soaking through the clothes, through the skin, into the soul. Young men stumbled groggily from one bar to another. Up the steep narrow streets that seemed almost European. Past the precarious little houses painted in pastel. Up and down the wooden staircases that sometimes took the place of streets, leading from one level of the town to another. This was the only state capital in

America where you needed a topographical map, as well as a street map, in order to find your way around.

When the pipeline came, the young men braced themselves and went to work. This was a new strain of flower child. Pipeline money had activated an ancient, buried instinct. These were flower children who wanted to get rich. Hippies with Rotarian hearts.

So they went north to the camps—Coldfoot, Old Man, Atigun Pass—and, weeks later, they returned. With money. Lots of money. They bought real estate, and boats, and airplanes. And, with what was left over, they bought cocaine. And gave some to Sandy, and to lots of other pretty girls who were their friends. Cocaine was everywhere. The materialistic flower children of Juneau used it to dry out their brains.

Sandy found a job with the Alaska legislature, which was in session from January through May. She worked upstairs, typing and answering the phone. Downstairs, in a committee chairman's office, elected representatives of the people, together with non-elected representatives of the press, were cutting up grains of cocaine with a razor blade. On a hand mirror, borrowed from a secretary. And snorting it up their noses through tightly rolled hundred-dollar bills. Then the representatives went back to the chamber to cast their votes, feeling much better, their alcohol hangovers now under control. They voted on the allocation of tens of millions of dollars. They made decisions that would change the very nature of their state. And spoke later, after the rush had worn off, about how destructive Juneau was; about how strongly they were in favor of the proposal to move the state capital; to build a new capital somewhere near Anchorage; someplace accessible by road. They said that if only they were not in Juneau, then they would not be acting this way.

Sandy did not have the status that would enable her to snort cocaine during the day, so she did it at night, hanging out with the in crowd of Juneau: those people who were making an effort to destroy themselves, instead of just letting it happen.

When she could not get cocaine she drank beer. Ten or twelve beers every night, mostly Olympia, sometimes a Bud, and somehow she did not get fat. No one could figure out why. Sandy thought it was the cocaine that kept her thin.

She lived in an apartment downtown, but seldom spent more

than four hours a night in her bed, unless there was someone there with her. She just could not take the risk of not being around if the action—the real action—were to return.

In the summer, Sandy had finally worked up the energy to leave. She had gone east, all the way to East Hampton, Long Island, where a boyfriend was working in a boatyard. She worked awhile as his assistant: hammering, sawing, repairing the boats. And balling her boyfriend's partner whenever she could. Within weeks, she grew bored with her boyfriend; bored with the East. She wanted to get back to Juneau, in case something exciting was going on. So in the fall she drove back across country in her little Datsun, stopping briefly in Hastings, where everyone thought she was living a glamorous life. Then she drove on to Seattle. And now here she was, with a rum and Coke and an old *Rolling Stone* on the ferry.

Vancouver Island was behind us now. Outside, there was wind, rain, and whitecaps, as darkness fell.

The *Malaspina* reached Ketchikan at three o'clock on Sunday afternoon. The sun was shining, the air crisp, and there was snow in the hills above the town. The hills were pretty, the way they almost always are above a waterfront, and the afternoon sun, glaring off the fresh snow, with the bright blue sky as a background, was good to see after gray Seattle and two days of gray sky and water, but Ketchikan was a squalid little town. Shabby low buildings and dirty streets. Barking dogs running in packs. Fat Indian girls with bad teeth. Sullen young Indian men leaning against unpainted storefronts, smoking and staring and not saying much. And old men stumbling around drunk. Sunday afternoon, nothing doing, winter coming on. And this was the fourth-largest city in Alaska.

There was a party that night in cabin 181—the cabin of the two heavy women with teased hair whom Eddie the Basque had met in the bar. I had wondered for a while, because of the way they dressed and the way they talked and because of all the makeup that they wore, if the two heavy women might have been prostitutes. But it turned out that they were just a couple of housewives from Wrangell who had been on a pre-winter Seattle shopping spree. Their husbands allowed them this once a year, in an effort to keep them reasonably sane. They had been gone for a week and seemed not very eager to get back. Neither to their husbands nor to the long wet months of Wrangell winter.

By the time I stopped in at the party, Duane Archer was on a top bunk, trying to kiss one of the women. Eddie the Basque was already sound asleep, passed out, with his head in the other woman's lap. He had been drinking pretty hard ever since Duane Archer had broken the news to him about the pipeline. But in a few hours he was going to have to drive his truck off the ferry and into a strange town in Alaska late at night and try to figure what to do next. With tears in her eyes, the woman in whose lap his head was lying was singing Eddie the Basque a lullaby.

"I always wanted a baby," she said in a thin, falsetto voice. Then she started to cry. Duane Archer had been putting Everclear into her drinks instead of vodka. Everclear was grain alcohol—180 proof—apparently quite a popular item in Alaska. "I always wanted a baby," the woman repeated, "but my husband said no because he didn't think I was emotionally stable."

Eventually, everyone from the party went to dinner. Except Eddie the Basque, who didn't wake up, and the woman from Wrangell who was holding his head in her lap. "I can't leave him like this," she said, "but I'll take a New York strip, medium rare, and a baked potato with sour cream, to go."

But half an hour later, when Sandy carried the food down to 181, the door was locked. And from inside there came sounds which indicated, to the practiced ear, not only that Eddie the Basque was no longer asleep but that he and the woman from Wrangell were well past the lullaby stage. Then it was 11 p.m. and the *Malaspina* was pulling into Wrangell in freezing rain. The other woman from Wrangell raced into the bar, hysterical.

"They're both asleep in there! With no clothes on! I can't wake up either of them! And how did he get that horrible scar on his stomach?"

Black coffee was rushed to 181. Cold water was applied in large doses.

"Hurry, hurry," the Wrangell woman who was awake yelled. "Her husband's even meaner than mine."

The *Malaspina* was grinding to a halt at the Wrangell dock. Passengers without vehicles—such as the two women—would disembark first.

Eddie was partly dressed by now and able to talk a little bit.

19

But it still seemed unlikely that he could make it down the stairs to his truck. Much less drive the truck off the ferry and into a strange, dark Alaskan town that was rapidly filling with freezing rain.

The women's problem, however, was more immediate. People already were starting to walk down the ramp and off the boat.

"I'll go first," the woman who was awake said, "and tell them that Phyllis is in the bathroom. I'll try to stall. But hurry. Hurry. We've got to live with these bastards all winter."

So ten minutes later Duane Archer and Sandy and the high state official and I came down the ramp. Propping up the second woman from Wrangell. The ramp was already slippery from the freezing rain. You could see nothing of Wrangell except a few lights here and there, and some cars and trucks that had got stuck on the ice as they tried to go uphill.

Then we saw five tall, silent, broad-shouldered men standing at the foot of the ramp with arms folded. Staring at the woman we supported.

"Phyllis, what the hell is wrong with you? Why ain't you walkin' by yourself?"

"It's slippery, honey."

But then she started to giggle, and then Duane Archer started laughing out loud, and, as he did, he took a bad step on the leg he had broken a year before in an automobile accident, and said, "Oh, shit," and slipped on the ice and slid to the bottom of the ramp. The five big men stood there, arms folded, staring at him, and no one made a move to help him up.

"Where's Joanne?" the woman said.

"In the car. She ain't fit to be seen in public." There was a pause. "And neither are you." Another pause. "And who the hell are these morons?"

By now Duane Archer had gotten to his feet. "Archer's the name," he said, offering his hand, which was ignored. "Restaurant and bar supply, Anchorage. Anything you folks ever need down here we can get it for you in forty-eight hours, air freight. From a coffee cup to a whole new kitchen. Wait a minute, I think I've got a business card."

But the five men—Phyllis's husband, and Joanne's husband, and Joanne's father, and Phyllis's husband's cousin Luke, and Luke's friend, whose name Phyllis could not remember—had no interest in restaurant equipment. They took her from us in mid-introduction, and stalked off with her, in the freezing rain and the darkness of Wrangell, toward whatever retribution lay in store.

It was at this point that we were suddenly distracted by the sight of a truck lurching off the vehicle deck of the ferry and skidding, almost sideways, down the ramp. Its horn was honking wildly and the driver was hooting and hollering above the horn. The truck hit the bottom of the ramp, spun on a patch of ice, and, with onlookers scrambling for safety, roared across the dock area toward the street.

The truck was bucking like a bronco as it shot past us, and Eddie the Basque was leaning pretty hard on the horn, but he still managed to get one hand free, to give us a big, sweeping wave of farewell as he too disappeared into the night.

Late the next sleepy gray morning the ferry turned up Gastineau Channel, and, before long, the ghostly silhouette of Juneau began to loom through sleet and snow.

Sandy, out on deck, bundled against the sudden winter, looked toward the city and the mountains.

Juneau again. For Sandy, the end of the line.

"Oh, Christ," she said. "This time I bet I never leave."

2 The Road

We reached Haines at 7 p.m. A hard rain was falling and the temperature was 34 degrees. Haines, in November, was not much. A few low buildings, heavy slush on the streets, a few drunken Indians in the rain. There did not seem to be any lights. A closed-up IGA store with the front window broken where someone, apparently, had thrown a rock. A cluster of Indians outside the one open restaurant and bar. Duane Archer and I went in for dinner. I had originally planned to get off the ferry in Juneau and fly to Anchorage, but now I was going to ride with Duane Archer in his truck.

The restaurant was not what you would call fancy—more just a plain old café. In November it was the only place to eat in Haines, and, at 8 p.m., we were the only people there. Formica tables, Alaskan prices—fourteen dollars for a thin and gristly rib steak, which went straight from the freezer to the pan. Served burnt on the outside, still purple and icy within. Salads with lettuce that was the color of freezing rain.

"See these glasses?" Duane Archer said. "Libby five-and-a-halfs. Sent 'em three cases. I remember when the order came in."

An Indian came stumbling through the swinging door that separated the restaurant from the bar. There were half a dozen Indians—and no whites—in there drinking. None of them sitting up very straight.

The Indian lurched toward our table. He wavered a bit, then pitched forward. I had to catch him to keep him from collapsing into our food.

"Fuck off, partner," Duane Archer said, barely looking up.

The Indian stood there, still weaving. There was drool coming from the corners of his mouth. His eyes looked like pieces of red linoleum. He smelled like a dead animal in the road. There seemed hardly a tooth in his mouth. He might have been, at a guess, between thirty-five and forty years old.

There was no way to tell what he wanted. Maybe money. For a drink. Or maybe just to say, welcome to Haines.

He made a little retching noise and Duane Archer shouted for the woman in the kitchen, who was serving as both waitress and cook.

"Charley. Get away from these folks. Come on, leave 'em alone."

The Indian made a few more noises.

"What's that? You don't feel well? Okay, Charley, just sit right down here, then, in this booth, until you start to feel a little better."

And she gently helped the Indian to a big booth in the corner. Where he sat, staring straight ahead through his linoleum eyes, and still making sounds with his mouth that might have been speech.

"No-good bastards," Duane Archer was saying. "It makes me sick. It really does. Shit like this is just ruining the state."

The woman had gone to the kitchen to cut us some pie for dessert. Blueberry pie, a dollar and a half a slice. A glass of milk to go with it cost a dollar. But coffee was only a quarter and they would refill your cup right through the winter, no extra charge.

"Just makes me sick to my stomach," Archer said.

Then the Indian began to fumble with his hands, somewhere down below the surface of the table. And a few seconds later, there came from his corner an unusual noise. The kind of noise that is not normally heard in restaurants that have fourteen-dollar steaks. A sort of hissing, splashing noise. And then we saw the stream of water, hitting the floor and forming a pool, which quickly grew larger, and which began to move across the aisle toward our feet.

"Jesus Christ!" Duane Archer yelled, jumping up.

It seemed to go on forever. As if the Indian had not emptied his bladder since midsummer. Halfway through, he could no longer sit up and began to slide sideways, and wound up, still pissing, stretched out on the booth, against the wall.

Duane Archer was screaming louder now and jumping up and down as if he had never seen urine before. Just then the waitress returned to our table with the pie.

"Forget the goddamn pie," Archer shouted. "We're getting out of here."

"Oh, Charley," the woman said calmly, putting down the pie. "You know you're supposed to use the bathroom."

The Indian looked up at her blankly. Then he toppled off the booth, onto the floor. The woman went back to the kitchen for a mop. We stepped out to the dark, empty streets of Haines, and slid a couple of blocks downhill, through freezing rain, to our motel.

The alarm went off at five-thirty. Then there was silence in the room. A silence that had not been there the night before. The sound of rain was gone. Of freezing rain, on the motel's tin roof. I opened the door and looked out. The rain had turned to snow. Big, soft, wet snow, at least a foot of it already, piling up fast. Falling heavily, without any wind. It wasn't too cold, maybe 20 degrees. At six o'clock we walked up the slippery hill to the café.

The café was brightly lit and steamy inside and smelling of coffee and ammonia. There were about a dozen men in beards and down jackets and woolen shirts, sitting in little clusters, drinking coffee and smoking and talking to one another in a stop-and-start, early-morning way. No one was talking about the storm. No one even seemed to think it was a storm. Just another Haines November morning.

We swung out of the parking lot at seven. Archer had his windshield wipers going strong, and his heaters—the regular heater and the auxiliary heater, about which he had made such a fuss in Seattle—turned up high. Clouds of his cigarette smoke filled the cab. Outside, there was darkness, not even the first trace of morning light.

I leaned back, unzipped my parka, unbuttoned my woolen shirt, and lifted my thermal undershirt off my stomach. I was already starting to perspire. The heater fans blasted dry, scalding air into my face. My first day on land in Alaska. I had dressed for a journey by dog sled, and had wound up in a hair dryer on wheels.

It took two hours to reach the Yukon border, forty-six miles out of Haines, climbing steeply toward Chilkat Pass. There was gray light now but it was still headlight weather, and no visibility beyond the sides of the road. Twelve miles beyond the border we reached the pass, at 7,200 feet. Having started at sea level at Haines.

By midmorning the snow had tapered off. To the west, there was a faint hint of blue sky behind a thin, wispy coating of cloud. And behind that, far off, a quick glimpse of what might have been a mountain. A big mountain. But just a hint of it—a suggestion of mountain—and then the gray came back to cover it again.

At Haines Junction, 159 miles out of Haines, we reached the Alaska Highway. It was a two-lane, mostly gravel road that covered 1,500 miles between Fairbanks and Dawson Creek, British Columbia. It had been built in nine frantic months by the U.S. Army Corps of Engineers at the start of World War II. The road was snow-covered, but the snow was packed smoothly and Archer said it was better than in summer, when the highway was potholes, flying gravel, and dust. On the snow, Archer could make fifty miles an hour.

In early afternoon, with the storm over and the sky clear, we came down a long, sweeping hill and around a big parabolic curve, and mountains suddenly jumped into view, rising from the shore of a long, curving lake. Kluane Lake: biggest in the Yukon Territory.

We stopped and I got out and walked around. The view extended for what seemed hundreds of miles in all directions. Nowhere were there any other signs of life. Just the mountains, the lake, and my breath forming clouds in the air. It was the biggest piece of emptiness I'd ever seen.

"Come on. Let's get moving," Archer called. "Before my goddamn engine freezes up."

It was getting much colder. With the heaters pumping hard, it still felt too hot inside the truck, but on the side windows the moisture had frozen. And my lips were drying, cracking, starting to bleed. Within minutes, just from the dryness and the cold.

We would go for half an hour seeing no one. Then a big truck would roar by the other way. A Sealand or Lyndon Transport truck, going eighty miles an hour through the snow. Taking up more than half the road. Rocking us with its velocity as it blew by. Then all would become empty and still again, except for the noise of the heaters and Archer's voice.

At a roadhouse at Burwash Landing, in midafternoon, we stopped for coffee and gas. The temperature was 12 below zero, the coldest air I'd ever felt. I left the overheated lodge after only a single cup of coffee. Erratic behavior; possibly even a breach of Yukon ethics; but I wanted some time out of doors.

There was a wall of mountains, towering high, across from the roadhouse, to the east. The tops were pink—like strawberry ice cream—as the late light reflected off the snow. The sun itself had gone behind the mountains to the west. I was wearing only street shoes, and within minutes, my toes began to hurt. The cold here was a force: a vital, physical force. Not just part of the background, as in an eastern, urban winter, but clearly the dominating partner in its relationship with man.

We made good time from Burwash Landing to the border. The pink mountaintops turned a soft purple and soon were just dark silhouettes against the sky. Outside the truck, the wind picked up and the chill factor resumed its long, inexorable slide toward deep winter.

It was dark by four-fifteen and just a straight-ahead ride after that. Not much excitement. Archer winding down a bit; still smoking incessantly, but talking less. I was no longer complaining about the heat; too busy rubbing Chap Stick on my lips. We reached Tok, on the Alaska side of the border, at seven o'clock. Tok was just a place where two roads met. The Alaska Highway continued northwest, another 200 miles to Fairbanks, and the Glenn Highway went southwest, 380 miles to Anchorage. At the Tok Lodge, where we ate dinner, there was a hand-lettered sign on the wall. It said: DINING ROOM CLOSED THANKSGIVING. BAR OPEN REGULAR HOURS.

26

This was Alaska, Archer said. First things first. Outside, the temperature had dropped to 17 degrees below zero.

Up at five-thirty again. There was a thermometer outside the motel office. I trotted down, in parka and long underwear. It had warmed up to 3 below. Uh-oh, Archer said. That meant snow.

We left right away, trying to beat it. No coffee, no breakfast, and three hours of darkness ahead. But the snow started as soon as we did, heavy and fast, without wind. A white sea of snow in the early-morning November black. Within an hour, the snow was hubcap high, and the road icy slick underneath. Duane Archer delivered a sermon on the virtues of four-wheel drive.

The crystals were dry and fine; lit up like sparklers by the headlights on high beam. Then the snow came so hard that Archer switched to low beam. Then he tried driving without lights, trying for the best visibility. There was no other traffic to worry about.

Half an hour out of Tok there was a sudden blur of big dark motion at the roadside. A moose. Moving much faster than I had thought a moose could move. Running down the road ahead of us, and swerving to the side as we passed. Big. Jesus. I had always thought of a moose as sort of an overgrown deer. Not at all. More like a muscular horse. Funny-looking, with that barrel of a body over those spindly trotting legs. Legs which looked spindly, at least from a truck. Up close, there was nothing the least bit spindly about a moose.

Gradually, gray light came. Low clouds, fog, the snow tapering off. A dull gray battleship of a day. Dawn through Mentasta Lake and Slana and Chistochina—these were not towns, really; just little dots on the map.

It was ten o'clock before we found a place to stop for breakfast. The snow by then seemed mostly behind us, but the road had turned bad: rough, bumpy, washed out in spots. We had to slow to fifteen miles an hour, up and down, bucking over washboard. The tundra was now spreading out from either side. And tiny, skinny little bushes shaped like trees. Evergreens that just were not able to grow tall. There was only a light coating of snow on the ground; covering hummocks, tussocks, land that looked flat; land that was flat until you tried to hike across it. And found those lumpy little tussocks constantly giving way beneath your boots.

We pushed on south, to Glennallen. Off to the left, Archer said, were the Wrangell Mountains. I looked at a map. Mount Sanford, at 16,000 feet, and Mount Drum, at 12,000, would be the closest; the most visible from the road. But not today. Today, mountains existed only in the mind.

Glennallen was the biggest town we'd seen since Juneau. Population 700. One hundred thirty-nine miles out of Tok. One eighty-nine still to go. Lots of religion in Glennallen. Lots of tacky little churches with strange, pentecostal, Bible Belt names. Crazed preacher babble on the radio. First time we'd had the radio on the whole trip.

Beyond Glennallen, we began to feel the pull of Anchorage. The ferry, southeastern Alaska, the Yukon, even Tok and the snowstorm were behind us. The destination was now within reach, and the destination became the focus of attention. Duane Archer began to talk about what he was going to do when he got home. About his children, whom he had left in the care of a sister-in-law; about the drink he would make, the fire he would build in his fireplace, the restaurant dinner he would go out to eat. I began to wonder what it would be like to see Tom and Marnie, the only people I knew in Alaska, after not having seen them for ten years.

We stopped for coffee at a lodge not far from Chickaloon. It was owned by a man who had moved out from Indianapolis to better resist the Russian invasion, which he believed to be imminent. He kept a loaded revolver by the cash register. Not because he was worried about theft, but in order to provide an appropriate welcome for the first Commie soldier through the door. He had bought all of his dishes and most of his kitchen equipment from Duane Archer.

"Say, Archer, you got any Communist products in that Anchorage warehouse of yours?"

"No, but I can order some for you if you'd like."

Duane Archer laughed. The owner of the lodge did not laugh. Some things were not laughing matters. The Communists, he had discovered, through reading material he had received in the mail, not only were profiting economically from selling their products in America, but were, in the process, infiltrating the whole nation with deadly germs. Secreted inside tins of Polish ham, inside goblets and crockery, on the surfaces of linens from Rumania. Horrible new viruses, which did not kill outright but caused victims to grow addicted to alcohol and drugs.

"We're going to be so weak in another ten years that they'll walk in and take over without a shot being fired." The man's voice was shrill. Archer nodded slowly. I kept an eye on the revolver. It seemed obvious that, no matter what happened elsewhere, Chickaloon would not be lost without a fight.

We drove down through Palmer in early afternoon, making good time. Palmer was the big farming town of Alaska. The federal government had sent farmers from Wisconsin and Minnesota to the Matanuska Valley during the Depression, giving them land and paying their transportation to get to it. Tough winters, but the land had turned out to be fertile. Not a long growing season, but an intense one. Almost constant daylight in the summer. A lot of things would not grow, but those that did grow grew big. Thirty-pound cabbages. Strawberries the size of a child's fist.

Palmer had about it the look of the plains, or even the Midwest. Except for the glaciers nearby, and the towering rise of the Chugach Mountains, which pressed close against it from the east. It was a town born of things that grew; not of lifeless minerals, or transportation needs. It seemed a town you could connect to. It seemed, I suppose, American, in a way the other towns we had been through had not.

After Palmer, a soft drizzle began. The temperature was rising. A gas station thermometer said 42 degrees. Hard to believe that the pre-dawn snow outside Tok had been only this morning; that last night it had been 17 below.

Just forty more miles. The outskirts of Anchorage ran full speed to meet us. Houses and stores, at first scattered, then clustered along the road. A four-lane road now, past the gates of Elmendorf Air Force Base, and the army base, Fort Richardson.

Suddenly, Duane Archer stopped the truck. A traffic light; the first since Seattle. And plenty of traffic to go with it. Lots of trucks, big, small, in between, hissing along through the drizzle. Quarter to three, on the afternoon before Thanksgiving. The sky a flat, pale gray. New construction, it seemed, at every corner.

"Anchor-town," Duane Archer said. "Christ, I've only been gone three weeks and half this shit wasn't here when I left."

3 Anchorage

In 1967, Tom and Marnie Brennan quit their jobs at the morning newspaper in Worcester, Massachusetts, and set out for Alaska, in search of freedom and adventure and whatever the future might bring.

They drove a brand-new International Harvester Travel-All, and were towing a houseboat on wheels, which they had just bought from a retired policeman for $1,500. Neither of them had been to Alaska before and neither knew anyone living there.

The trip took them six weeks, largely because the houseboat proved so difficult to tow. It would sway back and forth across the road, pulling the Travel-All with it. By the time they reached Chicago, Tom was drinking beer in the afternoons to steady his nerves as he drove. In the Black Hills of South Dakota they almost lost the houseboat over the edge of a cliff, and after that, Tom took to drinking beer in the mornings as well.

They drove to Edmonton, Alberta—already almost three thousand miles northwest of Worcester—and, beyond Edmonton, up past Westlock and north through Pibroch and Dapp and Jarvie and Fawcett and Flatbush and Chisholm; the flat western part of Alberta. Empty and bleak. North all the way to Lesser Slave Lake. Then west along the lakeshore, through Canyon Creek and Kinuso and Faust and Driftpile and into High Prairie: names that were like train whistles in the night. Up to McLennan and west again, across the plain, past Donnelly and Falher and Girouxville and Watino and Eaglesham and Codessa and on to Rycroft, where the road bent south; down through Woking and Sexsmith and Clairmont, and into Grande Prairie. Then west again: Wembley, Beaverlodge, Hythe, and Demmitt, to the British Columbia line. Then fifteen miles up to Pouce Coupe, and, just beyond it, Dawson Creek. And there, in Dawson Creek, they saw the sign: ALASKA HIGHWAY / MILE 0.

The real trip was about to begin.

Because of the houseboat, they were able to drive only fifteen miles an hour on the Alaska Highway. They were on the highway for twelve days. One thousand five hundred miles of two-lane road, of which the houseboat occupied a lane and one-third. More than a thousand of the miles were unpaved. Full of potholes and bumps, and shrouded in dust. Traffic was backed up behind them for miles. The houseboat bucked and plunged as if it had been set adrift in heavy seas. Dust covered everything: the inside of the houseboat, their belongings, themselves. With every bump, another dish would break, another lamp would fall over, another piece of furniture would slide across the houseboat floor. The dust obscured mountains, obscured the sky, obscured the road. For more than one thousand miles, in midsummer, they drove with their windows shut tight, because of the dust.

They reached Anchorage in the middle of August. They parked the houseboat at the Far North Trailer Park at Fifteenth and Debarr, which, at that time, was on the outskirts of the city. They got jobs at the big evening paper, the Anchorage *Times*. They proved to be very good at their work. Tom was soon offered the position of city editor. He declined, on the grounds that he did not yet know anything about the city. Marnie was offered the job of women's page editor. She accepted, figuring her knowledge of women was sufficient. They lived in the houseboat, at the trailer park, through the winter.

In addition to his reporting, Tom began to write a column about the Alaskan outdoors, which, as he had suspected, was quite different from the outdoors he had known in Massachusetts. He wrote about fishing for salmon, and hiking in the mountains, and flying in float planes, and moose hunting, and about his encounters with bears.

In spring, Tom and Marnie moved to a log cabin—a real log cabin—only a five-minute walk from downtown. Anchorage, Alaska: The Last Frontier. Five thousand miles from Massachusetts. It seemed to Tom and Marnie that their dream had come true. That they were pioneers. That adventure and freedom would always be theirs.

They towed the houseboat to a lake forty miles north of the city, to use on weekends. The following year they sold it to an accountant who had just moved up from North Dakota. He gave them $1,800, three hundred more than Tom and Marnie had paid. The accountant kept the houseboat for a year and then sold it for $2,400. By then, you see, the oil had been discovered and the boom was already underway.

The oil changed everything. It changed the whole state. Suddenly and drastically and permanently. Tom's and Marnie's were among the thousands of lives that it changed.

Tom had become the Anchorage *Times* man on the oil beat. The *Times* and its owner, Robert Atwood, were very much in favor of oil development. Atwood, actually, was in favor of development of any kind. He had come to Alaska in the 1930s and had married the daughter of the wealthiest banker in the state. He had taken over the newspaper when there were fewer than 3,000 people in the city. Now he wanted Anchorage to become at least Minneapolis, if not Chicago, in his lifetime. He wanted a million people in Anchorage. This had become an obsession. Oil development, therefore, was to be encouraged, because oil development would cause Anchorage to grow. Atwood had, it was said, felt much the same about World War II.

The Anchorage *Times* covered the oil companies the way *Osservatore Romano* wrote about the activities of the Pope. And it was under Tom's by-line that many of the biggest stories appeared. Thus, it was not surprising that when the oil was discovered at Prudhoe Bay, Atlantic Richfield, which owned 49 percent of it, offered Tom a public relations job.

He accepted. He figured covering the oil beat for the Anchorage *Times* was like working for an oil company anyway, and if he was going to work for an oil company, it might as well be for oil company wages. This was at a time in Alaska's history when many of its residents were trading in outmoded notions of adventure and romance in return for a substantially higher standard of living.

Tom lost weight and stopped smoking cigars and began to drink Fresca with his lunch instead of beer. He put his flannel shirts in a closet and bought some new suits and neckties. Soon he had to stop drinking coffee and start taking pills for his stomach. His hair began to turn gray. Within five years, he was Atlantic Richfield's director of public relations for Alaska.

Tom and Marnie had two children and moved out of the log cabin and into a bigger house a block away. From their living room they had a view of the park strip, and of Cook Inlet beyond it, and of Mount Susitna across the inlet, and, on clear days, of Mount McKinley, 170 miles to the north.

Tom was given a big corner office in the new ARCO building. Out his window he could see the Chugach Mountains and the inlet and all the new construction downtown. The office was only a ten-minute walk from the house, which was helpful, because Anchorage traffic was getting thick.

Tom traveled frequently, both within and out of the state. More and more he seemed to find himself in Houston and Denver and Chicago, as well as Seattle. And there were regular trips to Atlantic Richfield headquarters in Los Angeles.

But he and Marnie were putting money in the bank, so that someday they could buy a piece of land out of town. A place for weekends, where someday they might be able to build a little cabin. Some place they could go to, every so often, in order to escape the pressures of Tom's job and the fast pace of big-city life.

You just never know. You come to Alaska in search of freedom and adventure and whatever the future might bring. Sometimes the future brings oil.

I called Tom from Duane Archer's house, and he came to pick me up in early evening. We went up the Seward Highway toward downtown. Tom drove the old green Travel-All; the same vehicle in which he had come out from Massachusetts. Even after ten years in Alaska it still ran.

For a few miles, the Seward Highway was six lanes wide, the only six-lane highway in the state. I gave Tom the short version of my life and he gave me the short version of his. The Travel-All swayed from side to side as if it still had the houseboat behind it. Ahead, I could see city lights glowing in the dark evening sky.

We drove past the Atlantic Richfield building, its corporate insignia shining blue. Next to it was the headquarters of Phillips Petroleum; that corporate emblem a bright orange. The house was only a few blocks away, on a quiet street, which, in the dark, seemed as if it might have been in a suburb in the East.

Tom showed me to my room: a chilly front bedroom downstairs. I brought my things in from the Travel-All and piled them up in a closet and on the floor. I gave Tom a country ham and a bottle of Irish whiskey that I had brought with me from the East. He took off his jacket and loosened his tie and asked if I wanted a drink. He said Marnie and the kids would be home soon. It was as if he had just got off the 6:11 from Grand Central. The whole scene could easily have been taking place in Scarsdale. But in the morning I would be able to look out my window and see Alaska.

Thanksgiving morning. I took a long walk downtown. A low gray sky obscured the mountains. Cook Inlet seemed a slab of cold steel. There were ravens overhead and in the streets. The temperature was 28 degrees. A damp, raw day. Snow was expected by afternoon.

Tom and Marnie lived at the edge of the park strip, which was the edge of downtown. I walked to Fourth Avenue, the main street. There were very few people; very few cars. The Anchorage *Times* building, painted white; a couple of fur shops; some souvenir stores; a few banks—the Alaska Bank of Commerce, the National Bank of Alaska, the First National Bank of Anchorage, the Alaska National Bank of the North. A Woolworth's, a post office, a movie theater. Everything seemed sterile and deserted. As if it were not just shut down for Thanksgiving, but as if everyone who worked here had permanently fled.

The only place open seemed to be the Milke Way. A pink neon sign: CONEY ISLAND HOT DOGS. Five thousand miles from Coney Island. Next door there was a bar that was closed. A sign in the window said: RAINIER ON TAP, 75¢ A GLASS. In Anchorage, even in the mid-seventies, seventy-five cents for a glass of beer was such a bargain that they put a sign in the window to proclaim it.

Further down the street, by the Army-Navy store and the bail-bond office and the adult bookstore and the pawnshops, there was some action. Here the bars were open. The Eskimo and Indian bars. Goldie's, the Montana Club, bars like that. You could smell the stale beer and piss a block away. These bars did not close until five o'clock in the morning and opened again at eight. Even today; on Thanksgiving. Outside them, Natives leaned against walls, or lurched about aimlessly, looks of utter, sodden confusion on their faces.

Across the street from the Native bars, a new McDonald's was being built, the first in Alaska. The Anchorage *Times* was proud of this McDonald's, and hoped, editorially, for many more.

I cut down to Third Avenue, past fur shops, a travel agency, a car-rental agency, and the Anchorage Westward Hotel, which was the biggest in the city. It soon would be sold to a Native corporation. The federal government had given the Natives millions of acres of land and tens of millions of dollars, to prevent them from suing to block construction of the pipeline. Now Native corporations were buying up real estate and hotels and fish canneries all over the state, and beyond. One Eskimo corporation recently had announced plans to build a resort hotel in Hawaii.

I walked west along Third Avenue, back toward the inlet, past a small white house that was the office of Walter Hickel, once the governor of Alaska and Richard Nixon's secretary of the interior. Now he was back in Alaska, a rich and aggressive developer who wanted to be governor again.

I walked down a steep hill and into a section of private homes and condominiums, the most expensive part of a very expensive town. This was the section closest to the inlet, the section where the 1964 earthquake had hit hardest. The earthquake had torn up a lot of downtown. Further south, along the coast, it had been worse. Entire villages had been destroyed.

The construction by the inlet all seemed new. A lot of stained wood and plate glass. Big windows facing the inlet, pretending to be southern California.

It was eleven o'clock in the morning, and as light now as it was going to get. I was the only person on the street. Five minutes from the center of the city. It did not seem that anyone else was alive, much less awake.

I climbed back up a hill to Fifth Avenue, the other main street, along with Fourth. At the end of it there stood the Captain Cook Hotel, the big downtown hotel that was owned by Walter Hickel. A new addition would soon be built by the Hickel Construction Company, which was owned by Walter Hickel's brother. A block away, the Hickels were putting up a sixteen-story condominium, in which apartments would sell for $125,000 and up.

The Captain Cook was named, as was the inlet, for the British explorer. The outside of the hotel was the color of mustard that had spoiled. It did not blend well with the dark gray sky. I walked back toward the park strip, toward Tom and Marnie's house. The ravens were cawing and the wind was picking up. The inlet seemed even bleaker than before. The sky appeared to press closer to the ground.

The park strip was one block wide and fifteen blocks long, separating Ninth Avenue from Tenth. There were tennis courts, and a skating rink, and a shiny black locomotive for children to play on. In summer, there were band concerts, and people played softball and threw Frisbees and barbecued hamburgers and drank beer and flew kites. There was a soccer league which played its games on the park strip in summer. Yugoslavians, many of them cab drivers, wearing brightly striped shirts, shouting curses at the referees.

In winter, with darkness at two-thirty, the park strip was used for cross-country skiing and for the walking of dogs and for running, by people in sweat suits who wore scarves around their mouths against the cold.

Most years, by Thanksgiving there was snow on the ground. But this year, the park strip was colorless and dead; frozen hard. I walked quickly across it. The day was barely light enough for cars to get around without their headlights. Eleven o'clock. That would be four o'clock in the afternoon in the East. Time for Thanksgiving dinner if I were home.

Marnie cooked a turkey and a dozen people came to dinner, and, afterwards, the kids played and the grown-ups sang songs by the fire, but there seemed something strained and forced about the day. As if Thanksgiving in Alaska were artificial. Possibly it was because Alaska was so far from Plymouth Rock; or because a hundred years passed from the first Thanksgiving before Alaska was even discovered by the Russians. Or, maybe, just because Thanksgiving was a day for old towns, for home towns, and Anchorage was almost nobody's real home town.

I stayed in Anchorage for a week. The weather cleared; the temperature dropped. To zero, to 10 below. The Chugach Mountains came into view, rising abruptly, ten miles to the east of the city. The sunlight slanted in flat and hard, like a tackler in a football game. The sun was low on the southern horizon even at noon. You would meet someone downtown for a quick, early lunch and it would be dark by the time you were finished.

One thing I noticed quickly was that Alaska was almost an obsession to many of the people living there. It was not simply a place in which they happened to reside: it was a loved one, a family member, by which their emotions were monopolized; about which they fretted and dreamed.

Alaskans thought about Alaska, and talked about it, all the time. The world beyond its borders was called Outside—spelled, even in the newspapers, with a capital O. It was a world which Alaskan residents had willingly left behind, and what happened there now did not concern them, except insofar as a given event might somehow have an effect upon Alaska.

This seemed a unique phenomenon. One would not, for example, while wandering the streets of Toledo, expect to encounter such deep introspection concerning the meaning and essence of Ohio.

Anchorage was a boom town, nervous and greedy, afraid that the music would stop, afraid that the money would run out. A town of Texans and Teamsters and pickup trucks, bars and liquor stores, pawnshops and guns, country music, massage parlors, Baptist churches, public drunkenness, and an alarming rate of automobile accidents. But there were new restaurants, too, with wine lists and fresh flowers on the table. And new office buildings rising fast. With the oil had come the professional classes— lawyers and stockbrokers and real estate developers—grinning and bearing it; putting up with the winters; cashing in.

There had not even been an Anchorage until 1915. It had been founded as a labor camp, a tent city, a supply center for the railroad that was being built between Fairbanks, 400 miles north, in the interior, and Seward, 150 miles south, on the coast.

As one who came from a section of the Northeast that was steeped in three hundred years of American history, it was a shock for me to realize how close to its roots, to its origin, Anchorage was. For example: *the first white woman ever to have lived in Anchorage was still alive.* Nellie Brown. Living in a nursing home up in Palmer. Pretty far gone now, and deeply into the booze, so one would not gain much from talking to her, but she was the equivalent—chronologically, at least—of a Pilgrim who had reached the New World aboard the *Mayflower*.

As late as the start of World War II, there had been fewer than 3,000 people in Anchorage. Then the military arrived, and, after the war, commercial aviation, as Anchorage proved to be a convenient refueling point for planes that were flying the polar route. Then there was Alaskan statehood in 1959, and the discovery of oil at Prudhoe Bay ten years later, touching off the current pipeline boom, and that was the history of Anchorage.

To be in Anchorage was, in that sense, like being in Boston prior to the Revolutionary War; one had the feeling that one was a part of the prologue; that the real history was yet to be written.

The joke was—and I heard it at least a dozen times during the first week I spent in the city—that the best thing about Anchorage was that it was only half an hour from Alaska. When in Anchorage, in other words, you might as well be in Albuquerque; but get in your car, or, better yet, in your private plane equipped with floats or skis, and within thirty minutes you could reach country wilder than any that 99 percent of the American people would ever see.

Anchorage was a city that had got a late start; now it was trying to catch up all at once, skipping about two hundred years. It was poised on the edge, between its past, which was not much, and a future which was expected to be everything. Poised also between the "real Alaska," or, at least, rural Alaska, and the cosmopolitan capitals of the world.

From Anchorage International Airport, for example, one could fly nonstop to London, Paris, Tokyo, Frankfurt, Zurich. But also to places like Bethel and Barrow and King Salmon and Kotzebue. Places that were not reached by any road. Places that had zip codes but not necessarily running water. Places from which

Anchorage seemed impossibly civilized and sophisticated; not an outpost at the edge of a frontier, but, in fact, the very center of the universe.

One morning, I heard a traffic report on the radio. The report was delivered by a man in a helicopter, a demonstration of how modern and big-time Anchorage had become. But it was still a city very close to the edge. On this morning, for instance, the man in the helicopter said that traffic was backed up on the Glenn Highway east of town, due to a collision. A collision between a pickup truck and a bear.

4   The First Day North

The alarm went off at five-thirty. I dressed quickly but carefully, trying to remember every layer. Long underwear first, top and bottom. Cotton socks, then heavy woolen socks. Then I went to the bathroom and brushed my teeth. Too early to shave. Too cold and too dark. I didn't want to get wet; didn't want to be any more awake than I had to be. Back to the bedroom. Jeans on over the thermal underwear. Then a flannel shirt, and a woolen shirt over that. My Pendleton wool shirt from Eddie Bauer. Check for mittens, notebooks, sharpened pencils. Not pens. In Fairbanks, in December, ball-point pens had a tendency to freeze.

I stepped into my Snowpacks and went out into the dark to start the Travel-All. There were a couple of inches of fresh snow on the ground, squeaking against the soles of the boots.

The Travel-All was parked on the street, fifty feet in front of Tom and Marnie's house. There was an electric heater attached to the engine block. A short cord that led from the heater was connected to a long extension cord that ran from the basement of the house to the curb. The Travel-All had been plugged in overnight, in order that it might start in the morning. This arrangement was quite common in Anchorage.

The engine started easily. There was heavy frost on the windshield. I put the defroster on and went back inside to drink some juice. In the bedroom I laced the Snowpacks up tight, and slipped into my Eddie Bauer maximum-strength, ultimate, super-warm Arctic parka. It had a hood with fur around the edge. When the parka was zipped tight and the hood was pulled forward all the way, there was created, for three or four inches in front of the nose, a little tunnel that warmed the air before you breathed it. Not necessary, or even desirable, at zero or 5 below, but in Fairbanks, in December, who could tell?

The Travel-All defroster was not working well. I scraped the windshield. At 6 a.m. in December there were no other headlights to be seen; no other house lights yet lit. It was still a clear and starry night. I put the Travel-All in gear. The tires made fresh tracks through the snow. The temperature was 3 below.

Out through Spenard. Not much traffic, even on Spenard Road, at 6 a.m. Spenard was the most raucous section of the city. The rowdiest bars. The highest concentration of massage parlors per square mile. The bars had been closed for an hour. The massage parlors had not. They were open twenty-four hours a day.

I reached the airport at six-twenty, parked and locked the Travel-All. The terminal was modern, brightly lit. There were glass cases containing stuffed moose, wolves, and bears. The lobby was almost empty: just one large, ragged cluster of men, mostly bearded, mostly overweight, and mostly dressed in flannel or woolen shirts. They were bunched around the gate from which the seven o'clock Wien Air Alaska flight to Fairbanks would depart. There were only two or three people in suits and ties. Only two or three women. Not exactly the Washington shuttle from La Guardia.

Wien Air Alaska was one of the two major airlines in the state, the other being Alaska Airlines, which flew mostly to southeastern Alaska and which, in fact, was based in Seattle. Wien did not fly to southeastern Alaska but went to almost all other parts of the state. It was the airline founded by the Wien brothers, immigrants from Minnesota, who were among the first people to fly airplanes in Alaska. It had been Noel Wien, in fact, who made the first flight ever from Anchorage to Fairbanks, in 1924, as aviation brought the concept of relativity to Alaska: space and time suddenly being perceived as less than absolute.

There was a rumor that the plane might not go. The weather in Fairbanks had been very cold, and ice fog had set in. No flights at all had made it yesterday. Only two or three the day before. Ice fog was produced when pollution in the air—particularly exhaust from motor vehicles—began to freeze and turned solid. This happened in Fairbanks when the temperature reached 35 or 40 below.

The plane did take off, half an hour late. A Boeing 727, with every seat filled. Some people had been trying to reach Fairbanks for several days.

It would have been possible to drive, of course: an all-day trip, over an icy, snowy, two-lane road, with only about four hours of daylight. Or it would have been possible to take the train. But in winter the train ran only two days a week and took twelve hours to get from Anchorage to Fairbanks—without problems. And in winter there were very few trips without problems. An avalanche, perhaps, or maybe a moose on the tracks. Moose liked the railroad tracks because they were kept plowed and it was easier for the animals to move along them than through the deep snow in the woods.

I wound up in a middle seat between two bearded men who reeked of alcohol. Immediately, they went to sleep. We flew north in the dark past Mount McKinley.

After forty-five minutes, the pilot came on the intercom. He said he was going to begin circling Fairbanks. If a break came in the fog, he would land. There was enough fuel to permit ninety minutes of circling. If he was not able to land in that time, we would return to Anchorage.

A first, faint gray light now appeared. My seatmate stirred and glanced out the window. The engines droned as the plane banked and turned once again.

"What do you think?"

"Fuck, I don't know. I don't even care, man. Either way, as long as we walk off this baby. I don't care if it's Fairbanks or Anchorage, or fucking Paris, France." He shut his eyes and went back to sleep.

Circling and circling and the pilot back on the intercom, saying twenty more minutes and we'll have to turn back, and the gray light stronger now, and seeing low hills, pine-covered, snow-covered, no signs of an actual city, and then a flat, impenetrable gray cloud beneath us: Fairbanks, the airport, the ice fog.

The No Smoking sign flashes on. There is a change in the pitch of the engines. The plane plunges into the fog. No visibility now, just the feeling of going down fast. High-pitched scream of the engines, a little tipping motion back and forth, seats into the full upright position, the gum chewers chewing a little faster, the arm-rest grippers gripping a little tighter, a sudden swirling gray outside the window, land right there, snow, pine trees, fog again, see nothing, then ground below, only ten feet below, five feet, inches, a bump, a roar, and the plane is down, fog all around, can't even see the terminal building, the pilot leaning on the reverse thrust to slow us on the bumpy, icy runway, blue lights flickering past, we're in Fairbanks.

A cheer goes up.

The pilot comes back on the intercom. Announces that the temperature in Fairbanks is 49 below.

At first, the cold was less of a shock than expected. With no wind, the fog, initially, asserted itself more. It was gritty, metallic: not so much an odor as a taste. A fog made not of moisture, but of microscopic particles of foulness; a blanket of frozen filth.

There was, at first, a sense of numbness rather than a feeling of being cold. With parka zipped tight, hood forward, and no wind, there was little direct contact with the cold. The difference from Anchorage—the difference between minus 3 and minus 49— seemed not so much physical, at first, as metaphysical. A deep chill in the marrow of the soul. A sense of not belonging; an awareness that this was not a part of the world—of the universe— that man was intended to inhabit.

I took a cab downtown. There was snow piled high on both sides of the road, much more than in Anchorage. If Anchorage had been the edge, then this seemed the capital, the heart, of the bleak and foreign world that lay beyond. The icy, fogbound essence of Alaska.

Neon glowed, then vanished in the fog. The cab inched toward downtown at no more than fifteen miles an hour. Already, my eyes stung from the poisonous fog and from the cold. Forty-nine below. At 9:30 a.m. It would not be light yet in Fairbanks even if there had not been any fog.

"Forty-nine below," the cab driver said. "That don't sound too bad if you say it fast enough."

Then he laughed. In Fairbanks, they made jokes about the cold. They were proud of it. It was their greatest natural resource.

The driver said he had kept the engine of his taxi running all night, parked outside his house.

"What does it cost me? Five bucks in gas? I'll make that back on this trip." A lot of the taxis in Fairbanks had not started this morning. At 49 below, even plugging in was not enough.

The thought occurred that this was, in a sense, nature fighting back. The cold was, after all, in Alaska, the strongest weapon nature had. With Fairbanks—with all of Alaska—under brutal technological assault, here, for the first time, was evidence that it would not succumb without a fight.

In this sort of cold you did not think of normal things—upset stomach, fatigue, financial problems, whether there was life after death. You were able to think only of the cold: it monopolized every facet of your being; like first love, or news of a death in the family. Actually, the first time, it was a marvelous novelty. For the visitor, the Arctic dilettante, the cold was fun.

The cab reached downtown. At least the driver said it was downtown. In the ice fog there was no way to be sure. There was a sense of multi-story buildings nearby, but you could not actually see them through the fog. There were supposed to be four hours and twenty-seven minutes of daylight in Fairbanks on this date, but with the ice fog there would not be any daylight at all.

Out of the cab, it was as if I were no longer on earth, but on a distant, foreign planet; a planet that was much farther from the sun.

The pipeline public relations office was one flight up, in a shabby old building across the street from the Chena Bar. That was the one sign I could read through the ice fog. A neon sign. Chena Bar. With only the *R*—the last letter—lit. CHENA BAR. ENTERTAINMENT NIGHTLY. GIRLS GIRLS GIRLS.

In the office, there was classical music on an FM radio station, the University of Alaska campus station. They were playing Rachmaninoff. At 49 below, with the *R* of CHENA BAR flashing pink. In Fairbanks, in winter, they played a lot of music by Russian composers.

A pipeline public relations man was going to drive me to Pump Station Eight, so I could see how the pipeline would work. This was something I had arranged in Anchorage the week before. The public relations man was not happy. He was sick of Pump Station Eight, sick of the pipeline, sick of leading writers and photographers around by the nose. Besides, he was tired and cold: he had been up most of the night with his girlfriend in Anchorage, flying back to Fairbanks on the plane which I took; having to come back only because I was coming. Before the pipeline, he had worked for the Fairbanks newspaper. The pipeline was getting them all: the newsmen, the policemen, the short-order cooks. The trap was, first you fell in love with Alaska; then you had to work for the enemy— for the pipeline, for the oil companies, for the forces that were destroying what you loved—just to be able to remain.

For the PR man, all this would be over in a year. Then he would be able to move to London and to live for a year without even having to work. Just living off the money he was making now. But that would be next year. This was now. Forty-nine below. Heavy ice fog. And he had to drive, once again, out to Pump Station Eight, instead of remaining in his office with Rachmaninoff.

We rode for ten minutes, then went up a slight grade toward what turned out to be the edge of town. Suddenly it was a brilliant, clear day. A beautiful day. Soft, rolling hills, studded with evergreens, through the snow. The sky so bright it was painful. The sun, in late morning, low on the horizon to the south. Open land, uninhabited, rolling free, toward the sky, in all directions. From ice fog to no ice fog instantaneously. As if someone had pushed a projector button and changed a slide.

Pump Station Eight was thirty miles out of town, and still under construction. There were 170 men there working twelve hours a day, seven days a week, eight weeks at a stretch, then two weeks off. Earning up to $2,500 a week.

The pipeline was going to run almost 800 miles, from Prudhoe Bay, in the Arctic, to Valdez. There were going to be twelve pump stations along the way. The oil would flow in, get pumped, flow out. Something like that. To tell the truth, it was the cold I was interested in, more than the pipeline.

It was 35 below at Pump Station Eight. The sun was shining. We ate lunch, Polish sausage and rice, in a bright plastic cafeteria. Lots of pastry and pie for dessert. Liquor and drugs were supposedly prohibited in pipeline camps, and the workers were fed sweets instead.

After lunch, I climbed some winding metal stairs to the top

of an oil-storage tank. It was the highest point for miles around. Thirty-five below, a slight wind starting to rise, and, from the top of the tank, I could see the distant, flat sun setting over far-away mountains. There was a bright orange glare, then the onset of twilight, and a quick blue darkening of the pine trees and the snow. Then cold and stillness everywhere. Except for the machinery in the foreground. Except for the pipeline.

My feet got cold, even in the Snowpacks. I went back inside to the pump station manager's office. He was eating a cream-filled chocolate-covered doughnut. And why not? It had been almost an hour since his lunch. He smiled at me, at my red nose and at the frost on my hair. He offered a doughnut. I declined. He took another. The buttons of his flannel shirt were stretched tight across a stomach that had not been there, in such dimension, a few months earlier. He had a good job. As part of management, he did not have to live in the barracks. He drove back and forth to Fairbanks every day, one of the more exotic commuting routes in North America. He explained to me how the pipeline was a miracle of modern technology. He was quite sincere, quite proud of the work he was doing. I had met army officers like him in Vietnam. The pipeline, he told me, would be able to withstand an earthquake that registered eight on the Richter scale; it would be 99 percent operable even if hit by an earthquake that registered nine. Every valve on every pump could be remote-controlled from Valdez. He went into great detail about the purpose and function and virtual perfection of Pump Station Eight. Quite clearly, he had long ago convinced himself. Now he just about convinced me. What the hell, for eight billion dollars it should work.

But eighteen months later, when the first oil would finally flow toward Valdez, it would be here, at Pump Station Eight, that the most serious mishap would occur. Someone would forget to throw a switch, and the mechanical backup system would fail, too, and a spark would ignite oil and the whole place would blow sky high. The whole pump station. One man would be killed, a dozen would be injured, and thousands of gallons of oil would spill out, across the tundra.

It was dark now, and colder. The manager had work to get back to. My tour guide was eager to leave. We returned to Fairbanks at high speed. Through clear, brilliant night air; then, suddenly, back into the fog; swirling, stinking, bitter fog. I would be tasting it in the back of my throat for a week.

We parked behind the pipeline office, across from the Chena Bar, which, by now, was filled with drinkers. Fairbanks was a sub-Arctic blue-collar town. A town—even more so than Anchorage—of Teamsters and drunkards and pimps. And a lot of people getting rich quick. The population had gone from 12,000 to 60,000 in three years. Two-bedroom apartments were renting for $700 a month. There was virtually no police force left in the city. The cops had all quit to work pipeline security, at four and five times their previous wage. There were drugs and whores and trailer camps, and disputes among residents were less likely to be settled in small-claims court than by small-caliber—or large-caliber—pistol. Compared to Fairbanks, Anchorage seemed like San Francisco.

The pipeline man drove me to the airport, slowly, carefully, through the fog. It had warmed up to 46 below. No telling if the plane would get in.

The airport was a madhouse. People trapped by the ice fog had been trying to get out for days. And discovering that trying to get out of Fairbanks could drive you much crazier than simply not being able to get in.

My luck held. My plane came in, and I got my seat. A middle seat again, but I did not complain. There were people at the gate offering two hundred dollars for boarding passes. For a seat which cost forty-six dollars.

I was back in Anchorage by dinnertime, feeling like I had just returned to earth. It was only 5 below at the airport and the air was clear and I walked to the Travel-All with my parka unzipped.

5 Prudhoe Bay

The weather stayed clear; the temperature dropped. Down to 19 below, which is just about as cold as Anchorage gets. I did a lot of walking, between downtown and Tom and Marnie's house, and, even at those temperatures, I perspired inside my Eddie Bauer parka when it was zipped.

Tom returned from a trip to Los Angeles, where the temperature had been 86 above, and, the next morning, I flew with him to Prudhoe Bay. We flew north in daylight and this time I saw Mount McKinley. From the ground, in Anchorage, it had been a glowing pink triangle on the horizon; now it rushed up to meet us, massive and white.

Until McKinley, I had never gotten very excited about flying past a mountain in an airplane; it had always seemed like looking at a postcard of a mountain. McKinley was different: not graceful and elegant like the Matterhorn, but more a big defensive tackle of a mountain. A mighty spike, driven through the heart of the state. The Indians had named it Denali, which means The Great One. Then white men had come along and renamed it in honor of a Republican politician from Ohio who never had been more than a thousand feet above sea level in his life.

I stopped talking to Tom and pressed my face against the window. The morning sun was lighting the mountain white, but even through the plane I felt its chill. The plane kept moving but the mountain did not seem to go away. It was so big that it stayed with us for most of that first part of the trip. Only very gradually, very slowly, did it recede; very slowly, very gradually, we moved beyond it, beyond its field of force, toward Fairbanks.

The temperature in Fairbanks was 50 below and the ice fog impenetrable. We circled and circled. Frost glistened on trees; the sun was light brown through the fog. We circled for an hour, then the pilot gave up, and flew on toward Deadhorse, another hour to the north, the airfield that served Prudhoe Bay.

Tom told me a story about some people he knew in Cordova who had decided to spend a weekend shopping in Anchorage. Cordova is a fishing village on Alaska's southern coast, another place with no road in or out, so the couple took the Alaska Airlines flight to Anchorage, planning to return the next day. On the way back, however, Cordova was fogged in and the plane continued to its next regular stop, which was Yakutat. There was bad weather in Yakutat too, however, so there was no choice but to proceed to Juneau. Things in Juneau were even worse, so the pilot tried Sitka, the next port of call, and, when unable to land there either, flew on to Seattle, which was the flight's final destination. It seemed, however, that the weather in Seattle was very bad, and planes were getting in only after hours of circling. A bit low on fuel now, the pilot continued south to Portland, which, normally, was not even within Alaska Airlines' realm, and, even there, conditions were unsatisfactory. So, with no choice really, he flew on to the closest airport large enough to accommodate his plane at which he could be certain of good weather. And the couple from Cordova, who had only wanted to visit a couple of Anchorage department stores, wound up in Reno, Nevada.

Shortly after noon, we crossed the Brooks Range. And if McKinley had sent a chill into the plane, the Brooks Range threatened virtual frostbite. This was the most northerly mountain range in the world, the emptiest, least charted, least visited mountain wilderness on the continent. An endless choppy sea of mountains. Thousands of identical snow-covered ridges; jagged peaks, both unclimbed and unnamed. Slanting every which way, at odd angles, to the horizon on both sides of the plane. Stretching, it appeared, to the edge of infinity. Seeming themselves, perhaps, infinity's beginning.

These were mountains so remote that few within Alaska had ever seen them. So distant that few outside the state had even heard the name of the range. Unlike the Alps or the Andes, which have been inhabited for thousands of years, these mountains seemed as isolated as the surface of Mars.

Only a thin band of pink-orange light remained of the day. The ridges smoothed and flattened. We passed over the northern edge of the range. Now, not just McKinley and the huge Alaska Range; not just Fairbanks and the vast interior; now even the Brooks Range lay behind us. We had reached the North Slope: the final hundred miles of the continent; spreading north from the Brooks Range to the sea. That part of North America which could make you believe that the earth was indeed flat and that, at last, you had come to its edge.

Then the light was totally gone. We had left it behind to the south. We were north of all light now, in the realm of Arctic night. It would be another eight weeks here before the sun would rise again.

It was crowded, noisy, and hot inside the little wooden shack that served as the Deadhorse air terminal. And thick, as was most of the Alaskan indoors, with cigarette smoke. There were a couple of broken vending machines, and a window, closed for the weekend, which said Alaska National Bank of the North. When they called themselves Bank of the North they really meant it. The oilfield workers cashed their paychecks here before they left on vacation. To get bar money and whore money for Anchorage and Fairbanks. So they would not be bored while waiting for their flights to Honolulu or Acapulco, or Paris, France.

There were dozens of workers waiting to go to Anchorage on the plane which Tom and I had just left, but only a few were able to board. Most of the seats remained filled by passengers who had been unable to get off at Fairbanks. Some of the workers had been waiting four and five days in the crowded, noisy wooden shack;

days they had intended to spend in the sunshine; on the beach. They, too, were trapped by the Fairbanks fog.

We found a van that was going to ARCO base camp. We rode into the dark and all the flat land looked the same. There was nothing above the level of the ground that had not been built by man within the previous ten years.

The camp was like a brand-new college dormitory, or American officers' quarters at one of the big bases in Vietnam. Private rooms to sleep in, with each two rooms sharing a bath. Clean linen, hot water, and toilets in perfect working order. Free ice cream and soda machines in the lobby, and trays of pastry piled high. Men who were between shifts lounged around in flannel shirts, reading copies of magazines that featured pictures of women with no clothes on. Waiting for dinner. Waiting to see what that night's movie would be. Waiting for the next shift to begin.

We checked in with a guard at a desk. Tom got me a pass that I had to wear clipped to my parka at all times, so people could tell I wasn't a spy from Exxon, or something like that.

Normally, visitors to Prudhoe Bay were not permitted to stay overnight. They flew in before lunch, got the tour, and were flown out again before dinner. It was just too much of a nuisance, Tom said, and too expensive, to have visitors stay overnight. To feed and house one man for one day and one night at Prudhoe Bay cost Atlantic Richfield $165.

We drove in a small truck up a road that led away from the base camp. After a couple of miles, Tom said, "That's it." He had just driven off the edge of the continent. We were on the ice of the Beaufort Sea, which was a part of the Arctic Ocean. We drove eight miles out onto the ice. The truck was equipped with a radio so we could contact someone in case it broke down.

I was wearing my insulated rubber boots—the warmest ones—and had brought along my down pants. Tom stopped the truck and we got out and started to walk. There were chunks of ice sticking up five or six feet into the air; the pressure of freezing had squeezed the ice into bumps. It was 55 below, with a twenty-knot wind; the chill factor was 90 below. I wore a woolen face mask and pulled my parka hood forward as far as it would go. This cut down on visibility, but with the wind that strong there was no choice. Besides, there was little to see. I was more conscious of the sounds: my rubber boots crunching and squeaking on the dry snow which covered the ice; the distant hum of the ARCO machinery to the south; the hissing of my breath as I walked. My feet were perfectly warm, probably even sweating, though in ordinary shoes, or even ordinary snow boots or hiking boots, I would already have suffered frostbite.

We walked for maybe twenty minutes. On the surface of the frozen Arctic Ocean. In the dark, with stars out, at three o'clock in the afternoon, which was like midnight. Like midnight, perhaps, in outer space.

You cannot walk fast in all that bulky clothing, and you do not want to anyway, because if you start breathing too quickly the air does not have a chance to warm up in the little tunnel created by your parka and you can wind up with frosted lungs. It is not difficult to cope with the cold as long as you take adequate precautions, but there is no such thing as a small mistake. You forget one minor point and it can kill you. Everything must be done with great care, in orderly fashion. As in walking on the surface of the moon. You remember: I do this, and then this, and now this. Not in a natural rhythm, but in a slow, awkward, space-suit sort of way.

I remembered hearing about the soldier who had gone on winter maneuvers outside of Fairbanks. He had brought along a flask to keep him warm. He unscrewed the cap, took a gulp at 50 below, and dropped dead, his throat frozen shut. The alcohol had kept the liquid from freezing at that temperature, but the liquid, at 50 below, had produced the opposite of the desired warming effect.

We turned and walked back to the truck, using the faint lights of the base camp as a guide. It would be easy to get lost, walking on the frozen ocean in the dark. Easy to wind up heading away from shore, toward the North Pole. People had made it over the top, from Alaska to Norway, by dog sled. But on foot, with no food and unarmed, you would not get far; in addition to the cold, there were polar bears.

The truck motor was still running. We followed a bulldozer road back to shore, and reached base camp in time for dinner. Steak and potatoes beneath fluorescent lights; with five kinds of steak sauce, and three kinds of mustard on the table, and plenty of coffee and pastry and ice cream for dessert.

There was something so bizarre, so unnatural about it that I had no appetite. These men, stuffing themselves with pastry and money, at the edge of the earth. They were paid up to $2,000 a week, plus room and board, yet they rioted in the dining hall when informed that steak and lobster would henceforth be served on alternate nights, instead of both at the same meal.

For the first time since I had boarded the ferry in Seattle, I felt that I was no longer in touch with Alaska. Prudhoe Bay seemed in no sense except the geographic to be a part of it. This was just a lot of machinery hauled up and plopped down on the permafrost to make as much money as possible as quickly as it could. And the men were here only to make sure the machinery did its job. Alaska was not part of their dream. It had never been, for them, a goal, a destination; a frontier for them to explore as they explored new levels of themselves. It was just like Saudi Arabia, Indonesia, East Texas, the North Sea—a place under which oil happened to be. They were an occupying army, bloodless mercenaries, and in twenty years they would have all the oil sucked up and pumped south and their machinery would be taken away, or, if it seemed more economical, left to sit there, forever. It would not rot: things did not decompose in such weather. It was much too cold and too dry for rust. A discarded oil barrel would sit for hundreds of years; a scar in the tundra made by a bulldozer would not disappear for a century. This was, I reminded myself, the same technological mentality which had required astronauts to leave their garbage bags on the moon.

After dinner we drove down to where an oil rig was actually in operation, and I climbed up an icy metal ladder in the dark to a platform about a hundred feet above the ground, where a crew was changing the bit on a drill.

A problem with drilling for oil is that the bit of the drill becomes dull from grinding down through rock and ice, and must be changed after only a few hours of operation. The bit is at the bottom of many lengths of hollow pipe which are fitted together to form a long tube through which the oil can be pumped when the deposit is finally reached. The further down you get, the more lengths of pipe you have to use, and the longer it takes to change the bit. You have to pull up length after length of the pipe, disconnect one from another, and stack the lengths on the platform until you finally get to the bit itself. Then you remove the bit, put on a new one, lower it, and begin to replace the sections of pipe, each of which is about eight feet in length. It can take twenty-four hours—two complete twelve-hour shifts—to change the bit. Then, after as little as an hour and a half of drilling, you have to shut down and change it again.

I stood on the back of the platform for a while and tried not to get hit by the pieces of heavy pipe that were swinging around. There was a crane operator lifting the pipe, and a man on the platform disconnecting it. That would be his job for twelve hours —to disconnect the eight-foot lengths and stack them; a hundred feet off the ground; in darkness, except for the platform floodlights, and with the temperature 50 below and wind blowing. You need a couple of chocolate doughnuts after coming off a shift like that.

The chief driller was also on the platform. He is the man who operates the whole business when the bit is on. He is like the chief pilot for an airline, or a chief surgeon: his world is his fingertips and his brains. The good ones are said to be able to know just what is happening thousands of feet below the ground, just from their sense of touch, and can do all sorts of magical things to get the most oil out fastest.

This chief driller was from Mobile, Alabama, and planned to use his pipeline money to buy a string of condominiums on the coast of the Gulf of Mexico. He was complaining about the Eskimos. The oil companies tried to hire a lot of Eskimos so they would not be accused of racism or of not giving job opportunities to Alaskans, and the Eskimos were making a thousand dollars a week and most of them hadn't seen a thousand dollars in their whole lives before and it was destroying them. They would leave for their six days off—after eight days on—and not come back for six months. Or maybe only three months, depending on how long it took them to drink up the money they had earned. Back in their villages they could buy enough booze to send the whole place on a binge for a week, and often did, and everybody got sick and miserable, and sunk a little deeper into Eskimo existential despair, which is a bad and bottomless pit made deeper fast by alcohol; and now alcohol was available all the time because white man's money would buy it, and here, Prudhoe Bay, was a place to make all the money in the world.

So the Texans—and the guys from Shreveport and Tulsa and Mobile—who weren't particularly predisposed to like people with brown skin in the first place, saw these Eskimos not showing up and then not working when they did show up, and they didn't like it. And the thing was, the chief driller said, you couldn't fire the sons of bitches. It was damned hard to fire an Eskimo, the way they would file grievances and all, and with the requirement that a certain percentage of the people on the job had to be Natives, which up on the North Slope meant Eskimos. It was easier to keep them around, even if they would be late for their shift or want to quit early. They just didn't follow regimentation. Eskimos ticked to a different kind of clock, the chief driller said, and so there were all sorts of bad feelings.

Whaling season was the worst. In spring and fall, they would just up and take off for Barrow or Point Hope and might not come back for a month; not until the season was over and the whale meat all gone. Whaling season was their big event of the year; the pipeline could wait. The oil had been there for thousands of years; let it sit; there were, after all, only a few weeks a year to get a whale.

Sunday morning we went out to see the frozen barges. The barges had gotten stuck the previous August, when the polar ice pack had moved back toward shore sooner than expected. There were only about six weeks a year when the permanent polar ice moved offshore enough to let barges through. During this period, ARCO had tried to bring in tens of millions of dollars' worth of pipeline and Prudhoe Bay equipment. But the ice had moved to shore sooner than usual, and the barges had been frozen in place for the winter, which meant until the following July. Trucks had to drive out on the ice to the barges and unload them as new materials were needed. We climbed around the top deck of a barge, which offered just about the highest elevation available on the North Slope, except for drilling rigs.

The barges were like ghost ships. Like something the Ancient Mariner might have known. There were papers still on desks, frozen coffee still in paper cups. At 11 a.m., with the sky clear, and the snow reflecting what little light there was, the day was not completely dark. Even in December, there were a couple of hours a day when something much like twilight came into the sky, although the sun stayed below the horizon. From the top of the barge I could see the faint outline of the beginning of the Brooks Range, almost a hundred miles to the south.

Next, we drove to the headquarters of British Petroleum, the company which owned the other 51 percent of Prudhoe Bay. The BP operation was even fancier than ARCO's. BP actually had women in their base camp, working as secretaries and so forth. They also had a tree, and some plants, which they were trying to grow beneath a glass roof. And they had a heated swimming pool, glass-enclosed.

It must have seemed like such a stroke of genius to some vice-president back in London: *We'll put in a bloody heated pool!* The furthest-north swimming pool and the furthest-north tree in the world.

Well, they were. But the tree looked sickly and bent and forlorn, all alone under its glass roof, and, we were told, nobody ever wanted to go swimming. After coming off a twelve-hour shift at 50 below they just wanted to eat pastry and lie in their beds and look at dirty magazines and figure how many days until this stretch would be over, and how big the next check would be. Only once in a while, we were told, did somebody with a desk job fall into the pool by mistake.

6 Barrow

On Sunday afternoon, Tom and I flew from Prudhoe Bay to Barrow in a twin-engine Atlantic Richfield plane. We flew two hundred miles west, along the empty Arctic coast, in total darkness. The sun had set on November 18 and would not reappear until January 23. There was nothing to see out the window: no lights, no signs of habitation, no signs of life. In the winter darkness it was not even possible to distinguish the coastline. From the Brooks Range to the northern horizon and beyond, there was nothing but flatness and emptiness; ice and snow; darkness and cold.

Barrow was all alone; set apart; as far out on the edge as a place could be. Lying 330 miles above the Arctic Circle, it was Alaska's—and America's—northernmost settlement. With a population of 3,000, 90 percent of which was Eskimo, it was also the largest Eskimo community in the world.

"On Barrow's left," began a description in a Federal Writers Project book about Alaska, "is Siberia; on its right Arctic Canada and Greenland. Facing it are Leningrad, Stockholm, Oslo and London—on the other side of the Polar Mediterranean, the last of the Northern Hemisphere's great inland seas to await the coming of industrial civilization."

From Anchorage, Barrow had seemed even more foreign and remote than Anchorage had from New York City. Very few Alaskans had ever been there, and talking to Anchorage residents about Barrow was the equivalent of asking a citizen of Rio de Janeiro about some obscure river village up the Amazon. As nearly as I could determine, not even the two Anchorage newspapers had ever sent a reporter to Barrow. It was just too far away, too expensive to get to, and, from the perspective of Anchorage—which was the perspective of half the population of the state—there simply did not seem any reason to go.

From the perspective of Prudhoe Bay, however, a trip to Barrow was the essence of high adventure: a journey from the twenty-first century to the nineteenth; from illusion to reality; from the antiseptic soullessness of the ARCO and British Petroleum base camps to an authentic Arctic Eskimo whaling village, which might even turn out to be—who could tell?—the real Alaska that Alaskans did not seem to believe in any more.

We landed at 6 p.m. Our pilot said goodbye, then flew back to Prudhoe Bay for lobster dinner. We dragged our bags through the snow to the Federal Aviation Administration cabin at the far end of the airfield. A warm front had moved into Barrow: the temperature was only 6 below. Barrow claimed to have a taxi service, and, from the FAA building, Tom called a cab. We waited half an hour, then a genuine American-made automobile arrived, driven by a slender young Eskimo man who would not look at us, or speak to us, or help us load our bags into the trunk. Tom explained that racial tensions in Barrow were pretty high. The Eskimos were not fond of whites; especially now, with white money and white technology disrupting the quiet, self-sufficient life that the Eskimos had lived for centuries. For five dollars, however, the driver did agree to drive us six blocks, to the only place where an overnight visitor to Barrow could stay—the Top of the World Motel.

This was the new Top of the World. It had opened in June,

replacing the old Top of the World, which had been closed by the state board of health, and which, subsequently, had burned down. The Top of the World was not, strictly speaking, a motel. For a motel you needed motorists, and there wasn't a motorist—or even a highway that was open to the public—within five hundred miles of the Top of the World.

It was a modular wooden building, at the edge of the sea, up on stilts so the water would not wash it away. The sea was frozen now, of course, and there were big chunks of ice on the beach. We climbed a flight of wooden steps and entered the lobby. There was a smell of unflushed toilets as soon as we opened the door. The lobby was filled with Eskimos. Eskimos of all ages, slumped on chairs and on the floor; some sleeping, some just staring into space. In one corner there was a cluster of teen-agers, smoking cigarettes and giggling, as if they were waiting on a subway platform for a train. At the far end of the lobby, by the desk, there was a stuffed polar bear, rearing up on its hind legs, inside a glass case. The bear had been shot on the beach, outside the motel, two years before.

A young white woman, sleepy and sullen, was behind the desk. She said yes they had rooms. Sixty-one eighty for a single, pay in advance.

She locked the money in a box inside a safe. Then she told us there was no running water. There had not been running water for three days. The water was obtained from a freshwater lake and was delivered to the motel in a truck. The truck engine had been broken for three days, she said, and the only mechanic in town had been too drunk to fix it, and he was still drunk, and was acting as if he planned to stay drunk until spring. There would not be water until someone could be found to fix the truck. This might mean flying a mechanic up from Fairbanks. If the ice fog in Fairbanks should ever lift.

"Does this mean we can't use the toilet?"

"Oh, you can use it. Just don't expect it to flush."

She gave us more bad news when we asked how to get to the bar. The bar had been shut down since August, closed by the state police. Too many fistfights and knifings. The Eskimos of Barrow, apparently, did not handle their liquor very well.

We asked how to get to the restaurant.

The restaurant, she told us, was closed for the night.

"But it's only ten after six."

"That's right. The restaurant closes at six."

"Closes at six? What do you mean, closes at six? Who ever heard of a restaurant closing at six?"

She shrugged. "Mike wants it closed. Too much of a hassle keeping it open."

The girl left the counter and went back into an office where we could see a tall man with red hair and a red beard reading a paperback book. She closed the door. We were left standing in the lobby.

I went around behind the counter and knocked on the door. The man with the red beard came out. This was Mike.

"How come the restaurant closes at six?"

"Because I feel like closing it at six."

"Is there any other restaurant in town that might be open?"

"Nope. There's no other restaurant in town."

"Well, how about a grocery store, where we might get some food and something to drink?"

"Brower's store, across the street, but that's closed until tomorrow morning."

"Do you mean to tell me that there is no way to get anything to eat, or anything to drink in this town—not even a goddamned glass of water—until tomorrow?"

"That's right," he said. And he smiled, and stepped back into his office, and closed the door. The top of the world. The end of the line.

Tom and I took a walk through the town, to get our minds off our hunger and our thirst and to get away from the smell of the motel. There were Eskimos roaring up and down the streets on snow machines, and barking dogs running in packs. The houses of Barrow seemed to be mostly wooden shacks. Outside the shacks there were big piles of dog shit, frozen to the snow. And frozen whale meat, and caribou meat, cut into chunks. The town was only six blocks long, with the airfield at one end and the frozen Arctic Ocean at the other. There did not seem to be stores of any kind, and I saw no other white people on the streets.

We went back to the motel and shared a pack of wintergreen Life Savers that I found at the bottom of my duffel bag, and an old bag of peanuts left over from a Wien flight. After we ate them we went to bed. My room was overheated and the toilet smell was very strong. I lay in bed with the windows wide open, listening to the buzzing of the snow machines and to the incessant barking of the dogs.

In the morning we went to Brower's store. It had bright electric lights and long rows of nearly empty shelves. Eskimos in heavy parkas trudged slowly up and down the aisles. There were no drinks in the store, no soda, no juices, no milk. And very little food. Because of the ice fog in Fairbanks, no food had reached Barrow for a week. I finally found a dented six-pack of baby food orange juice, a can of sardines, and a package of cheese. They cost twice what they would have in Anchorage.

We walked back to the motel. The restaurant was closed and chained shut. There were about a dozen Eskimos in the lobby. Sprawling, leaning, smoking, dozing. Monday morning in Barrow, Alaska, in December. Nowhere to go, nothing to do. Life in the caboose of the world.

In Anchorage, Tom had introduced me to a lawyer who represented, among other clients, the North Slope Borough school district, the headquarters of which was in Barrow. The lawyer had mentioned that he would be flying to Barrow for the monthly meeting of the district school board and had suggested that we look him up if we made it to town. By midmorning Monday we had located him in the office of the school superintendent.

The North Slope Borough school district covered an area approximately the size of California, which made it, by far, the largest in the United States. The district consisted of Barrow, where 700 students attended school, and six villages scattered across the North Slope from Point Hope, three hundred miles west of Barrow, to Kaktovik, five hundred miles to the east, with a total additional enrollment of 400.

No roads connected any of the villages with any other, and all lay well above the Arctic Circle, the southernmost being at Anaktuvuk Pass, in the Brooks Range. Only three could be reached by telephone. With the others, the sole communication was by radio, and then only when conditions were right. "You might say," the superintendent remarked, "that busing is not one of our problems."

The mean average temperature in the district was 10 degrees above zero. During the previous school year, there had been 169 days when the temperature had been zero or below. For more than 60 days in winter there was no sun at all, but on the other hand, from May 10 through August 2 the sun was above the horizon for twenty-four hours a day and people taped tinfoil over their windows in order to be able to sleep.

Heating oil on the North Slope cost three dollars a gallon, and this was at a time when the average cost per gallon Outside was only a tenth of that. The cost of educating one high school student for one year in the district had been calculated at $20,000, which was approximately five times the national average. There was, however, plenty of money available, with 98 percent of the school district's funds coming from taxes which the oil companies at Prudhoe Bay paid to the North Slope Borough. "Our only problem with money," the superintendent said, "is thinking up enough ways to spend it."

The high school, with 300 students, had an athletic department budget of $250,000 a year. Most of it went to travel expenses. When Barrow High played an away game, it might be a thousand miles away. To go from Barrow to Juneau was like going from New York to Omaha. This year the basketball team had scheduled a game in Hawaii. Even for home games, Barrow had to pay traveling expenses for visiting teams; otherwise, nobody would ever come.

The superintendent was a short, stocky, energetic man from Oregon named John Anttonen. He had curly blond hair, a wry smile, which he employed frequently in the presence of visitors, and a slow, almost drawling manner of speech. He was married, with four young children, and he had been in Alaska six years. Before he came to Barrow, in June, his most recent job had been as superintendent in Yakutat, an Indian fishing village on Alaska's southern coast. His ambition was to become commissioner of education for the state, and he had taken the Barrow job thinking that, with its exaggerated challenges and responsibilities, the superintendency could move him considerably closer to that goal. Also, the job paid $54,000 a year, plus free housing, plus free transportation back to Oregon for himself and his family twice a year, which made John Anttonen, at thirty-six, the highest-paid school superintendent in America. Assuming you considered Barrow to be part of America, which, despite its having a zip code and an area code, and the fact that American dollars were used, John Anttonen was finding it increasingly difficult to do.

It was certainly not like Oregon, or Yakutat. True, in Yakutat it rained a lot, and you might wind up, over a winter, with, say, 300 inches of snow, but there were good streams and mountains and fine thick forests all around, and the people—Indians, not Eskimos —given a more livable environment, had not turned so quirky and strange. Certainly, they'd had more affection and respect for their school superintendent and his family. In Barrow, when John Anttonen's children walked the streets, they were called "honkies" and cursed at, and spit at.

The feeling of racial hatred in Barrow was deep and strong. This was not country where the white man belonged, and the white man had come, since the earliest whaling days, only to take; only to better his own life; never to do anything for the Native. It was the same now—in the minds of most Natives—with the oil. The white man had come to take away. To get rich from something that was underneath the Native's ground. And the same with the teachers: white men who came to get rich for a couple of years, telling Eskimo children that they didn't brush their teeth enough and that they should wash harder behind their ears.

For John Anttonen himself, Barrow was not so bad; he was there for a purpose, and he was working sixteen hours every day. For his children, however, and for his wife—his high school sweetheart in Moses Lake, Oregon—Barrow, which had at first seemed like it might be such a great adventure, had become, with the onset of winter, a dungeon, into which they had been cast as punishment for crimes they hadn't realized they'd committed.

Already, only a month after the sun had gone down, the children were moping, sulking, frequently sick. To avoid the cold and the darkness and the animosity, they stayed indoors as much as possible. In their dark, cramped apartment. With coughs and runny noses, and memories of Yakutat. The youngest child, Anttonen said, kept asking what had happened to the sun.

Tom said he had to go back to Anchorage, on the Wien flight that would be leaving Monday evening. John Anttonen invited me to stay. He said I could sleep on the couch in his apartment. I moved my bag from the Top of the World to the school district office, and then went to visit the principal of Barrow High School, who, like John Anttonen, was midway through his first year on the job.

The principal's name was Ted Healy. He was a stocky, fast-talking man in his mid-thirties, with the sort of features that are sometimes described as ruggedly handsome. He had been assistant principal of a junior high school in Eureka, California, before coming to Barrow. After six years of marriage, with no children, Ted Healy like so many other Alaskans and, particularly, like so many other whites in Barrow, had recently been divorced. Barrow had seemed as clean a break with his past as he could make, he said, but, of course, he'd had no idea what it would be like.

"Well," he said, "my first surprise was that I had to get my bus driver's license, which, in California, very few principals have. The thing is, our Eskimo bus drivers just won't get out of bed on winter mornings. If I want these kids in school, I have to get them myself. What I'm told is, most Eskimos just hate to get up early. We've pushed the starting time back to nine forty-five, but we still have a serious late problem. The thing is, the kids wander around the streets until one or two o'clock every morning, which is something that definitely did not occur in California.

"I guess the big thing I've had to adjust to, in terms of running the school," Ted Healy said, "has been in the area of discipline. Up here, you just have to be more relaxed. For instance, you have to accept the fact that the kids are going to arrive in the morning with a six-pack of Coke under their arms, and it's the Coke, not books, that they'll carry up and down the halls between classes, and by the end of the day, the whole six-pack will be finished. We'd never let a kid drink six cans of Coke during the school day in California. Here we're thankful that it's Coke and not beer.

"The whole attitude toward school is totally different from anything I've ever seen before. I remember, my first day, the first hour, in fact, that school was open, I had a kid come into my office and say, 'I don't like school this year, it's too boring.' I said, 'You've only been here an hour.' I couldn't believe it. I mean, in California, that just would not have occurred.

"Marijuana has turned out to be a much bigger thing than I'd expected. Marijuana and alcohol both. I'd been told the use was widespread, but still, I was completely unprepared for what I found. I've had no choice but to take a lenient attitude. If they're caught smoking marijuana in the cafeteria at lunchtime, for instance, they're sent home, because they won't be any good for the rest of the day anyway, but there's no follow-up. There's no punishment. If we started punishing them just for smoking, none of them would ever come to school. And, besides, as it is, the whites up here are unpopular enough.

"Actually, my own attitude toward marijuana has changed considerably. A year ago, if I'd caught my own nephew using it, I would have had him put in jail. Now, I even smoke it myself. It's not bad. I can see why the kids enjoy it. And, listen, after seeing what alcohol does to these people, if there were some way to discreetly arrange it, and if I thought it would actually help them stop drinking, I'd buy the marijuana for them myself. Which, for me, is quite a change in attitude."

Academically, too, Barrow High School had proved different from the school in Eureka, California. To make school more relevant to the lives of the students, John Anttonen had instituted courses in such things as Skidoo Shop, which was snow-machine repair; Parka and Fur Sewing; Small Engine Repair & Maintenance; Eskimos in Fact and Fiction; Science of the North Slope; Inupiat Studies, which was a course in the Eskimo dialect spoken in Barrow, and a one-semester, one-half-credit course called Native Land Claims, which was probably the most relevant subject of all. "The history of the Alaska Native Claims Settlement Act will be studied," the course description said, "and the terms of the settlement in land and money. The rights, responsibilities, and benefits of [the act] to Native people will be emphasized, as well as the current corporate structure of the Arctic Slope Regional Corporation. Students will understand their role as stockholders in the Native corporation."

"The funny thing is," Ted Healy said, "of all the courses, by far the most popular is driver's education. Even though, up here, there's really nowhere you can drive."

On a personal level, he said, the two most shocking aspects of life in Barrow were the drinking and the violence, which, quite obviously, were not unconnected.

"This year," he said, "there have been, I believe, twenty-three murders. In a town of only three thousand people. They've all been Natives, just like all the suicides have been Natives. Some of them still commit suicide the old way. They walk out on the ice with the wind at their back, until they're too exhausted to walk further. Then they turn and start walking back, into the wind. Before long, they collapse and freeze to death. But a lot of them now just blow their brains out. I don't know how many suicides there have been. And things like rape and assault I don't think the police even bother to count. The boys just drag the girls out on the ice and rape them and beat them up and leave them there.

"We had a killing just a couple of days ago. A nineteen-year-old kid who just graduated from the high school last year. He got drunk and picked up a knife and stabbed his sister and his cousin. Killed them both. He doesn't know why. He had nothing against either of them. Supposedly, he feels terrible now. He says the drinking just made him go crazy. But I'll tell you what I'm worried about: sooner or later these kids are going to get tired of killing one another, and they're going to start killing whites. Their anger, and their despair, mixed with alcohol, is a very, very dangerous thing.

"To be honest, though, as far as the drinking goes, it's not just the Eskimos. It's all of us. I would say, conservatively speaking, that I'm drinking ten times as much, at least ten times as much, as I drank back in California. It worries me, sure, it worries me. But I figure I'll be able to cut down again once I leave. And, in the meantime, it helps the time pass. Besides, everyone is doing it, night after night. It's the kind of thing that just sneaks up on you, and, after a while, you don't even bother to fight it.

"As a matter of fact, stop by tonight if you get a chance. We've invented a really potent new drink called Border Buttermilk. I won't tell you what's in it, but, hey, three of those and you'll swear the sun is starting to rise."

That evening, however, I attended the monthly school board meeting with John Anttonen and the lawyer from Anchorage. I went first to Anttonen's apartment, which was connected to the high school building by a series of long, winding corridors that smelled of garbage. The apartment had electricity, and, because the school district had its own water supply, it also had—unlike the Top of the World Motel—running water and a toilet that flushed. There was an eight-track stereo in the living room, and, in the kitchen, a microwave oven and a large pantry, filled with food that had been shipped in by barge the previous summer. A year's worth of ketchup and evaporated milk and Campbell's soups. But the apartment was cramped and poorly lit, and there were few smiles on the faces of its occupants.

The school board was composed of seven members, all Eskimos. Four lived in Barrow, and three had to fly in from villages. One came each month from Anaktuvuk Pass, in the Brooks Range, by chartered plane. Round-trip fare from Anaktuvuk was $1,100, which the school district paid every month.

"I go to conventions down in Seattle," Anttonen said, "and people start talking about budget problems, and, you know, there really isn't anything for me to say."

Anttonen's only budget problem was that the board members always insisted on spending more. This was just their second year of running their own schools. Before that, the schools had been administered by the Bureau of Indian Affairs, out of Washington. Schooling in Barrow had lasted only through eighth grade. For high school, children from the town, and from the villages, had been shipped to Bureau of Indian Affairs schools which were sometimes as far away as Oklahoma. Now, after so many years of having had nothing—of having gone so suddenly, due to the provisions of the Native Claims Settlement Act, from a position of powerlessness to a position of total control—the Eskimos of Barrow wanted everything all at once, and were convinced that the oil money would enable them to get it. Temporarily at least, they were probably right. Under such circumstances, if John Anttonen proposed a budget reduction, the board members considered it a racist act. A white man not wanting to spend money on Eskimo children.

There was, as an example, the trip to Hawaii by the basketball team. When a Barrow High School athletic team traveled, it went with a full complement of players, cheerleaders, and fans. This meant, for Hawaii, that not only fifteen players would make the trip, but a dozen cheerleaders as well and thirty or forty students to do the cheering. Now there was a motion before the board to increase the amount of money allotted for the trip, so that parents of the players also might be able to go to Hawaii. John Anttonen tried to explain that, strictly speaking, in financial terms, this was imprudent, but the board voted unanimously in favor of the motion. Anttonen shrugged, and moved on to the next item on the agenda. This was only December, after all, and he was in the first year of a two-year contract, and to teach fiscal restraint to people who were suddenly receiving tens of millions of dollars for doing nothing would take time.

The meeting lasted until after 1 a.m. In Barrow, when a number of people have gathered indoors, and they are warm, and there is fresh coffee, and the sun will not rise for another six weeks, there is little inclination to hurry things.

After the meeting, certain influential community leaders were invited back to Anttonen's apartment for drinks and snacks. Such hospitality was de rigueur. They ate caribou sausage and cheese and crackers, served to them by John Anttonen's wife, and they sipped Anttonen's whiskey and they got themselves pretty thoroughly loosened up, and they kept talking until almost 4 a.m. There was no way to hurry them. That was not the Eskimo style. You should want your guests to remain with you as long as possible, not to rush out into the cold. For a white man to hurry his Eskimo guests—or to suggest even that he might be less than totally devastated by their departure—would be considered the grossest form of insult. Definitely not a viable approach for the new school superintendent to adopt.

So John Anttonen and his wife had to sit up and listen and keep the glasses full. And the Eskimo leaders talked on and talked on. Telling tales not of Far North adventure: of killing the walrus or the whale; or of the struggle against the fearsome polar bear. But talking instead of ratables, and the new borough taxation program, and of what investment advice the regional corporation had recently received from its San Francisco-based consultants. The creases still fresh in their mail-order Brooks Brothers suits, the Eskimo leaders planned the Arctic of tomorrow.

Later in the morning, after a few hours' sleep on a couch, I went to see the mayor of Barrow. The mayor had a white man for an adviser, a Texan, who had taken up residence in Anchorage but flew to Barrow frequently to whisper in the mayor's ear.

The Texan, whom I had met the night before, had thought that perhaps I might devote an entire book to the mayor of Barrow and make him famous. After a few drinks, and a bit of marijuana, the Texan had begun to speak of how the mayor of Barrow could someday become vice-president of the United States. To me it seemed a bit farfetched, but the Texan spoke forcefully about the prospect. It seemed probable that he told the mayor the same thing on occasion, even without the marijuana or the drinks, which might have been one reason why the mayor liked having him around.

The Texan emerged from the mayor's inner office and said the mayor could see me briefly. The Texan seemed considerably less effusive than he had been the night before. I went in. The mayor was sitting behind a desk. A thin, spare, balding man; he seemed almost Oriental.

The mayor said that the problems faced by Barrow were severe, but the opportunities and challenges were invigorating, and his administration was striving for prosperity and progress. He spoke softly, with a strong, guttural Eskimo accent.

The mayor said he eagerly awaited the completion of the new town hall. This was a building on which the mayor was spending $12 million. There would be wall-to-wall carpeting in all the offices and a closed-circuit TV system for interoffice communication. This was, I reminded myself, in a town that had not had fresh water for four days.

The Texan sat at the mayor's left hand. He said Hubert Humphrey had thought very highly of the mayor. The mayor watched to see if I wrote this in my notebook. He was a low-key individual, but he had very sharp eyes. I found it hard to imagine him in the national limelight, but, then, I had only been in Barrow for a couple of days, and I was not being paid to so imagine.

The mayor said that any time I had questions about the operation of municipal government he would try to find an assistant to explain things to me; but he personally was generally too busy for the press. He suggested that I tour the construction site of the new town hall. I believe he was able to perceive that I regarded him primarily as an object of curiosity, almost as a tourist attraction. He kept looking at the Texan, who assured him again of my renown and said that my writings could open a whole new world of opportunity for the people of Barrow and for their duly elected political leader.

The mayor frowned and pursed his lips. He fell silent. He began to stare out the window at the darkness. The interview apparently was at an end.

The Texan assured me that I was welcome to remain in the outer office and absorb atmosphere but said that, unfortunately, due to a pressing schedule, direct conversation with the mayor would now have to cease.

I left the municipal office and walked to the other end of the town. Past all the dilapidated, tilted, shabby wooden shacks in which the people of Barrow resided. Past all the dogs and little kids and snow machines. There were dogs everywhere: barking, whining, running in packs. Shitting and pissing all over everything. And the people filling up big buckets with their own waste and dumping them out onto the snow.

I walked past the new town hall, which was almost completed, and, nearby, past the site of the new headquarters of the Arctic Slope Regional Corporation, which was vying with the mayor for political and economic power in the town. The regional corporation headquarters would be, like the town hall, a two-story building at the edge of the sea. Having heard that the mayor was planning a closed-circuit television system for the town hall, however, the regional corporation had decided to go him one better. In its new headquarters, the Arctic Slope Regional Corporation would have an elevator to travel between floors. An elevator. In Barrow, Alaska. The first elevator north of the Arctic Circle in North America. The furthest-north elevator in the United States; quite possibly the furthest-north elevator in the world. Let the mayor have his closed-circuit TV. He would still have to climb a flight of stairs to get to his office every day, whereas officers of the corporation could come in for board meetings, or for conferences with investment analysts from San Francisco or Boston or Chicago, and could simply say to the uniformed operator: "Two, please."

It was just about noon: maximum daylight, which was a dusky, late-twilight sort of thing. Eskimo kids wandering the streets. Hanging out, hanging around, nothing to do. Twenty below and darkness at noon. The only kind of winter they'd ever known. A lot of them in school, but a lot, apparently, not bothering to go.

Everyone in Barrow seemed to have a snow machine. At least one, maybe two. The people would roar up and down the streets on them, and would leave the motors running while they went inside to shop or to visit, and the machines would send fumes and racket into the air. Besides the one or two working snow machines for each adult, there seemed to be three or four already broken. Discarded machines, which cluttered yards, porches, vacant lots, and even the tundra at the edge of the town. If a machine of any kind broke in Barrow, it was thrown away, not repaired. Though, more often than not, the owner didn't even bother to throw it away. He would just let it sit there where it died. And buy a new one. Plenty of government money, and oil money, for that. The old machines would sit there for years, for decades, scarcely changing. Abandoned, broken cars would sit in front of houses, their interiors stuffed with plastic bags containing garbage. I peeked at the odometer of one: it registered only two thousand miles.

I kept walking past all the houses and past the Top of the World Motel and right out onto the ice on the ocean. I walked maybe half a mile out. It was hard to judge distance, staring straight ahead, plenty warm in my parka, looking at the darkness to the north.

The ice was chunky and rough, full of big bumps and ridges. I picked my way among them, hoping I would not meet a polar bear. One had been seen a couple of days earlier, crossing the Point Barrow road.

I walked slowly around the bigger chunks of ice. As if by walking slowly I was somehow giving myself a better chance against a bear. I reached a large flat chunk of ice which rose about four feet above the surface. It was rough enough on the sides for my boots to catch hold and I was able to climb up on top.

From this vantage point, I looked slowly in all directions. No bears. Nothing moving. Nothing alive, out on the ice. To the north, the emptiness; the void. To the south, the edge of the continent. The edge of life in North America. From the mayor, from the electric typewriters in the municipal office building, from the talk of closed-circuit TV, it was only a fifteen-minute walk to reach this.

The day was dull gray, with a slightly brighter light to the south. From half a mile out, the racket of the snow machines seemed more the distant buzzing of a chain saw. Smoke was rising from dozens of chimneys: the skyline of Barrow.

I could see occasional headlights as trucks passed along the shore road that led out to Browerville, a smaller cluster of houses across a lagoon from the main part of the town. The road then went five miles north to Point Barrow. At Point Barrow there was a DEW line station, and the Naval Arctic Research Laboratory, where a few scientists studied aspects of Arctic biology and charted the movements of polar ice. This was the edge. The ragged edge.

But from half a mile out there seemed a warmth, a feeling of life to the shacks all jammed together like that. I would turn and face north: toward the void. The absence of life. The choppy ice extending another thousand miles, to the North Pole, and beyond.

Then I would turn and face Barrow. There was now a faint trace of color, a thin orange rim to the far south. With smoke and traces of ice fog mingling at the edge of the town.

From that distance, half a mile out, Barrow was, for the first time, almost appealing. It was the edge, but, from this perspective, for the first time, it seemed not the end but the beginning.

It was as if I had walked off the edge of the earth and were now floating free, in the void, staring back. The smells and noise and the shabbiness receded, and Barrow became a still life: the dawn of man.

That afternoon I borrowed a school district truck from John Anttonen and drove to the naval laboratory at Point Barrow. It consisted of a large airstrip and a group of Quonset huts. At one end, behind the huts, were cages where animals were kept, wolves and wolverines and Arctic foxes. In a cage inside a hut there was a polar bear. Various studies were being performed concerning the metabolism of these creatures.

It was 2 p.m. Thirty below. No wind. Totally dark. My boots squeaked on the dry, granular snow as I walked. My breath froze in the air and coated the fur of my parka hood white.

I spoke to a young man named Derek who took care of the animals. He said the polar bear was fed raw meat twice a day. Derek had grown up in Montana, the son of a man famous for his studies of bears. This job seemed a sort of apprenticeship: start with polar bears, then work your way up to grizzlies.

Derek introduced me to his girlfriend, Kate. She was from Iowa, by way of Oregon, and she had come up for a summer job and had stayed on. She said she did not find it lonely or boring and she did not mind the darkness and the cold. She was twenty-one years old and very pretty. She and Derek went cross-country ski-ing every day, no matter how bad the weather was. She was get-ting in shape for a climb of Mount McKinley in the spring. She was going to lead an all-woman group up the mountain.

This was an intriguing thing about Alaska: the people you met, particularly outside of Anchorage, were doing the kinds of things, or planning to do them, that people in the East just did not do. You meet a pretty girl on a weekday afternoon and it turns out she has just finished feeding a polar bear and is preparing to climb Mount McKinley. It was as if the boundaries within which the normal range of human activity occurred had been, in Alaska, not just extended, but removed.

I had been told that there was another writer in Barrow, a man by the name of Duncan Pryde. He was said to be with the new university, Inupiat University of the Arctic, which had just opened its doors—or door, rather—and was Barrow's fist brush with higher education. Duncan Pryde had been a best-selling author in Canada and now was chairman of the university's Inupiat Lan-guage Department. I went looking for him late Tuesday afternoon, and found him, eventually, though Inupiat University of the Arc-tic was a little hard to locate in the dark.

Actually, it was just one building, an unpainted wooden shack. One of the many unpainted wooden shacks at the edge of the frozen sea, only in front of this one there was a sign which said: INUPIAT UNIVERSITY OF THE ARCTIC.

Inside, there was a large room with a stove in the center and a few small, unheated offices in the back. The doors to the offices were kept open in the hope that some of the heat from the big room might drift inside. At a desk in one of these offices, sur-rounded by cardboard boxes filled with books, and by several brown-paper bags that held his clothing and other belongings, and by a dozen smaller metal boxes containing index cards which were the raw material from which he hoped someday to write an Eskimo-English dictionary, I found Duncan Pryde, a pale, thin, thirty-eight-year-old Scotchman with pus oozing out of one eye.

"Have you got my check?"

"I beg your pardon?"

He stared at me as closely as his bad eye would let him. "Oh, never mind. I thought for a moment you might have been the new treasurer, or comptroller, or whatever in God's name they're calling him this week, the man who's supposed to pay me. Oh, well. Come in, come in, whoever you are, and I'll see if I can't scrounge you up a cup of tea."

Duncan Pryde had been raised in an orphanage in Scotland and, at the age of fifteen, had run away to join the British merchant navy. Three years later, an eye injury forced him to leave the service and he went to work at a Singer sewing machine factory in Glasgow. There, one Sunday, he saw a newspaper advertisement placed by the Hudson's Bay Company.

"Fur Traders Wanted for the Far North," it said. "Single, ambitious, self-reliant young men . . . Must be prepared to live in isolation . . ." Within weeks, Duncan Pryde found himself at a remote and isolated trading post deep in the Canadian Arctic, living intimately among the Eskimos, gaining the experience which would eventually form the basis of *Nunaga: Ten Years of Eskimo Life*, a graphic account of his Arctic exploits.

He asked me plainly, "Do you desire my wife?"

I still played it cautiously, and said, "Oh, she's very desirable. Any man would desire her, a woman as good-looking as your wife."

"Do you like her?" he persisted.

"Sure I like her."

Then, looking right at me, and with Niksaaktuq hanging on every word, he said, "Do you want to make love with her?"

I was still very cautious. "Well, she's not my wife, you know."

Nasarlulik grinned and said, "Well, Niksaaktuq likes you, and I like you, too, so if you want to get my wife (and that was the term he used) then go right ahead."

Duncan discovered rather quickly that he was unusually well suited, both physically and mentally, to the harsh, unrewarding environment. As time passed, he acquired great expertise in both Eskimo survival skills and the Eskimo language. He acquired, too, a sense that the Arctic was where he belonged. For Duncan, in fact, the frigid wasteland turned out to be the home he'd never had. And it provided him with many adventures.

We pushed on through the day without losing any more dogs, but we knew it was just a question of time. We didn't make very many miles, and the dogs were visibly weakening. Palvik and Iksis were as worried as I was. That night we tried to feed the dogs the dry dog food. We held their mouths open and pushed the stuff down their throats, but as soon as we let a dog go he just spat and coughed the stuff up. They just wouldn't take it dry. We even tried urinating on it to soften and warm it, but they wouldn't take it. Their refusal to eat proved what really alarming shape they were in.

The next day was a nightmare. If anything, the weather had deteriorated. . . . Eight dogs died that day. They dropped in their tracks.

Duncan spent ten years in the Canadian Arctic, becoming absorbed, almost totally, into the Eskimo culture. He traveled thousands of miles by dog sled and, in the brief Arctic summer, by canoe. There were a number of trips from which he almost did not return.

I cried: "Erik, what the hell are you up to?" and poked my head out of the tent. . . . I found myself talking to a polar bear, about six feet away, its head down in the canoe, lapping up the seal blood. . . .

I began reaching down behind me with one arm, feeling around for my rifle. . . . The bear turned toward me then and reared up. Its teeth were as long as my fingers. I still wasn't sure what it would do, but it was so close that if it decided to come my way, there would be little time for me to do anything. I shot it right through the heart with a 250/3000, and it flopped over against the canoe with a high-pitched scream like a woman's.

His years of travel throughout the region, and his remarkable mastery of Eskimo dialects, had made Duncan a familiar figure, and a respected one among the Natives. In 1966, he was elected to a seat on the Northwest Territories Council, an extension of the Canadian Parliament. His campaign had included the slogan "Every Eskimo Woman Ought to Have a Little Pride in Herself," and his opponent—aware of the fact that Duncan's fascination with the varieties of Eskimo dialect was exceeded only by his attachment to a variety of Eskimo women—contended that, with only a slight change in spelling, many of them already did.

Duncan won easily, however, and, unfazed when up for re-election two years later, urged his constituents to "Vote for Daddy." Certain missionaries were not overly fond of Duncan's approach, but no one could deny the authenticity of his Arctic experience. He had come to know the Canadian Eskimos, their culture, and their language as well as any white man of his era.

While in Yellowknife, serving on the Northwest Territories Council, Duncan met and fell in love with an Indian beauty queen, Miss Northwest Territories of the previous year. After ten years in the primitive, isolated Arctic, Yellowknife seemed, to

Duncan, an uncomfortably crowded and cosmopolitan place. And, after ten years among Eskimos, he found it strange that he should have fallen in love with an Indian woman. But love it was, and marriage soon followed. The wedding was the major social event of the Yellowknife season.

Within a year, a baby girl was born, and suddenly, Duncan Pryde, Arctic adventurer, found himself living in a wooden frame house on a quiet side street in Yellowknife, Northwest Territories, where mail was delivered every day, and where a newspaper was published and television broadcasts received, and where, in the course of one day, he could get into conversation with more non-Eskimo people than he had spoken to during the ten preceding years.

What Duncan wanted to do was go back to the Arctic. His wife did not. She was an Indian and didn't like Eskimos; Eskimos had become family to Duncan Pryde. He considered Yellowknife too crowded and large; she thought it too small and remote. She wanted to move to Edmonton, then maybe Vancouver. Some nights she even spoke of San Francisco. There was no telling where she would have them wind up. But wherever it was, it would be a long way from fur traps and sled dogs and steaming mugs up in icy trading posts at Perry Island or Gjoa Haven or on the shores of Pelly Bay, where Duncan had lived the most intense years of his life.

To pass the time in Yellowknife, Duncan wrote the book about his experiences in the Arctic. He put everything in: the polar bears and the dog-sled trips and the sex with the Eskimo women. He wrote smoothly, with great authority, and with a vivid sense of detail. *Nunaga* was published in 1970, and, to Duncan's astonishment, it became the number-one nonfiction best seller in all of Canada. Duncan became, for a time, a celebrity. He traveled all over Canada, from Victoria to Halifax, on a book-promotion tour. He became a regular on the Canadian talk-show circuit. Once, he even went to Los Angeles for an appearance on the Merv Griffin show. He came across as witty and humble on television, and everyone found his Scottish burr a delight.

In May of 1972, Duncan's fame reached its peak: his picture appeared on the cover of the Canadian edition of *Time* magazine.

In other ways, however, Duncan's life was beginning to complicate itself. Self-discipline, in matters of finance or of the flesh, had never been one of his strong points. There were tax problems in the aftermath of *Nunaga*'s success, and increasingly severe difficulties with his wife. By 1974, the marriage was coming apart, and that summer, back in Yellowknife and not knowing what to do next, Duncan met another beautiful girl, this one from the University of Edmonton, the daughter of a prominent Canadian surgeon. She had a summer job in a resort hotel outside of Yellowknife. Duncan spent a good deal of the summer in her company, and by the time she returned to Edmonton she was pregnant.

Duncan's wife filed for divorce. Before a judge who was an old family friend. The judge awarded all of Duncan's assets, present and future, to his wife. This caused a variety of painful complications, arising mainly from the fact that Canadian tax authorities had already awarded most of the same funds to themselves. By the fall of 1975, it had suddenly become desirable—one might even have said essential—for Duncan to depart not only Yellowknife but Canada, on short notice.

He went first to Anchorage, because it was the closest city he could think of that was still the Far North but was not Canada. In Anchorage, he was punched in the eye one evening while attempting to negotiate with a prostitute. The eye became infected. It was the same eye that had been injured in the merchant navy years before. Apparently, a dormant viral condition had flared up. Duncan flew north to Barrow, with his clothes, his books, his index cards, and with several tubes of ointment for his eye.

He had known nothing about Barrow. Just that it was as far north as a person could go and that it was not in Canada. In addition, the Barrow Eskimos spoke the one Inupiat dialect with which he was not yet familiar. By living among them, Duncan felt, he would be able to complete his dictionary, which, in turn, would establish him as a worldwide authority on the Eskimo language and would enable him to build a new life. Besides, temporarily at least, Barrow seemed a good place in which to hide.

Duncan's arrival, in September, had coincided with the opening, such as it was, of Inupiat University of the Arctic. Its founder, a recent arrival from the Lower Forty-eight, had convinced the mayor, and the Texan who advised him, that what Barrow really needed—almost as much as it needed a $12 million town hall— was its own university. An Eskimo university, the first in the world. Just think, the founder said publicly, of the prestige. Privately, as events would demonstrate, he might have had certain other motivations.

The founder obtained, from the mayor, a wooden shack. He put up his sign. He ordered office equipment and stationery. Very flashy stationery, with "Inupiat University of the Arctic" in bold blue letters across the top, and a logo that portrayed both a spouting whale *and* the midnight sun.

Using this stationery, he applied to the oil companies and to the federal government for various grants. There was no way the oil companies could refuse, not while preparing to dredge up billions of dollars in profits from Prudhoe Bay. And the federal government turned out to be an even easier mark. Barrow was so isolated, so remote, that the government dealt with it only on paper. And, on paper, Inupiat University of the Arctic had been made to appear an extremely meritorious undertaking.

When Duncan arrived in September, the founder sensed immediately the fund-raising potential of his credentials. Arctic adventurer, best-selling author, expert on Eskimo linguistics. Duncan was appointed to a full professorship on the spot. And made chairman of the previously nonexistent Inupiat Language Department.

Duncan moved into his office with his index cards, and the founder applied for fresh grants. There were, of course, no classrooms at Inupiat University of the Arctic; just the one wooden shack with the sign out front, from which applications for funds were processed and mailed.

The mayor occasionally seemed impatient, but the founder explained to him that the creation of such a noble and significant institution as Inupiat University of the Arctic required great care and extensive planning, and could not be rushed.

It was many months before anyone outside of Barrow got around to examining the structure of the university. By then, the founder was on an extended vacation in Hawaii, reachable only through his attorney.

All that, however—the FBI investigation, the indictments, the conviction on eleven counts of obtaining money under false pretenses, the appeal—was in the future. For now, Duncan Pryde, sitting alone in his unheated office, with pus oozing out of one eye, still believed that Inupiat University of the Arctic was for real. He had not eaten for two days. He had no money. He had run out of medicine for his eye. He had just been evicted from his house because he had not paid the rent.

For the past several nights, in fact, Duncan Pryde had slept on his office floor, using his hand-woven parka as a blanket, and, comforted by little beyond the remembrance that, in the past, he had endured circumstances even less appealing, and the expectation that, someday soon, the founder would return, students would enroll, classes would begin, he would start to get paid, and he could then commence in earnest the process of restoring order to his life.

I still had my can of sardines and a small piece of cheese in my parka. I gave these to him. In return, he presented me with an autographed copy of his book.

Most of the teachers in Barrow lived, as did John Anttonen, in apartments that were connected to their classrooms by a network of corridors. This made it possible for one to go inside when school started in late August, and not to emerge again until June, when it was time to go home. It was like living in a fallout shelter, shielded from a poisonous atmosphere: with artificial light, tape-recorded music, and canned food from the *North Star*, the barge that brought supplies to Barrow once a year.

A few of the more adventurous, or less fortunate, actually lived in houses in the town, and it was to one of these houses that I went to dinner Tuesday night. It was an unpainted wooden frame building with electricity but without running water.

The living room, which also served as dining room and kitchen, was crowded, smoky, and hot. There were eight people and one dog inside. They were smoking marijuana and drinking whiskey and beer. These were people who had no choice but to spend almost every evening with one another, and numbness seemed the key to survival.

They were unusual people, the whites of Barrow. They had to be: else why would they have been there? They had come seeking adventure, or high wages, or, more frequently, escaping from problems outside. Recently divorced, in many cases. Needing a fresh start, someplace distant. Trying, once more, to pull their lives together, against what seemed lengthening odds.

Whatever had been their reasons for coming, Barrow was not at all what they had expected to find. They had known it would be strange, foreign, remote, dark, and cold. But so grim? So squalid? So totally alien? And such hostility, even hatred, from the Eskimos? Whatever the problems back home may have been, after three months in Barrow, they seldom seemed worse than the solution.

The whites of Barrow found themselves, as winter closed in, forced into strange, tense, dependent relationships with one another. With people to whom, outside the Arctic, they might not have even bothered to say hello. It was not surprising that by February or March—sometimes much sooner—a number of people, and situations, got out of control. This was a Catch-22-style arrangement: to survive as a white in Barrow, you needed an unusual degree of psychological stability. But to have come to Barrow, as a white, in the first place, you already had displayed an extraordinary absence of the same.

The door to the house banged open. A large, bearded man stepped inside.

"Got her going. Got her going. We finally got the motherfucker running again."

It was the water man—known also as the Mad Russian. He had been bartender at the Top of the World until the bar had shut down. Now, having made a deal with the mayor, he had the water concession for the town, leasing a truck with a 2,400-gallon capacity. He drew the water from a freshwater lake and sold it to residents—and to the Top of the World—at eight cents a gallon.

For the first time in almost a week, his truck was running. He was on his way to the lake and said he wanted company, so I went with him. It was only once we had started—bucking and bumping up the icy, narrow road—that he told me why he wanted company.

"Last time I was out here, last week, just before this motherfucker broke down, I saw a big goddamn polar bear as soon as I stepped out of the truck. Now, tonight, see, what we're gonna do is, I'm gonna take my power auger out on the ice and start drilling, and you're gonna stay by the truck with this rifle, and if you see a bear coming, just honk the horn and flash the lights and fire that fucking rifle over his head."

The Mad Russian—the water man—was not really a Russian. Just as Eddie the Basque was not a Basque. But he was of Russian descent. And in the Arctic, in December, with his size and his beard and his voice, which roared even louder than the engine of his truck, he could have passed for a bodyguard of the tsar.

We reached the lake and drove onto the ice. It was a very cold night and getting windy. I didn't know how I could spot a polar bear, even if there was one, with my parka hood pulled so far forward over my face.

The water man dragged his auger to the spot where he wanted to drill. The auger was a big machine that you started by pulling a cord, the same as on a power mower.

I stood there with the rifle in my hands, feeling the tip of my nose getting cold. The water man pulled the cord, cursed, and pulled again. I must have stood there for half an hour, with my nose getting numb, watching the water man pull the cord. There were no polar bears, but no power in the power auger either. The motor had frozen. We rode back to the house to eat dinner.

The water man said he was living in the house with the people from the school district for a while. He was married, and had a small child, but he had just sent his wife and child down to Fairbanks.

"I was getting too pissed off, you see? Too uptight. I was afraid I was gonna hurt them. Hurt them bad. So I just sent them down. To get them out of my hair for a while. See if I can't get calmed down. I'm really tense, really tense, all the time. It scares me. Things were never like this in California. I've got a wicked fucking temper, man, and I can't really control it like I should. Like right now, man, I'm really pissed off about that auger. As far as you can see, I'm probably just an ordinary guy, a real calm guy, but underneath my surface, man, I'm really boiling. I don't know. First the truck is fucked up for five days. Now the auger. How am I gonna make any money selling water if I can't get the water out of the lake? Wow. I just hope nobody pisses me off at dinner tonight. 'Cause I can feel myself getting ready to blow."

It was not, however, the water man who blew at dinner. It was a man named Wade Smith from the borough municipal office, and he blew not at dinner but before it.

They were still drinking and smoking dope when we got back. The potatoes had just gone into the oven and the caribou steaks were defrosting in the sink. The tip of my nose had turned white and was numb—the beginning of frostbite. I warmed it by holding a hand over it until I could feel it start to sting.

Wade Smith was there with his wife. They were a little older than the rest of the people in the room. Possibly they had fewer illusions. This was their third year in Barrow, and they had a child, a ten-year-old daughter, who attended the Barrow school. It was very unusual for white people, especially with children, to stay in Barrow that long.

Wade Smith had been drinking pretty hard and had seemed already groggy when the water man and I had gone out. Now he appeared considerably worse. His face was a deep red, his eyes were glazed, and he was locked in an argument with someone from the school district business office. Something to do with purchasing orders. The kind of thing which can seem very important in Barrow, in winter, when for months you have no contact with anything else.

Suddenly Wade Smith jumped up and threw his glass on the floor. He started to scream. Then he charged at a man named Casey, who was our host. Casey had just put the caribou steaks on to fry.

Wade Smith shouted horrible curses and flung himself at Casey and tried to knock the frying pan off the stove.

"Seven-thirty! Seven-thirty! It's already seven-thirty and now you're just starting to cook dinner!"

Other people jumped up and grabbed Wade Smith and held him still.

"You know I eat dinner at six o'clock! You miserable, flatulent son of a bitch. You overweight mongoloid bastard. You invite me over here, knowing I eat dinner at six o'clock, and then you deliberately don't even start cooking until it's already seven-thirty!"

His face had turned purple. "Deliberate!" he was shouting. "You've done this deliberately. Well, you're not going to get away with it. No, you're not getting away with it this time. I won't eat dinner here! I won't eat your food! I'm leaving here now and I'll never set foot in this house again."

He broke loose from the hold he was under. "Come on," he snarled at his wife. "We're going home."

She had sat there quietly through it all, as if this was not the first time such a scene had occurred. Now she said no, she would not leave. She had come for dinner and she was going to remain until she had finished her meal. She had been married to Wade Smith for fifteen years. She had grown up in Chicago, and had lived, for most of her adult life, in Phoenix, Arizona, until Wade Smith had lost his job there three years ago.

Wade Smith told his wife that if she didn't come with him immediately, then she was a disloyal harlot and a slut and that he would go home and load his rifle and shoot her through the forehead the minute she walked in the door. Then he reached out and slapped her across the face.

A couple of people pushed Wade Smith out the door and Casey went back to frying his steaks and a couple of other people tried to comfort Wade Smith's wife.

She remained very calm. She went to the phone and called her daughter and told her to get into bed and to pretend she was asleep when her father came in. And not to worry if she heard him cursing and yelling. Wade Smith's wife said she would be home as soon as she had eaten. Then she hung up. She made herself another drink. She said she wasn't worried about the rifle, because she had hidden all the ammunition a couple of weeks earlier, the last time a scene like this had occurred. What did worry her, though, was that it was only December.

The caribou steak tasted fine, like beef tenderloin. There were baked potatoes, onions, corn, and Olympia beer to go with it. Toward the end of the meal, I heard a low roaring noise in the distance. It was the sound of the Wien plane coming in, the plane that would be leaving, within the hour, for Anchorage.

Suddenly it seemed that I had been in Barrow half my life. I said, "Listen: I've got to get out on that plane." No one asked why. Everyone understood. They would all have gone too, if they'd been able.

The water man drove me to John Anttonen's apartment, where I scooped up my things, and then to the airfield. There were still a couple of vacant seats on the plane.

I boarded quickly. And was airborne, out of Barrow, climbing steeply above the flat, empty tundra; above the ice and the wooden shacks and the polar bears; heading south, toward the Brooks Range, toward Fairbanks, toward Anchorage and Tom and Marnie's house on the park strip where the Johnny Carson show would be on television.

A month or so later I was in the Army-Navy store on Fourth Avenue in Anchorage and saw a tall, thin, dark-skinned man whom I recognized as someone I had met briefly while in Barrow. It was Bill Vaudrin, the president—though not the founder—of Inupiat University of the Arctic.

He was an intense man of French-Indian descent, with powerful eyes. In Duncan Pryde's office he had stressed to me that he was not primarily a university administrator. He was, he said, a poet, and translator of Tlingit Indian legends, particularly those which used the raven as a symbol. He was a man with a strong mystical streak. He said he felt deep pulls within him that might move him suddenly in an unexpected direction. He said he had made few conscious choices in his life; that he had an inner fire burning at all times, and sought always the direction of the greatest light and warmth.

I had thought at the time that his mystical compass must somehow have malfunctioned—Barrow in midwinter was not exactly the essence of light and warmth—but before I'd had a chance to pursue the question, he had darted out the front door, saying he was in the midst of an extremely complex and acrimonious misunderstanding with his girlfriend.

Now he was in the Army-Navy store in Anchorage, buying woolen socks and down pants and a Coleman lantern. I approached him at the cash register. He said he was no longer living in Barrow. He had resigned as university president and was now staying in a cabin north of Anchorage, training a dog team for the 1,100-mile Iditarod Trail sled dog race, which was held each March along a course that went from Anchorage to Nome.

Duncan Pryde, he told me, was no longer with the university either. Duncan had been fired for insubordination to the founder, leaving the university without an Inupiat Language Department, and, more to the point, leaving Duncan, apparently, without hope of ever getting paid.

John Anttonen, however, had come to the rescue, hiring Duncan to teach Inupiat language classes at Barrow High School. This, unfortunately, lasted only for a matter of days. There was an incident, a—how might one put it?—carnal incident, involving Duncan and marijuana and female students. Parents complained. They demanded Duncan's removal from the classroom. John Anttonen acceded to their wishes, but, unwilling to let Barrow's only resident best-selling author starve to death, awarded him one of the school district custodial jobs, which, in the past, had gone exclusively to Eskimos. The author of *Nunaga: Ten Years of Eskimo Life*, former two-term representative to the Northwest Territories Council, former husband of the former Miss Northwest Territories, former guest on the Merv Griffin show, was, in other words, now the janitor at Barrow High School. With his eye infection, Bill Vaudrin said, even worse.

The next day, in the Anchorage *Times*, I read that Bill Vaudrin, thirty-one years old, former president of Inupiat University of the Arctic, had been killed on the Richardson Highway when the car he was driving struck a moose.

7 Nome

Arthur MacIntosh owned the weekly paper in Nome. If he was mad at you for some reason, he would put it right there in his paper, whatever it was you had done to make him mad. At one time or another, Arthur MacIntosh had been mad at just about everyone who lived in Nome. At least at every white man. Four-fifths of the people in Nome were Eskimos, and Arthur MacIntosh left them pretty much alone, except for putting the ornery ones into "Police News" whenever they would get themselves arrested.

Usually, Arthur MacIntosh was mad at the Nome city council. A bunch of do-gooders. Busybodies. Meddlers. Talking progress all the time. Goddamnit, if a man couldn't go to Nome, Alaska, to get himself away from progress, where could he go? Arthur MacIntosh had already been in New York City, Washington, D.C., and St. Louis, Missouri, among other places, and he had experienced all of the progress that he cared to.

What the city council had done this time to make Arthur Mac-

Intosh mad was vote to pave Front Street, the one main street that Nome had. It ran north and south, along the beach, at the edge of the Bering Sea.

Most of Nome's bars were on Front Street. So was the newspaper office. And so was the Nugget Hotel. These were just about all that Nome consisted of. Two thousand five hundred people— only five hundred whites—on Alaska's dreary western coast. One hundred and fifty miles below the Arctic Circle, five hundred miles northwest of Anchorage—five hundred miles, as a matter of fact, west of Hawaii—closer to the coast of Russia than to Fairbanks. In a town like this, Arthur MacIntosh said, why the hell pave the main street? Nome had been mud and dust and mosquitoes in 1899 when the first boats full of gold rushers washed up on the beach, and what was the point of changing it now?

Arthur MacIntosh knew all too well what the point was: to make the town more attractive to tourists. Wien Air Alaska flew a few planeloads in every summer. Mostly sorry old folks who had just missed the last bus to Mount McKinley. They walked up and down Front Street and choked on the dust and watched Eskimos puke on each other. Then the mosquitoes got to them and they ran for their rooms—sixty-four dollars a night at the Nugget—and pleaded with Wien to fly them out.

Arthur MacIntosh knew more than he wanted to about the tourists. Too damn much. He had, in fact, married one of them the previous summer. A schoolteacher from Cleveland. He met her at the Bering Sea Saloon, where she had gone to get away from the mosquitoes. The Bering Sea Saloon was just across the street from the newspaper office. In Nome, you were never more than a few steps from a bar.

The schoolteacher told Arthur she was interested in absorbing local color. So Arthur bought her a bunch of drinks and told her stories, some of which even happened to be true. Then she bought him a bunch of drinks while he remembered more stories he could tell. She thought he was wonderful: an Arctic adventurer with the soul of a poet laureate. When the Wien tour left the next day, she stayed behind.

The marriage lasted until October, which was longer than anyone in Nome thought it would. By then, with winter darkness setting in and the icy Siberian winds starting to blow, Arthur was beginning to repeat himself and the schoolteacher was coming to recognize that Cleveland might not be such a bad place in which to grow old after all.

The thing about the city council was, in response to Arthur's campaign of vitriol, insult, and personal invective against them, the bastards had put a parking meter in front of his office. Right where Arthur parked his truck, in order to load it, on the days when he delivered the paper. It was not only the only parking meter in Nome, it was the only parking meter north of Fairbanks. In fact, as far as Arthur was able to determine, it was the northernmost goddamn parking meter in the world. What was worse, the sons of bitches had sent away for a whole big book of parking tickets, just in case Arthur ever neglected to put in his dime.

I went to Nome for New Year's Eve. It was another of the Alaskan towns to which there wasn't any road. To get there from Anchorage you had to fly first to Fairbanks and then through Kotzebue. The plane went only three days a week in the winter, and Nome was at the end of the line. It was built right on the beach, on Alaska's bleak and treeless western coast—subject to floods; battered by storms, which blew unchecked across the Bering Sea; and raked, almost constantly, by biting winds. The few whites who lived there saw themselves as keepers of the flame: the last of the unbridled romantics, in whose hearts and minds the gold rush lingered on.

In the summer of 1900, at the peak of the gold rush, there had been thirty thousand people in Nome. People like Rex Beach, the novelist; Tex Rickard, who later built Madison Square Garden; Tommy Burns, a future heavyweight boxing champion of the world; Doc Kearns, who became Jack Dempsey's manager; Wilson Mizner, the playwright, screenwriter, and developer of Florida real estate; and Wyatt Earp, who was fined fifty dollars that summer for assaulting a policeman on Front Street.

The town had been named by mistake: a nineteenth-century map maker, misreading an old naval chart, had interpreted the notation "? Name"—a query as to whether a particular point of land had a name—as "C. Nome," or Cape Nome, and he so marked the point near which the town of Nome was later founded.

There had been, however, no mistake about the gold. It was there, in great quantity, in the creek beds that led down to the coast. The first discoveries were made in the summer of 1899, just as the Dawson strikes, the biggest of the Klondike gold rush, were petering out. In May 1899 there had been only two hundred people in the vicinity of what soon would be Nome, but by late summer there were two thousand. By winter, there was an established town on the site, with twenty saloons, sixteen lawyers, twelve general merchandise stores, eleven doctors, six restaurants, six lodging houses, six bakeries, five laundries, four wholesale liquor stores, four hotels, four bathhouses, three secondhand stores, three watchmakers, three packers, three fruit, confectionery, and cigar stores, two paper hangers, two photographers, two tinsmiths, two sign painters, two meat markets, two dentists, plus a brewer, a boat shop, a bookstore, and a massage parlor.

There was a general atmosphere of tolerance about the town. Five prostitutes were confined to a makeshift jail on the second floor of the city hall when they refused to pay an assessment of $17.50 levied against them by municipal court, but it was reported that "they enjoyed themselves, singing French and American songs lustily, and making the dogs howl." The most severe hardship imposed by winter isolation was that the price of beer rose to one dollar a bottle over the bar.

The social highlight of Nome's first winter was, unquestionably, the arrival of Ed Jesson with newspapers from San Francisco and Seattle. Jesson traveled from Dawson City by *bicycle:* an eight-hundred-mile journey that took him more than a month, as he tried to keep his wheels in the narrow tracks made by dog sleds. The Indians at Fort Yukon had never seen anything like it: "Geasus Christ," one of them said, "white man he set down, walk like hell." When Jesson arrived, the dance hall was taken over for a public reading of the newspapers, which continued through the night, punctuated by outbursts of cheering as news of victories in the Spanish-American War was announced, and by many toasts drunk to Admiral Dewey and the battleship *Oregon,* and by the repeated tossing of hats in the air. More relevant to Nome's future, however, were stories of the thousands of people already flocking to the Seattle docks, clamoring for space aboard the first northbound boats of the spring.

The first wave brought ten thousand people to Nome. They dumped their belongings on the beach and went quickly inland to search for gold. Except for those who were so disillusioned that they returned immediately to their ships when they found that the beaches of Nome consisted of sand, and not of gold dust, as they had been led to believe. One man was reported to have jumped ashore, grabbed some of the sand in his fingers, and shouted, "I knew it was all a hoax." He then returned to his ship, remarking that he was "glad to get out of the damned country."

For those who stayed there was, in a few cases, astonishing wealth, but for all there was turbulence, danger, and unprecedented opportunities for debauchery. The town, said Doc Kearns, smelled like beer, whiskey, unwashed bodies, and cheap perfume. An aroma complemented, not infrequently, by gunpowder. A new doctor arrived and recorded that the first sound he heard as he stepped ashore was that of a gunshot. Fired by a gambler at the Northern Saloon—Tex Rickard's bar—as a means of expressing displeasure at a cut of the cards. A prospector named Will Ballou turned up for three days and reported that each day there was a killing. He said, "We had a dead man for breakfast every morning."

One new arrival penned this description of the scene:

We reached Nome, that human maelstrom, at night. We could see from afar the twinkling of the lights and their reflections dancing in the waters of the sea. We proceeded through the main street, and if ever pandemonium raged, it raged there. The streets fairly swarmed with a heterogeneous mass of people. Drunken gamblers grovelled in the dust; women, shameless, scarlet women, clad in garments of velvet, silks, laces, of exceedingly grotesque character but universally *décolleté*, revelled as recklessly as any of their tipsy companions. From the rough dance halls the scraping of a fiddle rose above the noisy clattering of heavy boots that sounded like a chariot race in an empty garret. Dust settled around about us like a heavy fog. We waded through rivers of it before we reached our hotel. There were thirty thousand inhabitants in Nome at that time, of nondescript character. Cultured, intelligent men hobnobbed with the uncultured and ignorant. The one touch of nature that made them all akin was the greed for gold.

It was the kind of town where Jimmy the Goat won $14,000 in a no-limit faro game at the Hub Saloon and, when someone started shooting in protest, so many new players were attracted by the sound that the game had to be shifted to the more commodious Northern Saloon in order to accommodate them.

By August 1900 there were more than a hundred saloons in Nome and it sometimes seemed as if the whole population of the town was inside them all at once, that no one was out looking for gold. There were marked cards and loaded dice and, three days in a row, a dissatisfied customer tried to set fire to Dick Dawson's Second Class Saloon. The social scene was further enlivened by the arrival of Miss Short and Dirty—one of the Far North's most renowned prostitutes.

Wilson Mizner, who years later would describe his days in Hollywood as "a trip through a sewer in a glass-bottomed boat," was known, in Nome in the summer of 1900, simply as the Yellow Kid—a nickname which implied no lack of courage, but which had to do rather with the technique Mizner had developed, while working as a saloon cashier, of pouring a bit of syrup in his hair in order that, as he weighed out gold dust from a miner's poke, he would be able to brush a hand through his hair and cause a few particles to remain.

Jack Hines was there in the summer of 1900, too. Nome's Merry Minstrel he was called, a man with a fine tenor voice. The following year, a Russian count named Podhorski absconded with Hines's young wife and Hines tracked him from Alaska to New York City and back to Nevada before shooting him three times through the heart. While testifying in his own defense, Hines sang some sad love songs for the jury, which was so moved that it voted quickly for acquittal.

Even Swiftwater Bill Gates came to Nome. He was a prospector, gambler, and entrepreneur who once, in Dawson City, infatuated with a show girl named Gussie Lamore, and aware of Gussie's passion for fresh eggs, had purchased, for $2,800 in gold dust, every fresh egg in Dawson City, and had then informed Miss Lamore that her only means of satisfying her craving in the morning would be to satisfy several of Swiftwater Bill's through the night.

As a not necessarily disapproving young minister who arrived in the summer of 1900 phrased it: "You see more, live more, in twenty-four hours in Nome than in a cycle of Cathay."

I got into town at one o'clock on the afternoon of New Year's Eve. There were Christmas lights strung across the main street, hung on thin wires which bucked in the wind. Snow was falling; the end of a three-day blizzard. It was not yet totally dark. The sky looked heavy and gray and powerful. The wind blew in hard from the sea.

I walked down Front Street to the newspaper office. The paper was published daily, said its masthead, "except Monday, Tuesday, Wednesday, Thursday, Saturday and Sunday." Arthur MacIntosh was in the back room. He had once been a copy desk man for United Press in St. Louis, New York, and Washington. But he was in his sixties now, and had been in Nome for more years than he cared to remember.

He had a full beard, rheumy eyes, and long, unkempt hair that was the color of an overcast winter sky. He was unsurpassed at the art of looking grizzled. When he gave up drinking, which was often, it meant that instead of drinking whiskey all afternoon, he would drink beer; with just an occasional shot of brandy on the side.

Once, a camera crew from public television visited Nome for a day and Arthur MacIntosh became the star of their show. As the camera zoomed in tightly on every craggy feature it could find, he nodded sagely and remarked that the way you could tell a real Alaskan was by how many plane crashes he'd survived.

Actually, as Arthur confessed later, that was not true. The way you could tell a real Alaskan was by how many marriages he had survived. Arthur, having walked away from three of each, was qualified by either standard.

Despite the fact that he'd given up drinking, Arthur agreed to come across the street with me to the Anchor Saloon. I noticed the parking meter as we walked past. Its base encased in concrete, it still stood in front of Arthur's office. But it was bent like a pretzel now, from having been bashed with a sledgehammer, and the coin box was riddled with bullet holes. Attached to the top of the meter was a large "Out of Order" sign, which Arthur had stayed up late to print in the back of his newspaper office. Just after he'd finished smashing the meter with the hammer and shooting the coin box full of holes. In the good old days, he said, he would have let the meter be, and shot the city council members full of holes.

Arthur ordered a brandy and a beer. He was giving up drinking at the Anchor, he said, and not at the Vitus Bering Café, because Bobby Joe Morgan, the owner of the café, had insulted him. The embarrassing part was that Arthur did not know what the insult was. It had been late at night, and the Vitus Bering, as usual, had been full, and Bobby Joe Morgan and Arthur, as usual, had been in an argument about something or other, with both of them talking kind of loudly, when Bobby Joe Morgan, who basi-

cally was not a very pleasant man, made a remark which Arthur
was not quite able to hear.

Everyone else, however, apparently heard it clearly enough,
for as soon as Bobby Joe Morgan finished, the other customers
began to hoot and holler and stamp their feet and clap their hands
and to point fingers and laugh at Arthur MacIntosh. So he knew
that, whatever it was, it was not only nasty but clever. And he
knew that to ask Bobby Joe Morgan to repeat the remark would
only make matters worse.

Not knowing the specifics of the insult, however, Arthur found
himself unable to muster an effective retort. And so, with derisive
laughter ringing in his ears, he drew himself to full height and,
calling upon his last reserves of dignity, announced that there
were some things which a gentleman simply could not be expected
to tolerate; that an uncrossable line had been crossed; that the
breach of conduct, of trust, of decency, had been so severe that, in
future, Mr. Arthur MacIntosh would simply take his trade elsewhere, which, in Nome, meant to the Anchor, which was two
doors away.

Today, however, Arthur did not want to stay at the Anchor for
too long, because he knew what the evening would bring. For the
publisher, editor, star reporter, photographer, advertising sales-
man, and deliveryman of Nome's only newspaper, all of which
positions Arthur filled, New Year's Eve meant significant work. He
would have to drive out to the Roadhouse and take pictures of the
upper-crust party.

This was the city council crowd, the Rotary types, the bankers
and lawyers and judges, and the sorry sons of bitches who sold
insurance. And Leslie Robertshaw, that priggish little fellow who
owned the drugstore, and who wanted to become mayor, and to
make all the bars in town close up at midnight. Hell, what Robertshaw really wanted—him and most of the ministers in the town—
was for Nome to vote itself dry, the way Bethel had done and the
way Barrow was going to try to, but he could not come right out
and say so, because he would never become mayor that way.

The upper-crust party cost fifty-dollars per couple to get into.
The men wore suits and ties and the women wore long, out-of-
fashion dresses that had been in a trunk for a year. There would be
a four-piece orchestra, featuring an accordion, and a midnight
supper of overcooked beef. The music would be strictly wedding

reception. The party was being held at the Roadhouse because the Roadhouse was practically the upper crust's private club. They had gone and built it for themselves two miles from town, on a road that went nowhere, just so they could separate themselves from the Front Street crowd, which they considered uncouth. Well, of course the Front Street crowd was uncouth. Arthur had no argument there. But wasn't uncouthness—or at least the option of being uncouth—the whole point of living in Nome?

He would have to go out there, in a matter of hours, and take pictures of all those silly bastards dancing around. Wearing their party hats and tooting their horns. Then he would have to fill up the whole next week's paper with the pictures. Because if he didn't, they might stop advertising in his paper. Unfortunately, the upper crust owned most of the businesses in Nome, except for the Front Street bars, and without their advertising neither the newspaper nor Arthur himself, in his present capacity, could long survive.

The whole situation was enough to make a man gloomy. Especially on the afternoon of New Year's Eve. When you are past sixty and living in Nome, there is no way to pretend that you have not reached the end of the line. Arthur MacIntosh ordered another beer, and drank several brandies along with it, in an attempt to keep the chill of depression from setting in.

Then, because he knew what the evening would bring, he left the Anchor and walked back across the street, which was in total darkness now, at 4 p.m., except for the Christmas lights. He cursed wearily at the parking meter, as was his habit, and then climbed the steps that led to his office. He walked straight through the front office, where the classified advertising was accepted, and where, occasionally, someone would sit down and try to type out a story, and he walked through the second room, where the engraving equipment was, and the typesetting machine, which was no longer used, now that the newspaper was printed offset, and he entered his little private office in the back, where, ever since the schoolteacher had moved back to Cleveland, Arthur MacIntosh had been sleeping on a cot.

There were bookshelves above the cot, and more bookshelves, overflowing with books, lining the walls of the room. On a table near the cot there was a hot plate. Also a jar of instant coffee, a few cans of soup, a box of crackers, and half a dozen dirty coffee mugs, with rings from the bottoms of the mugs on every surface.

Arthur thought briefly of trying to read, but instead closed his eyes and was asleep within minutes. One hundred and fifty miles to the west, across the International Date Line, the new year had already begun.

The Vitus Bering Café was only half full at 7 p.m. on New Year's Eve. There were more whites than Eskimos, which was the way Bobby Joe Morgan wanted it. He did not care for Eskimos, which made life a bit awkward from time to time, since Eskimos made up 80 percent of Nome's population. It was not prejudice, Bobby Joe maintained; it was simply a matter of business. The Eskimos did not know how to drink. They would come in, have three whiskeys, and then slump over, unconscious, on their barstools. Or fall from their stools to the floor. Drooling, and pissing in their pants, and throwing up, and blocking access to the bar for the white folks of Nome, who knew very well how to drink, and who kept practicing constantly, to make sure they would never forget.

Bobby Joe Morgan himself was tending bar. He was dressed all in black for New Year's Eve. Black cowboy hat, black western shirt, tight black pants, and highly polished black cowboy boots. Around his neck he wore a silver medallion. On one hand he wore a diamond ring. He was thirty-five years old, and he had once very nearly made the Oakland Raiders as a defensive back. Instead, he had come to Nome, where he could pretend he was the bad guy in a western.

His girlfriend of the season stood next to him behind the bar. He made her work when he was working, so she would not be able to fool around with anyone else. She was wearing a low-cut black evening dress, a silver necklace, and diamond earrings. She was the prettiest white woman in Nome. Not infrequently, Bobby Joe Morgan would be involved in altercations with patrons who, in his opinion, had looked at the girlfriend too long or too covetously. Even by Nome standards, Bobby Joe Morgan was said to have a quick temper.

I was taking no chances. I was looking at Cal Cramer, the former jockey, who had worn his painter's overalls into the bar, and at Brian Devlin, twenty-three years old, of Killarney, Ireland, who was wearing his chef's uniform. Despite the fact that it was

New Year's Eve, both of them had been claiming—apparently for several hours—that they were just about to leave the Vitus Bering and go to work.

Cal Cramer had once ridden horses in California for Bugsy Siegel and other members of the mob. His specialty had been winning only when told to. Bugsy Siegel had been a gracious and generous employer in many ways, but was not a man with much tolerance when it came to having his instructions misunderstood.

As he grew older, and came to recognize that most of his better horses were behind him, Cal Cramer began to drink a bit more than he should have. This was unfortunate for two reasons: first, it caused him to put on some weight, which was a serious problem for a jockey, and second, he began to have difficulty remembering just when it was that he was supposed to win a race and just when it was that he was supposed to lose. In time, Bugsy Siegel dispensed with his services—though not, happily, with Cal himself—and he drifted out of the racing world, and out of California, and, for a number of years, continued to drift throughout the West, taking such employment as he could find, including one stint as a cook in a Montana mining camp, at a time when United Mine Workers president Tony Boyle was there. Compared to Tony Boyle, Cal Cramer said, Bugsy Siegel was one of the greatest humanitarians that Western civilization has ever known.

After many years, and a chain of circumstance, coincidence, and good and bad fortune that even he was no longer able to unravel, Cal Cramer, near sixty now, found himself in Seattle, painting houses. He found himself also reacquainted with his one child: a daughter from a marriage to a Hollywood starlet long ago.

The daughter was grown now, and working as a supervisor of stewardesses for Alaska Airlines, and happened to mention to her father one evening that the airline planned to repaint and renovate the interiors of the tourist hotels which it operated in various Alaskan towns.

Billing himself as not just a painter but also an interior decorator, Cal Cramer had bid on the job. His was by far the low bid. He was in trouble over some gambling debts in Seattle, and was less interested in making a profit than in just living out of town for a while. Preferably, far out of town.

Cal Cramer had been in Nome for three weeks. He had spent

all of his nights, and most of his days, in the Vitus Bering Café. By now, he could hardly distinguish day from night. He had not yet started to paint. The way he figured it, he might not have to. Through a couple of Seattle bookies with whom his credit was still good, he had made a large bet on the Rose Bowl football game, which would be played on New Year's Day. If his team won, Cal Cramer would be able to go home.

Brian Devlin, on the other hand, had no desire to go home. He just wanted his pipeline job back. Through a friend at Aer Lingus, the Irish airline, who had a friend at British Petroleum, Brain had obtained a lucrative cook's job at Prudhoe Bay. He had left Ireland fully expecting to return a millionaire. His plan was to come back to Killarney, and to buy the hotel at which he had once worked as an apprentice. Or maybe he would open a gourmet restaurant in Dublin. Or maybe live on the Continent for a while —an Irish chef running a three-star restaurant in the heart of Paris. That idea had great appeal. All ideas, in fact, had great appeal, insofar as they helped him to keep his mind off the reality of his situation. Having been fired for drunkenness at Prudhoe Bay, Brian was now stranded in Nome, working for minimal wages at the Nugget Hotel. The wintertime chef at a summer resort. An extremely backwater summer resort. On the most forsaken edge of what seemed to Brian to be the most forsaken place in all the world. Ah, sweet Jesus, the fates could be unkind to a man.

But very soon now, after probably just one more drink or maybe two, Brian Devlin would walk down to the Nugget and begin preparations for the big New Year's Eve midnight banquet. Featuring lobster tails and filet mignon flown in from Fairbanks. The most opulent feast west of the Roadhouse. Brian's first major challenge and, along with the big New Year's Day brunch, the meal with which his comeback would begin.

When Brian did leave the Vitus Bering Café an hour later, however, it was to go not to the Nugget Hotel kitchen, but to his room. He returned in ten minutes with a scrapbook which he had brought with him from Ireland. The book contained photographs of what Brian considered to be his finest meals. Page after page, in full color, of coq au vin, salmon mousse, asparagus soufflé.

Cal Cramer and I looked through the scrapbook as Brian described, in great detail, the circumstances that had surrounded the preparation of each meal.

"This kid," Cal Cramer said, "knows the secret." He was speaking as an old mining camp cook.

"What's the secret?"

"You feed the eyes, you feed the stomach. That's all you got to know to be a chef."

Brian turned the page. To a close-up of ham slices in aspic. I left, temporarily, for some fresh air.

I walked around town for a while, then along the road to the Roadhouse. It was a warm night, maybe 20 above. The road ran right along the coast. Dogs were howling and the moon was out. Siberia was just across the ice.

What had made Nome a good choice as a place to spend New Year's Eve, I reflected, was that in no other town in America had such a high percentage of local history involved saloons. There was, for example, the tale of Big Jim Wilson, proprietor, during gold rush days, of the Anvil Saloon.

Wilson weighed more than three hundred pounds and, even in Nome, was considered an exceptional drinker. On Christmas Day 1900, he threw a party at the Anvil with free drinks for the house. When finally the party ended, he found himself still in a partying mood. He gathered together those few of his acquaintances still ambulatory—including his girlfriend, Ione; Wilson Mizner, the Yellow Kid; a man who was nicknamed the Hobo Kid; and another who was called the In-and-Out Kid, which referred either to his card-playing tactics or to his sexual habits, no one was ever sure which—and the group began a tour of other saloons, with Big Jim still insisting that every round for everyone was on him.

Sometime during the morning of December 26, the party returned to the Anvil, where it seemed that the excess was beginning to take its toll, even upon a man of Big Jim's herculean capacity. He remained conscious, but was no longer able to stand, and as one witness later described: "His puffy face seemed ready to explode."

Girlfriend Ione, however, insisted that the party go on. She persuaded Wilson Mizner to start singing. In addition to his other talents, Mizner, who was six foot three and weighed two hundred twenty pounds, was said to possess the best baritone voice in Alaska. At Ione's request, he sang a war ballad called "Tom and

Ned," one of Big Jim's favorites, a number which brought tears to Big Jim's eyes and powerful emotion to his heart. Emotion which was, perhaps, a shade too powerful.

Wilson raised a glass to toast Mizner—"My oldest friend, and the best damned songbird in Alaska"—downed his drink, and then collapsed forward out of his chair, falling face first to the floor. He was unconscious, and breathing only irregularly, but Ione rejected all suggestions that a doctor be summoned. Perfectly normal, she said; this was the way Big Jim ordinarily concluded an evening with friends. She then persuaded Mizner to keep on singing, and, given the attention which his powerful baritone could command, it was some time before anyone noticed that Big Jim no longer was breathing at all. That he was, in fact, dead.

At this point, a doctor was summoned; a formal pronouncement of death was made; and Big Jim's carcass was dragged, feet first, and for the last time, through the front door of his saloon.

The party was over. In more ways than one. As Mizner went toward the bar, to pour a final, commemorative round, girlfriend Ione stepped into his path. From somewhere deep inside her evening dress she pulled out a will. Big Jim Wilson's last will and testament. Which stated quite clearly that, in the event of his demise, Ione would become sole owner and proprietress of the Anvil Saloon.

Christmas was over, she told Wilson Mizner. From now on there would be no more drinks on the house.

Back on Front Street, I stopped at the Nugget Hotel. The lobby seemed in need of repainting. There was a big crowd at the bar. In the dining room, all the tables were set, but the kitchen was silent and dark.

I got back to the Vitus Bering Café just in time to see someone ring a big bell above the bar, which meant he would buy a drink for everybody in the house. To celebrate the start of the new year. It was midnight. Already six o'clock in the morning in New York. People shouted "Happy New Year" to one another. Bobby Joe Morgan stood motionless, next to his girlfriend, behind the bar. Making sure no one tried to give her a New Year's kiss.

Cal Cramer and Brian were still at the table where I had left them. An empty Irish-whiskey bottle lay on its side. Brian was staring nostalgically at a color photograph of a stuffed bass. There were tears in his eyes, and he was mumbling something about shallots.

Cal Cramer wished me a happy new year. He said if I were a horse he would have remembered my name. He said he could remember the name of every racehorse he'd ever ridden, but with people he did not do so well.

Just then the door to the Vitus Bering Café opened and the manager of the Nugget Hotel rushed inside. He had a piece of filet mignon in one hand and a bright red lobster tail in the other. Both were frozen. He cursed violently and flung the meat and lobster at Brian Devlin. It seemed apparent that the midnight banquet would be delayed.

"Don't worry about it, kid," Cal Cramer said. "You feed the eyes, you feed the stomach. They can always pass your scrapbook around the room."

I woke up at eleven the next morning. It was light out, a bright, sunny day. I walked to the Nugget Hotel coffee shop; not to be confused with the dining room, where they were cleaning up the remains of the banquet and preparing for the big New Year's brunch.

I ordered a reindeer burger for $4.25. Reindeer burgers were fifty cents cheaper than hamburgers, I suppose because there were a lot more reindeer around Nome than there were cows.

The Rose Bowl football game was on the radio, over the Armed Forces Network. Cal Cramer, who was still wearing his painter's overalls and said he had not yet been to sleep, was sitting at a corner table, listening.

The sun was so strong outside that a venetian blind had to be pulled down over the big plate-glass window that looked out onto Front Street. At half time, Cal Cramer's team was three touchdowns behind. I went with him for a walk on the ice.

The sun was not far above the horizon. It was a bright orange color, almost Day-Glo. All of Nome seemed to recoil from its harsh light. The ice was crowded with Eskimo children. The little ones were playing tag and hide-and-seek, hiding behind big chunks of ice. The bigger kids were riding around on snow machines, or ice fishing through holes which they had cut back in the fall and at which they worked each day to keep open.

Cal Cramer stayed on the ice to watch the sunset, which came at about quarter to three. Then he went back to the coffee shop. His team had lost the Rose Bowl game by twenty-seven points.

He went immediately from the coffee shop to the lobby. At the rear of the lobby there was a closet, inside which he had stored paints and his other equipment. With fingers that trembled—from alcohol, perhaps, or from age, or from lack of sleep, or possibly from his just having lost one of the larger wagers he'd ever made— Cal Cramer pried the lid off a five-gallon can. Then he spread some drop cloths on the floor, poured the paint into a tray, dipped a brand-new roller in the paint, and went to work.

At the Vitus Bering Café, Bobby Joe Morgan was passing his black cowboy hat around the bar. Not for people to put money in, but so everyone could see how big the hole was.

At six o'clock that morning, just after locking the front door, Bobby Joe had climbed the stairs to his apartment above the café. His girlfriend was already waiting in the bed. He undressed with the light on, and with his back to the window that faced Front Street. He took off his black shirt and his black boots and his black pants, and then his underwear, which was not black. The last thing he took off—it was a custom—was his black cowboy hat.

Just as he lifted the hat from his head, two shots—from a .357 Magnum, a gun powerful enough to kill a bear—were fired from the roof of a building across the street. One bullet went past Bobby Joe Morgan's shoulder and shattered a mirror on the far side of the room. The other made a large, ragged hole through the crown of his hat, approximately three inches above the top of his skull.

There were no suspects. Probably half the people in Nome owned .357 Magnums, and as was remarked more than once around the bar, probably half the people in Nome would just as soon see Bobby Joe dead as alive.

The sun had set on New Year's Day and it was dark again on Front Street when Brian Devlin came into the Vitus Bering Café. He was pale, and walking unsteadily, and he was not wearing any shoes. He didn't know where his shoes were. He couldn't remember the last time he'd had them on. But bygones were bygones, he said. When the stores opened the next day he could always go out and buy a pair of shoes. For now, he said, the thing to focus on was the New Year's Day brunch. The big noontime brunch, the preparation of which would mark the true beginning of his comeback, or, as the Nugget Hotel manager had put it the night before, his last chance.

What he needed, Brian said, was just the lightest touch of Irish whiskey. Just a wee drop or two to set him right. And then, shoes or no shoes, he would be off to his kitchen and to work.

He continued to talk in this vein for several minutes before it first occurred to me that he was serious. Brian Devlin actually believed that it was morning. That it simply had not yet got light. He didn't realize that he had missed the daylight. That brunchtime was long past. And that it was already dark again.

8 The Village

The town of Bethel sits where the Kuskokwim River—a river which flows for eight hundred miles—begins to widen and to empty into Kuskokwim Bay. This is in the southwestern part of Alaska, about five hundred roadless miles, and three mountain ranges, west of Anchorage. It is good fishing country, and unparalleled for the hunting of waterfowl, but it is not much to look at either from the air or from the ground; either from a distance or up close.

The population of Bethel is about 3,000, making it approximately the same size as Barrow and Nome. It is as run-down as Barrow but without the distinction of being in the Arctic. And it was founded by missionaries, not by gold seekers, and is thus lacking in the lusty traditions of Nome.

Bethel is, in fact, the only town in Alaska with a Hebrew name. Chosen by the Moravian missionaries who arrived there in the late nineteenth century, to find an Eskimo village called Mumtrekhologamute. Life was difficult enough without that, so they changed the name to Bethel, after a passage in Genesis, wherein "God said unto Jacob, arise and go up to Bethel, and dwell there . . ." which seemed to indicate, to anyone who had spent time in Bethel, Alaska, that Jacob was not, after all, one of God's chosen people.

It is, in short, a shabby, dreary town, in flat, dull, river delta country—a part of Alaska that might as well be Kansas, except for the summer mosquitoes and winter cold.

Bethel is, however, the administrative, commercial, and transportation hub for the dozens of Eskimo villages that are scattered across western Alaska like pieces of birdseed thrown in a yard. The little places that the Moravians did not get to, and that retain, therefore, the Eskimo names that no white man—with the possible exception of Duncan Pryde—can properly pronounce: Kongigamak, Kwigillingok, Kvigatluk.

It was in one such village, a Russian Orthodox Eskimo village with a population of only 200, that Olive Cook had lived for the first eighteen years of her life. Until she had written to the senator's office, and he had found her a job in the Department of the Interior, and she had gone off to Washington, D.C.

In the village, Olive Cook had not given much thought as to what sort of place Washington, D.C., would actually be. Just that it would not be the village was enough. In the village, in the summer, fishing was the main occupation. Catching salmon and whitefish, then drying the fish, and smoking them, and putting away enough to ensure that there would be food for the winter. In the winter, in the village, there seemed to be no occupation at all. Just endless miles of snow, and endless days of empty, sterile, bitter cold and, worst of all, from Olive Cook's point of view, isolation.

She was of that generation of Eskimo—the first such generation—for whom the ancient tasks, the centuries of culture and tradition, had lost their meaning. The white man and his technology, and the Eskimo's new awareness of the outside world, had put the primitive society under a pressure that it seemed unlikely to survive. And it was the teen-agers and young adults—like Olive Cook—who were feeling the pressure most acutely. For them, the village of their birth was no longer, necessarily, the place where they would have to spend the rest of their lives.

Olive Cook had been to Bethel frequently. She had once even

traveled to Anchorage, and had seen there a way of life involving automobiles and movie theaters and restaurants. A way of life that enabled people to heat their homes simply by turning a dial; that permitted them to consume food which they had not had to kill themselves; and that gave them money, apparently, for doing no more than sitting in a warm building all day, playing with pieces of paper, and talking to each other on the telephone.

Olive Cook, by the time she was eighteen, was sick of the village. Sick of fish, sick of snow, sick of seeing the same thirty or forty wooden shacks every day and the same two hundred people every week. And sick, most of all, of sleeping, as she had done since her infancy, in the same room as her parents: the bedroom half of the two-room wooden shack on the riverbank in which she and her parents and her two younger brothers and her younger sister had always lived.

Nothing in Olive Cook's experience, however, or in her education or in her genetic heritage, had prepared her to cope with Washington, D.C., in July. The temperature was 96 degrees and the humidity was over 90 percent. The temperature remained in the 90s for most of her first month in the city, a factor which—in combination with homesickness, culture shock, and the responsibility of working for the first time at a job with fixed hours, in surroundings that were totally alien to all she'd ever known—brought her to the edge of nervous breakdown.

She was aware, for the first time in her life, that she was a member of a racial minority. And, in Washington, seemingly a minority of one. She did not fit in with whites and she did not fit in with blacks, and there was not what one could call any Eskimo social network in the city.

She was an attractive young woman, but in Washington, as one of the thousands of attractive young women with government jobs, Olive Cook inspired few second glances.

To make matters worse, her job—a low-level clerical position for which she was inadequately trained—proved to be less than rewarding. What she did for most of the day was to sit at her desk and wonder what was going on all around her.

And what she did for most of her nights was either to go back to her cramped, unattractive apartment, and wonder why she had ever wanted to leave the village, or, more frequently, to go out to a party, where, due to her nervousness and her inexperience and her feelings of isolation and insecurity, she would drink too much too quickly, or, if the opportunity presented itself, smoke so much dope that, temporarily, she would no longer care where she was.

Except for eating salad, there was little about Washington that she enjoyed. And while the salads were marvelous—for eighteen years she had lived in a place where the nearest thing to fresh greens had been packages of Doublemint gum—all the lettuce in Washington was not enough to overcome the sense of loss and confusion she felt.

The village had always seemed so stifling, so confining, and the life she would lead were she to stay there had seemed as barren and bleak as the frozen winter tundra which began outside her family's kitchen window and stretched on, unchanging, for hundreds of miles.

Yet as empty as Eskimo life had once seemed, it had become clear to Olive Cook that the ways of her people were almost infinitely more rewarding than the existence that was available to a single Eskimo girl from a small, backward village who had made the mistake of moving to Washington, D.C.

At least that seemed clear some of the time. At other times Olive Cook felt that there was nowhere she belonged. And nowhere she would ever belong. That she would not be able to go home again. But that neither would she be able to remain in the white man's world.

There were times—in fact, it may have been most of the time—that Olive Cook felt she would always be lost and confused. That she—and many others of her generation—had been cut loose forever from the moorings of Eskimo life and were doomed to drift endlessly on seas that they would never come to know.

By December, Olive Cook had decided that she needed to go back to the village for a while. To go home for Christmas. Not so much for the white man's Christmas of December 25, but for the Russian Orthodox Christmas festival—the Slavic—which was celebrated for a full week in early January. Her village was one in which the Russian Orthodox religion—which had been brought to the region two centuries earlier by the first white men to travel there—had endured. And where the week of the Slavic celebration was considered to be at once the most festive and the most solemn time of the year.

It would be, for Olive Cook, an opportunity to try to come to some sort of terms with herself. With her Eskimo heritage. And with whatever it was that she intended to do with her life.

She arranged for a two-week vacation and flew home. Through Chicago, to Anchorage, and then to Bethel; and then on a Delaire Flying Service charter flight—in a single-engine plane that landed on skis instead of wheels—to the village.

After she had been back for a few days, I called her on the village telephone. There was only one phone for the village—in the home of a man named Yeako Slim. It was a business. He would come fetch you if you received an incoming call, but on outgoing calls he took a commission.

I called one Sunday afternoon in January when it was 30 degrees below zero and dark in the village. I asked to speak to Olive Cook. The connection was not terribly good. Yeako Slim said something which I did not understand. Then, apparently, he went to get her.

It was a ten-minute walk from Yeako Slim's shack to the shack, at the south end of the village, where the Cook famliy lived. And then Olive had to put on her parka and her boots. Altogether, it took her more than twenty minutes to get to the phone.

She told me, as she had first told me in Washington, on the October night when I had met her, that it would be okay if I came to visit for the Slavic. I said I would fly out the next day.

Bethel was an hour and twenty minutes from Anchorage. The Wien terminal was a big wooden shack. There was a large, pushy crowd waiting for the plane, a mixture of Eskimos and whites. Waiting to board the plane and fly out of Bethel and back to the twentieth century.

In Alaska, the airplane does not just cover distance. It is also a time machine. You get on in Anchorage, an aggressive, if tacky, late-twentieth-century American city, and get off, eighty minutes later, not just five hundred miles away, but also fifty years back in time. No plumbing, only occasional electricity, and with the few streets of the town not yet paved.

The Wien terminal was a couple of miles outside of town. The Delaire Flying Service was right in the middle of the town, in a small wooden shack on the bank of the river. The river, of course, was frozen and covered with snow. The Kuskokwim is a big river by the time it reaches Bethel, maybe half a mile wide. The Delaire plane was a single-engine six-seater which used skis in the winter and pontoons in the summer. The fare to the village was thirty-two dollars but that could be divided among however many people happened to be making a given trip. I was lucky. There were three Eskimo women already waiting for a flight. That made it only eight dollars apiece. There was no schedule. We would go when the pilot turned up, and when the plane was in shape, and when they could fit this trip in among the shuttles back and forth to other villages. In the small Eskimo villages of Alaska, you call for the airplane the way, in a city, you call a cab.

It was a clear and windless day, with the temperature 20 below zero. By now, I had grown used to such temperatures. The sun glowed orange to the west. The village was at the same latitude, with the same amount of winter daylight, as Anchorage. Which was about the only thing that the village and Anchorage had in common.

The plane landed smoothly, on skis, on the river that served as the main street of the village.

In the distance, I saw a figure walking slowly up the river. A bulky figure, in a parka, maybe about a hundred yards away. The figure waved an arm. I waved back. This was Olive Cook, I assumed. She had heard the plane—in the village, you could not help but hear the plane—and had come out to see if I was on it. I picked up my duffel bag by one end, and, dragging the other end through the snow, I headed toward her.

"Hey, you crazy guy, you really nuts, you know that? I never thought you would come. How long you staying anyway? It's very crowded here for the Slavic. I think you just be in the way." Then she laughed. A bit hysterically, I thought.

"Look at that bag. What you got in there? You got presents for me, I sure hope. I don't know where you going to put a big bag like that. We don't have no extra space in our house. When you going back? When you tell that pilot to come for you? Oh boy, you crazy guy, I don't know what you are doing here."

We walked down the river to her house. Most of the village had been built on the east bank of the river. The Cook family, and one or two others, lived on the west bank, so in summer to pick up their mail, or to use the telephone, or simply to go out and visit, they would have to cross the river in a boat. In winter, of course, it made no difference. The river was like a six-lane highway right through town.

The house was an unpainted wooden shack. Olive pushed open the door and we stepped inside, accompanied by billows of steam.

"Take off your boots, you!" This was Olive's mother. Glaring at me, and pointing to a pile of boots by the door. In my socks, I stepped into the room that served as kitchen, living room, and dining room, and as bedroom for Olive's younger brothers and her cousin.

The room contained a wood-burning stove, a big table, and a couch that folded out to be a bed. There was a basin to wash in. Water was obtained by melting ice. There was a small storage closet, separated from the kitchen by a curtain. At the rear of the storage closet there was a bucket. This bucket was the Cook family's toilet. Every couple of days, they dumped it outside and started again. In spring, when breakup came—when the snow melted and the ground thawed and the river started flowing—the winter's waste pile would gradually disappear. As would all the other waste piles around the village.

There was a second, smaller room. With a bed in one corner for the parents, a bunk bed next to it, a bunk bed at the other end, and a cot pushed up against a wall. Normally, five people slept in this room. The parents, Olive, her sister, who was fourteen years old, and a male relative who lived with the family much of the time.

Olive's father was sitting cross-legged by the stove, working intently with a knife. A bald and bloody carcass lay beside him. He looked up, nodded once, went back to work.

"What's the matter?" Olive said. "You never seen anybody skin a fox?"

There was fur, blood, gristle, and bones all over the floor. Olive's father worked silently, with head bowed. He was a short man, of medium build, with a crew cut. Her mother was taller, lighter in color, less Asiatic looking.

"Hey, what do you think?" her mother said. "This is some kind of hotel? What you come here for with that big bag?"

"It's not so big."

"Yeah, where you think we gonna put it? We don't have no space in here."

"Hey, goddamn you," Olive said. "I sure hope you brought us some vegetables."

But no, I had not brought vegetables. I should have. I had thought of buying vegetables and fruit in Anchorage. But then I had been in a rush to catch my plane.

Olive's father put down his knife, wiped his bloody hands on his pants, and sat down at the table to eat lunch. Olive's mother put a bowl in front of me. She filled it with a light brown, pasty substance. There was a plate of pilot bread—thick, flat crackers—to go with it.

"I hope you like moose soup," Olive said. "That's all we eat here in the winter."

Actually, this was not quite true. That night, for dinner, following an afternoon during which Olive took me on a walking tour of the village, there was moose stew. The difference was, moose stew had gristly joints of moose in it, while the soup was just moose-flavored gruel.

As soon as the evening meal was over, Olive's father went back to the floor, where, now that he was finished skinning fox, he had started to build a blackfish trap.

Blackfish were oily little fish that swam all winter long in the river that flowed through the village. To catch them, you lowered the trap into the water through a hole in the ice, and pulled it out the next day. The trap was made of freshly cut wood, which was peeled, cut into strips, and then woven together to make a basket. A cone was placed over the open end. The fish would swim into the basket but then would be unable to get out.

It was a painstaking, intricate process, but Olive's father worked quickly, with total concentration, his sharp knife flashing, his stubby, worn fingers handling the wood the way a professional blackjack dealer handles cards.

The children had disappeared right after dinner into the other room of the house. Olive was helping her mother wash some clothes. They had an old-fashioned washtub, with a wringer that had to be cranked by hand.

By 9 p.m. Olive's father had almost finished the trap. Just two or three more strips to weave into place. His breathing was steady and rhythmic. He sat with head bowed, legs crossed, nothing moving but the masterful hands. To watch him work was to see not just the heart of a separate culture, but, it seemed, the essence of a dying age.

All over Alaska, Eskimos were giving up, moving to the cities, signing on for government aid. Taking jobs on the pipeline, or staying home and cashing welfare checks. Some, the more adaptable, had begun going to school to learn white men's trades: real estate, construction, and other forms of profitable entrepreneurship.

But here, in the village, was Al Cook. A survivor. Impervious to the assaults of time and progress upon the sacred traditions of his people.

His expression had not changed; he had not uttered a sound for more than an hour. The blackfish trap had come to seem an extension of himself. Then, suddenly, Olive's eight-year-old brother ran in from the back room.

"Papa, Papa!" the boy shouted. "Hurry up! Hurry up! 'Six Million Dollar Man' on TV!"

Al Cook dropped his knife. He tossed the almost completed blackfish trap aside. He jumped to his feet, his face animated for the first time all day. Grinning and chattering and rubbing his hands in anticipation, he hurried toward the other room, following his son.

"Oh boy," he said. "Hurry up." Motioning for me to accompany him. " 'Six Million Dollar Man' on TV."

Television was new. This was its first winter in the village, which had been chosen as part of a pilot project. Ostensibly, to see if the introduction of television would improve the quality of Eskimo life. Although some considered it a not so subtle form of genocide.

For the villagers, television was the biggest innovation since the airplane. Even bigger, in a way, since the airplane affected the lives of a comparatively small percentage of the population, whereas television influenced every life.

No more were ancient stories told late into the night. No more the quiet visits, the dances, the little games. Now, not even a blackfish trap was more important than a program as exciting as "The Six Million Dollar Man."

For the first time in history, the Eskimo had been given an opportunity to live vicariously. And he had seized it and was clinging to it for dear life. No matter that very few of the viewers could understand the dialogue—the English spoken was too quick, and the accent, to the Eskimo ear, was too foreign—the picture alone was enough. After centuries of staring into the flickering fire through the night, the village people could now stare at electronic images that flickered in a variety of adventurous ways.

It was television, I soon discovered, even more than the celebration of the Slavic, around which the life of the village seemed to revolve. There was only one channel—from Bethel. It broadcast a mixture of commercial and educational programs. The children watched "Sesame Street" each afternoon. Little Eskimo kids coming off the tundra and sitting three feet from the screen. Learning to count from one to ten in Spanish. Gone was the symbolism of the raven and the bear. The new gods were Big Bird, and Bert and Ernie.

It did not matter what program was on. After centuries of changeless frozen winter, where the only thing that moved for miles around was the snow when the wind happened to blow, it was now possible to turn one switch and this magic machine would bring a seemingly infinite variety of hallucinatory images before your eyes. It was almost a form of peyote.

"Starsky and Hutch." "Charlie's Angels." "Mister Rogers." The residents of the village loved them all. One afternoon, the entire Cook family sat transfixed for half an hour watching "Book Beat" as Robert Cromie directed questions at Saul Bellow.

I slept on the folding couch in the front room. The eight-year-old was next to me. His cousin slept next to him. A younger brother slept on the floor. Olive's parents got up at 6 a.m. Her father went outside and attached a sled to their snow machine. Her mother made coffee, then went to help with the sled.

"Where are they off to at this time of day?" I asked Olive.

"To Bethel."

"To Bethel? By snow machine? But that must be fifty miles away."

"Yeah, so what? Otherwise, how we gonna get our food for the Slavic? You think we can phone up and they deliver?"

Most of the food the Cook family ate was obtained by hunting or fishing. They caught fish in the summer and smoke-dried what they did not eat. In the fall, they froze the fish they caught. They also shot ducks and geese, and at least one moose every year. For incidental foods, there was a small store in the village, which had its goods delivered by charter flight from Bethel, after a Wien flight from Anchorage, and after a longer cargo flight, or shipment by barge or truck, from somewhere outside of Alaska. It was all this lugging around that made a can of string beans cost $2.50.

For the Slavic, however, the village store was not enough. For the Slavic, and maybe one or two other times during the winter, Olive's parents would travel all the way to Bethel by snow machine to do their shopping. Then all the way home the same day. This could be done only in winter, of course. In summer, there was no way to reach Bethel on the ground.

When the sled was attached, Olive's parents came back inside. They ate crackers with jam and drank coffee. Then they told their children what the chores were for the day. I gave Olive's mother some money for the food, in place of the vegetables I did not bring from Anchorage. She thanked me, they put on their parkas, and they were gone.

"How much did you give her?" Olive asked.

"Thirty dollars."

"Yeah, why don't you give her more, you rich white man? You come out here and eat all our food and take up all our space with your goddamn duffel bag, I trip over it every time I go in to take a piss. Why are you here? Didn't you know I was just drunk and stoned when I invited you?"

I shrugged. This seemed just Olive's way of saying good morning. I spread some butter and jam on a piece of pilot bread for my breakfast. Kool-Aid was the only thing to drink. The little kids drank Kool-Aid all the time, and chewed gum constantly, and told their mother to be sure to bring back the Sugar Pops. I think they saw commercials for sugared breakfast cereals on TV.

"Now what are you going to do, goddamn you? I got to do the wash. I am not here just to entertain you. Why don't you go play with the kids, that's all you are good for. Go on, don't bother me, I don't have no time for you. I got to be nice to you yesterday just because my mother and my father are around, but today they are gone and I wish that you were gone, too."

Then, inexplicably, she broke into a grin and leaned close to me and squeezed my arm and said, "Hey, don't worry. I just get a little upset, that is all. I'm only fooling. It's okay. You stay here as long as you want."

She did another load of wash, she mopped the floors, refusing my offers to help, and she tried to make a spaghetti sauce that afternoon, to show her parents the kind of food she ate in Washington. The sauce was doing well, too, until she decided that, having no meatballs, she should instead add little pieces of moose.

That night, there was a basketball game against a team from a nearby village to the north. The game was played in the school gymnasium. The gymnasium had a low roof, and the baskets were only nine feet high, but, otherwise, basketball was basketball, anywhere in the world.

Olive and I sat in the second row of folding wooden bleachers. The bleachers were only half filled. Another sign of the impact of television. Before TV, it had been standing room only for every game.

It was apparent from the start that the village team was outclassed. The opponents were bigger, stronger, faster, and had a guard who hit twenty-foot jump shots. The score, at the end of the first quarter, was 28–16.

Between quarters, the village players seemed embroiled in hot debate. There was much waving of arms, and voices were raised. Then, while some of the players sat back down on the bench in disgust, two members of the team walked over to where Olive and I were sitting.

"You play basketball?"

"A little bit. Long time ago."

The two players were about five feet six inches tall. No one on either team was more than three inches taller. I was over six three in bare feet.

"You play now. For us."

"No, I couldn't do that. I mean, look . . . I don't even have any sneakers."

"You play in socks."

"No, I think I'll just—"

"Goddamn you!" Olive shouted. "You play!"

So I played. For the whole second quarter and for part of the third. Until finally the village players had to admit that I was not such a great white hope after all. At least not in socks.

I scored four points. I got three or four rebounds. I committed a couple of fouls. And I slipped and fell about a dozen times on the highly waxed floor.

I might not have helped the village team, but I did prove to be a favorite with the crowd. They didn't react when I scored, but each time I slipped they gave me a standing ovation.

Midway through the third quarter time was called. The village team now trailed by twenty points. There was another heated discussion among my teammates. In their own language. A decision was reached and announced: "Okay, you, now go sit down." I was replaced by a kid five foot two.

The Slavic began the next day. It did not seem a very structured affair. Village leaders would carry a prayer wheel and incense into a home, followed by whoever was participating at any given time. As many people as possible would crowd into the house, and then, for twenty minutes or half an hour, they would chant prayers and sing ancient Russian hymns. When the singing was over, food would be served. And that was the problem. The praying and the singing were not so bad: exotic enough to be interesting for a while, and kind of stirring, really, when you realized how closely in touch these people still were with the days when the only white men in Alaska were the Russians.

But after the singing came the food. Sometimes there would be moose soup. Sometimes fermented seal meat, which was worse. But always as a staple, there was something called Eskimo ice cream. This was either seal oil or Crisco, whipped to a batter-like consistency, and laced heavily with a particularly noxious and bitter type of berry.

Unfortunately, you were expected to eat it. To pass a bowl back unfinished would have been considered not merely rude but, under the circumstances, almost blasphemous. And this stuff was served at every house.

At each house, also, the children were given bags full of candy. For three days, no one under the age of fourteen in the village ate anything else. And no matter how much they ate, their reserve supply seemed to increase. They would have candy enough, by the conclusion of the Slavic, to last them until freeze-up again the next fall. That they would have any teeth left was a doubtful proposition.

It was by far the most awesome, revolting, and chilling orgy of sugar consumption I'd ever seen. No Halloween, no Easter Sunday, no Christmas vacation in even the most permissive or uncaring American household could have begun to approach what Slavic meant to Eskimo children in western Alaska. And the parents did not seem bothered by it in the least. It was history, tradition; this was the way it had always been done. Not even a recent warning from the Russian Orthodox bishop, based in Sitka, that sugar consumption during the Slavic should be curtailed had any effect. No wonder that by the time he reached puberty, the average Eskimo child had fewer teeth in his mouth than a Boston Bruins defenseman.

Over the next twenty-four hours it became obvious that Olive Cook did truly regret having invited me to the Slavic. She had never expected that I would come, she was deeply embarrassed by my presence—I was, other than the schoolteacher, the only white person in the village—and she would feel immense relief when I departed. In addition to that, I couldn't take any more Eskimo ice cream.

I walked over to Yeako Slim's house and phoned the flying service in Bethel. They said they would send out a plane the next morning. I paid Yeako Slim a dollar for the call. There was a sign on the wall which said: PLEASE TRY TO AVOID SCRIBBLING ON TELEPHONE LOGS. SHOW SOME RESPECT. If you made a call, you marked down where you called and how long you talked. Then, every once in a while Yeako Slim would make you pay. It was like owing money at the grocery store.

It was cloudy in the village that day, and the temperature was up close to zero. The Cook family was busy, preparing for the arrival of the Slavic procession at their house. In the afternoon I took a long walk across a frozen lake.

The village ended right in the Cook's backyard. From there you could go seventy-five miles west and, in winter, not see another living thing. The seventy-five miles would bring you to the western edge of Alaska. The edge of the continent once again. The Bering Sea, and Russia beyond it. You could go a hundred miles north and not see another living thing. Until you hit the frozen Yukon River at a place called Pilot Station. This was the Yukon, which had started in Canada, a thousand miles to the east, now almost at the end of its run.

And from the village, in no matter what direction you went,

you would have to cover pretty near a hundred miles before you came to any land that rose more than one hundred feet above sea level. Most of the people in the village had never been that far from their homes.

In the evening, in the Cooks' house, all was ready for the celebration of the Slavic. The children were dressed in their finest clothes. Their hair was combed, their faces washed. Olive's mother and father had finished the cleaning and the preparation of the food. There was no more to do but to wait for the procession to arrive.

. The eight-year-old went out to see how much longer it might be. He came back saying two more houses, and then ours. That meant maybe an hour, maybe two. The family crowded into the bedroom and turned on the TV. The program was a public television production of *Macbeth*. The little boy thought it superb. Lots of sword fights. Olive's father felt it was not quite as good as "The Six Million Dollar Man," Macbeth, of course, not being bionic.

Macbeth was followed by a special: "Christmas from Disneyland." A one-hour program which had been broadcast across the rest of America three weeks before. Disney characters singing Christmas carols; Mickey Mouse riding in a sleigh. Glittery decorations strung from palm trees.

The entire Cook family was ecstatic. They had heard about this place called Disneyland, and now here it was, right in their home, for them to see.

I don't know if it was Anita Bryant who was the hostess, but someone like that. It was classic Disney, "Silver Bells," "Frosty the Snowman," "Rudolph the Red-nosed Reindeer." In the village they had real reindeer practically outside their back door, but this was better. This was TV.

A chorus of children dressed as snowballs was standing in front of a phony cathedral, singing "Santa Claus Is Coming to Town," when, very softly, in the background, the first faint sounds of the approaching Slavic procession could be heard.

The worshippers had left the last house on the other side of the river, and now were walking slowly across, spinning the prayer wheel, waving the incense, singing the ancient Russian processional hymn. Fifty or sixty people, keeping a centuries-old tradition alive.

They crossed the river and started up the path toward the

front door. The singing was coming now in rich, mellow tones through the frigid night air.

Olive's mother got up and turned off the television. Disneyland vanished. The Slavic procession arrived, as it had been arriving among these people for two hundred years.

Olive jumped to her feet and angrily threw a dish towel against a wall. "This goddamn Slavic ruins everything," she yelled. "You can't even watch real Christmas on TV."

In the morning, when I left, Olive came with me, even though there were three days left of Slavic. Her decision was sudden: she packed in a hurry, laughing and crying, as the pilot waited impatiently by the plane. For a couple of days, she said, she'd stay in Bethel, where there were people she wanted to see. Then she would go to Anchorage, where she wanted to spend a few days being drunk. Eventually, she would go back to Washington, to the Department of the Interior to try again; but this time with less enthusiasm than despair.

9 Juneau

Sandy had found Juneau almost unchanged. Physically, there were differences: the new Federal Building, a concrete block with windows like gun turrets; and the big new State Office Building, which seemed ridiculous, because the capital was due to move in a couple of years; and a new Hilton hotel had opened, and the downtown movie theater had closed, and there was a lot of new home building and a new shopping center out by the airport. But, in its essence, Juneau, like Sandy herself, was pretty much the same when she returned as it had been when she had left. The bars stayed open until early morning and everybody Sandy knew stayed in them. Cocaine was even more prevalent—and more expensive—than it had been. A lot of the guys—and some of the girls—had gone up and worked the pipeline for a while. Everyone had money, plenty of it; but everyone still wanted more.

Sandy had moved into a house on Star Hill, an old place that had been divided into several apartments. It was as high up on the hill as houses went. Out the front door, the neighborhood, and the city, ended abruptly. There was a little flight of stairs leading into the woods. With a sign that said: TRAIL TO MOUNT ROBERTS— SUMMIT 3.5 MILES.

From her bedroom, on the second floor, at the rear of the house, Sandy had a good view down the long, sloping streets toward the water. A view of Gastineau Channel, and of Douglas Island, across the bridge.

The house was eight blocks from the center of downtown. To walk down took less than ten minutes. To walk back up took more than twenty. It was so steep that at one point, on Fourth Street, the pavement stopped and the street continued as nothing more than a flight of wooden stairs.

Ross and Karen were living in the house on Star Hill, though not together. Ross was one of the few men Sandy had met since she'd been back with whom she had not gone to bed. It was just something they had agreed not to do. For one thing, she could tell he was still too much in love with Karen, and besides, Sandy figured she needed at least one friend around town who did not know what she looked like with her pants off.

Karen had an apartment on the second floor, across from Sandy, while Ross had moved into one of the little basement apartments. It was cheaper down there, and Ross had received a further reduction on the rent by agreeing to act as the building's superintendent. This meant, for instance, that if the drain of Karen's bathtub should become clogged by strands of her long brown hair, Ross would come up and unclog it. Which he was used to, because for much of their first year in Juneau, as well as for the two years before that, Ross and Karen had lived together.

Karen was from Reno, Nevada, and Ross was from Anaheim, California. They had met in college, at Cal State Fullerton, and, along with their friends Hippy Shark and Barely Human, they had decided to go to Alaska on the ferry. Being the state capital, Juneau had seemed a plausible destination. If they liked it, they would stay for a while; if not, they would go somewhere else. They were just out of college, and not much seemed to be happening in the world, and they were in no hurry to get on with their lives.

Once in Juneau, Ross and Karen remained a couple until the

middle of winter. When they split, it was nothing personal; Karen just wanted to be independent for a while. Juneau had turned out to be an extremely confusing place, and she thought she might be better able to cope with it if she were freed from the pressure of a relationship. She was reading a lot of feminist literature at the time. Karen moved into a cabin with a young woman who had just broken up with the man with whom *she* had come to Juneau.

No doubt about it: Juneau was a tough town on couples. The way Ross figured it, you felt so cramped, so confined by the imminence of the mountains, and by the impossibility of getting out of the city by road—especially if you had just come from the automobile world of southern California—and so oppressed by the constant, nagging, relentless precipitation, that you had to break out in some way. Some part of you, in some way, had to give; and, in most cases, right after the self-discipline and the ambition went, the next thing to go was the relationship.

But the other thing about Juneau was, while people were always breaking up, very few ever left town. So it was best that the split be amicable, because with only four or five bars to go to, no matter what you were doing or who you were doing it with, you could not help but run into your former partner, or partners, with his or her new mate, or mates, practically every night of the week.

Booze helped, of course, in that kind of atmosphere, and so did dope. Except when they had the opposite effect, and somebody beat up somebody, or stabbed him, or tried to burn down a house. But this happened rather less often than might have been expected, considering the isolation and the climate.

Even by Juneau standards, Ross and Karen's split seemed incredibly amicable. No matter who else they went out with, or what else they did, they still met for dinner once a week. Just the two of them, away from the crowds, in one of Juneau's more expensive restaurants. They kept few secrets from one another, and told few lies. They still enjoyed each other's company more than they enjoyed the company of anyone else. It was apparent that they were still quite in love. But Karen had her independence thing to work out, and both of them, by now, were a little afraid of Juneau, and of what it could do to them, and so they felt it was safer to stay apart.

Even so, when Karen's cabin burned down, and when her friend moved into an apartment with a new boyfriend, and when

Ross told Karen about the vacant second-floor apartment in the house on Star Hill, she agreed to move into it, even though Ross was already living in the basement.

Karen was pale and thin and very pretty. She had a soft voice, a gentle nature, an alert mind—when it was not numbed by drugs or alcohol or lack of sleep—and a sharp, self-deprecating sense of humor. She worked half days in the darkroom of a commercial photography establishment. When she was not working, or drinking, or taking one sort of drug or another—or reading feminist literature—Karen wrote poetry, and took photographs of Juneau, and made charcoal sketches on a large drawing pad she had bought. She had artistic talent, but not much confidence in herself, and she had not yet figured out how the creative impulses she was feeling could be successfully integrated into the haphazard, self-destructive sort of life—with its alternating bouts of excess and lethargy—which she was leading in Juneau.

Ross was a thin, cordial, easygoing person who had spent most of the fall and winter pretty drunk. His problem was that he had this college education and this love for Karen and these memories of southern California, and now he was in Juneau, in winter, apart —but only two floors apart—from the woman he loved, and getting paid only to fix bathtub drains. He was still in the process, as they say, of getting it together. Not an easy thing to do in Juneau, where the chronic dampness, and the widespread manic-depression, tended to make things—and people—come apart.

About the only thing to which Ross applied himself seriously was his weekly class at the airport. Ground school. Which would give him the textbook knowledge that would prepare him to learn how to fly a plane. That was his goal: to be a pilot, a commercial pilot, probably, for one of the Juneau air services. Since it seemed that about 20 percent of the adults in Juneau were pilots of one sort or another, this did not seem an unreasonable goal.

Ross was spending a lot of time with Harvey, a tall, stringy-haired fellow from Jackson, Wyoming, with whom, as it happened, Sandy was intending to go to bed as soon as she was able to find the time. Harvey was pretty wasted looking and scruffy, even by the generous standards of Juneau, but until a few months earlier he had been a pilot for one of Juneau's leading flying services.

That had ended when Harvey inadvertently turned a seaplane upside down in Gastineau Channel. He had been on a return flight, with no passengers in the plane, and he had, perhaps, rushed his approach just a bit, in order to get down to the Triangle and meet a connection for some cocaine, but even after he had explained this, the flying service took the position that Harvey might just as easily have flipped the plane over with a full load of passengers aboard. Besides, the salt water had not done the engine any good.

So Harvey was now an ex-pilot, except for when he could borrow a plane for private use, at which times he would take Ross up and teach him how to do flips and loops and stalls and all sorts of things that he had not yet been taught in ground school. Ross figured if he could survive Harvey's lessons, he would survive anything that he himself might do while at the controls.

After his flying career had ended, Harvey became a partner in a house painting business and hired Ross to work for him. When weather permitted, Ross spent sixteen or eighteen hours a day painting the exterior of Juneau houses. Weather, however, had not permitted since early November and might not again permit until May; so, in the meantime, while waiting for the weather to permit, and while waiting for Karen, his true love, to work through her need for independence, and while waiting to finish ground school so he could actually and officially learn to fly, and while waiting to get just a slightly tighter grip upon himself, Ross spent most of his time drinking beer. Occasionally, he spent time being sick, which would cause him to stay out of the bars for a while, and lie around his basement apartment, from which he couldn't see the sun even on those rare days when it did shine.

Sometimes, Hippy Shark and Barely Human would come to visit. Those two—living on a boat down in the harbor—had become so totally assimilated by Juneau that there were times when Ross did not even recognize them when he saw them in a bar or on the street. But mostly, when he was sick, Ross stayed alone. He would play his guitar in the basement. This was something he was very good at, but like Karen with her art, he lacked confidence, and so played only when alone, or very drunk. His other activity, when he was sick, was reading books. Fiction, mostly. James Michener, Irving Wallace, Herman Wouk. Just so it was long; just so it would kill some of the vast amount of time there was to kill in a basement apartment in Juneau in the winter, while waiting for Karen's drain to clog again.

I flew to Juneau on a Saturday night, on the weekend before the state legislature opened its annual session. The plane was filled with legislators and staff members, girding themselves for the coming ordeal. Bourbon seemed to be the method most in favor.

Until very recently—until the oil and the pipeline—there was little of consequence for the Alaska state legislature to legislate about. The big decisions affecting the state were made in Washington, and Washington federal agencies carried them out. A legislator would come to Juneau for a binge, for an affair, or, if he got lucky, for a quiet but lucrative arrangement with a lobbyist.

It was an informal, easygoing way of life. On Saturday night, the governor would walk down from his residence, buy a few rounds of drinks at the Red Dog, and sing a few country and western songs. "Your Cheatin' Heart" was one of his favorites, and only a few of the legislators took it personally. Another favorite was "Release Me" . . . "Please release me, let me go" . . . which was understandably popular in Juneau in midwinter. It was also a song which, eventually, the voters of Alaska took to heart, as the governor discovered when he ran for re-election.

But things were different now, at least in some ways. Not only was the present governor a teetotaler, but the legislators found themselves with genuine business to conduct. The atmosphere still ranged from informal to raucous, and still only 10 percent of the legislators were attorneys—by far the lowest percentage of any state legislature in the country—but the stakes had grown immeasurably. Alaska had a lot of money to spend now, and it was the legislature that decided how to spend it. Sometimes the sessions now extended into June, which had been a major impetus behind the proposal to move the capital. To build a new capital city, somewhere within driving distance of Anchorage. That proposal had passed in a statewide referendum, and, in a later ballot, the voters had even selected the new site: about seventy road miles north of Anchorage, near the tiny settlement of Willow. But even if the legislature ever did get around to appropriating the billions of dollars that would be required to build a whole new city in the wilderness—a sub-Arctic equivalent of Brasília—it would be years before any government business would be conducted there. In the meantime, the legislators would have to continue to try to cope with life in Juneau.

There were those who believed there was a cause-and-effect relationship between the nature of Juneau and the irrational behavior that seemed so often to be engendered there. That the sheer, unbending intensity of it all—the weather and isolation, set against a backdrop of such magnificence—caused the human nervous system to overload.

It was not simply that actions which anywhere else would have been merely ludicrous were given special poignance by their juxtaposition with such a setting, but that Juneau's particular bittersweet and haunting loveliness might actually be responsible for such behavior. That outbursts of excess—generally involving alcohol, narcotics, or members of the opposite sex—were the only valid response, or possible response, to such an excess of beauty and wretchedness as was provided by Juneau itself.

There was one school of thought which held that it was less scary to fly into Juneau at night, when you could not see the closeness of the mountains. On the other hand, if the passengers could not see the mountains, neither could the pilot. And the Alaska Airlines crash a few years earlier—in which sixty-two people had been killed—had come at night. In truth, there was no good way to fly to Juneau; just drink what they sell you and hope for the best.

On the night I flew from Anchorage, in mid-January, it was snowing so hard that daylight would not have made a difference; you couldn't have seen a mountain had it been noon.

It was a ninety-minute flight, with a two-hour time change along the way. Juneau was on California time, two hours removed from most of the state, which was another reason given for the proposed transfer of the capital. The time difference between Juneau and Nome, in fact, was as great as the difference between Juneau and New York.

The plane landed safely, and I rode into town on a bus. Through rich, thick snow that was piling up quickly on the ground and on the evergreens that were so much a part of Juneau's setting. The lights of the city glowed, soft and muted, in the distance. Against the black velvet backdrop of the mountains: Mount Juneau and Mount Roberts the two big ones, to the bases of which the city clung. The fresh snow gave the scene an Alpine charm that was deceptive. By Monday morning the snow would turn to sleet. By Tuesday it would be back to rain again. And then once more, for the residents of Juneau, it would come to seem that the wet gray days would never end.

Actually, the natural place for the city to have been located was twenty miles north, at the old Indian settlement of Auke Bay. The weather was less onerous, the land was more open, and Auke Bay itself was even better than Gastineau Channel for the harboring of boats. But it had been gold—the almost accidental discovery by Joe Juneau and his partner Richard Harris, a pair of drunken stumblebums who were practically pushed into the creek by their Indian guide before they noticed the gold was there—that had led to the founding of Juneau. And it had been gold that had led to its growth.

At one time, across the channel on Douglas Island, there had been twelve thousand people working at the Treadwell mine, the biggest of its type in the world. And by the time the gold had dwindled, the government had grown up to take its place. So that Juneau did not become a ghost town, like Skagway to the north, or like Dawson City in the Yukon, or even, to some extent, like Nome. Juneau continued to prosper; in some ways a very lucky place. And what set it apart from any other Alaskan community, what gave it, even more than the natural beauty of its setting, an unmistakable identity and flavor of its own, was the fact that it was the only one of the gold rush cities of Alaska not to have suffered a major fire in its central business district.

The town had been founded in 1880, and within the seven-block radius that had formed the original downtown, sixty of the buildings constructed in the first twenty-five years were still standing. There were almost one hundred fifty others that had been built prior to the start of World War I. Thus, in Juneau, the sense of history, the closeness to roots, was palpable; not abstract, as in Anchorage, which, although in existence for only sixty years, had long since paved over any traces of soul it ever had.

As one walked through Juneau—in the snow, in the sleet, in the rain—past all the pastel houses, up and down the wooden stairways, and through all the narrow, winding streets, this atmosphere, engendered by the presence of so many of the original structures, combined with the natural setting—the steepness, the mountains above, the water below—constantly asserted itself. Juneau staked out its own territory in your consciousness. To be there was to feel a sense of surroundings so powerful as to seem almost an extra dimension.

The feeling, however, was bittersweet: the sweetness in the

beauty, the bitterness in the weather that so often obscured it. The sleet, the mist, the rain, the inevitability and relentlessness of wet weather. Spend a week in Juneau, especially with a couple of sunny days, and you think you would like to live there for the rest of your life. But stay for three months, especially in winter, and you would give a year of your life just for a weekend out of town.

From the house on Star Hill, I walked around a corner and back along a narrow, winding road. The road led into Silverbow Basin, an area from which gold had once been mined. The road was closed in winter, covered with snow, with only a snow machine track to walk along. Tons of soft, wet snow hung precariously from a mountain for several hundred feet above the road. There were avalanches here every year. Below the road, a sharp precipice dropped several hundred feet to a creek. Across the creek, a thick wall of evergreens rose steeply up the lower portion of Mount Juneau. There was no trace of civilization. No sound of the city. The landscape all around was undisturbed. Ten minutes from the house on Star Hill.

Another day, I walked down the hill to the channel, and across the bridge to Douglas Island, and south a few blocks to a point where, at the edge of a newly developed residential neighborhood, a trail began. The trail—in winter it was only a snow machine trail—led deep into the forest that covered the island and eventually to the top of a ridge on the western edge, from which, if it were not too snowy or rainy or foggy, one could see across another channel, to the next island to the west, Admiralty Island.

It was a full day's walk across Douglas Island and back through the snow; and once on the trail not a living creature larger than a bird was encountered. There were bears on the island, of course, but in January they were assumed to be hibernating.

The thought occurred, as I walked, that for all the traveling through Alaska I had done, I had not yet come very near what I had perceived, at the beginning, to be its essence: the direct experience of vastness, isolation, and cold. I had spent many hours in exotic locations, in the company of unconventional human beings, but I had not yet established contact with the land. Before the winter ended, I wanted to spend some time with it alone.

10 Crescent Lake

The Federal Writers Project book on Alaska, published in 1939, reprinted a diary found next to the body of a man who had lived the last six months of his life alone in a cabin in the Alaskan wilderness.

Oct. 4th, 1917. Getting sick packing, now looking for camping place. Cold in the lungs with a high fever.

6th. Less fever, less pain, but getting weak.

7th. Feeling better but very weak.

9th. Getting a little stronger.

10th. Going to build a house. Will not be able to pull canoe up this fall, got to wait for the ice.

13th. Shot a glacier bear.

14th. Shot a goat.

17th. House finished.

18th. Taking out some traps.

20th. Made a smoke house.

21st. Shot one goat.

25th. Shot one lynx.

27th. Shot a wolf and a bear cub.

28th. Winter has come. Strong wind, two feet of snow.

Nov. 4th. Shot one lynx.

6th. Made one pair of bearskin pants.

8th. Sugar is all gone.

13th. Made two pair of moccasins.

18th. Finished one fur coat of bear, wolf, and lynx.

21st. Finished one sleeping bag of bear, goat, blankets, and canvas. Rain for several days.

22nd. Left eye bothers me. Shot one goat.

26th. Shot one lynx while eating breakfast.

27th. Made one pair of bearpaw snowshoes.

Dec. 1st. Getting bad. Cold for several days, river still open.

4th. River raised six feet in 24 hours.

6th. Slush stiffening, slowly making ice.

7th. The wind is so strong that you can't stand upright. River froze except a few riffles. Too much snow and too rough for sleighing. Snow getting deeper now.

15th. Very cold and strong wind, impossible to be out without skin clothes.

19th. Snowing but still very cold. Riffles up in the bend still open. Can't travel. Don't believe there will be ice a man can run a sleigh over this winter. Very little grub, snow too deep and soft for hunting goats. Stomach balking at straight meat, especially lynx.

21st. Shot a goat from the river.

25th. Very cold. A good Christmas dinner. Snow getting hard. River still open in places above camp.

26th. Broke through the ice. Skin clothes saved the day.

31st. Finished new roof on the house. One month of cold weather straight. Last night and today rain. Stomach getting worse.

Jan. 8th, 1918. River open as far as can be seen. Health very poor.

12th. Lynx moving down the river one or two a night; no chance to catch them.

15th. Goats moving out of reach. Using canoe on the river.

16th. One lynx. Weather getting mild.

20th. Rain today.

22nd. One lynx.

28th. One goat, been cold for a few days, no ice on river.

Feb. 1st. Cold weather nearly all month of January. Lynx robbed my meat cache up river. Salt and tea but once a day. Gradually getting weaker.

5th. Colder weather, feeling very bad. Just able to take care of myself.

10th. Milder, feeling very bad. Heavy fall of snow.

15th. Good weather continues, feeling some better.

24th. More snow. Living on dry meat and tallow.

26*th.* Shot one goat from the river.

Mch. 2*nd.* Shot one goat.

11*th.* Starting for Dry Bay, believing the river open. Out about one hour and struck ice. Can't go either way. Too weak to haul the canoe. Snow soft, no game here.

25*th.* Trying to get to the house. River is frozen in places and rising. The sleigh is now only three miles from there, but open river and perpendicular cliffs keep me from getting any farther. At present cannot find anything to eat here. Eyes are getting bad.

28*th.* Eyes can't stand the sun at all. Finest kind of weather.

Apr. 1*st.* Got to the house with what I could carry. Wolverines have been here eating my skins, robes, and moccasins, old meat, and also my goatskin door. They tried to run me last night, came through the stovepipe hole showing fight. Heavy fall of snow. Canoe and some traps down the river about five miles, close to Indian grave mark. Camp about halfway.

3*rd.* Still snowing. Cooking my last grub, no salt, no tea.

4*th.* Shot one goat, using all but three of my shells. Can't see the sights at all.

7*th.* Wolverine working on camp below carrying away my things. Ate part of my bearskin pants. Packed the old .30-.30 out into the brush. Eyes getting worse again, don't even stand the snow.

10*th.* Wolverines at my bedding and one snowshoe. In the tent, getting shaky in the legs. A five-mile walk a big day's work.

12*th.* Seen a fox track today. Birds are coming too. Fine weather.

15*th.* The no-salt diet is hitting me pretty hard. Eyes are getting worse, in the bunk most of the time.

17*th.* Rain yesterday and today.

20*th.* Finest weather continues again, cooking the last grub, got to stay in bunk most of the time—my legs won't carry me very far. My eyes are useless for hunting, the rest of my body also useless. I believe my time has come. My belongings, everything I got I give to Joseph Pellerine of Dry Bay; if not alive, to Paul Swartzkoph, Alsek River, April 22, 1918.

V. Swanson.

From the apartment I had just moved into, I walked to the Forest Service office on Fireweed Lane and picked out a cabin at Crescent Lake, on the Kenai Peninsula, about a hundred miles south of Anchorage. I planned to spend three days there alone. It was late February, and although winter still had a long way to run, there was already more light in the sky.

I had moved out of Tom and Marnie's guest room, finally, and into a one-bedroom apartment in a brand-new two-story building called a six-plex. The apartment was near Fifteenth and Gambell, just behind the ball field at Mulcahy Park, where the Anchorage Glacier Pilots baseball team played their home games in the summer. It was about a fifteen-minute walk from Tom and Marnie's and about twenty minutes from downtown. There were three liquor stores within a five-minute walk of the apartment, all of them open from 8 a.m. to 2 a.m., seven days a week. The liquor store was where you went to buy your paper on Sunday morning. To buy a quart of milk, you had to walk more than a mile.

My one-bedroom apartment, unfurnished, rented for $350 a month. I borrowed most of the furniture I needed from Tom and Marnie and bought the rest secondhand. The apartment next to mine was occupied by the night bartender at the Petroleum Club, who snored loudly through most of the day. I was one flight down, below street level, and had no views of Cook Inlet or Mount Mc-Kinley, but from my bedroom window, if I stood on tiptoe, I could look out past a vacant lot and see the Chugach Mountains. That would change with the first hint of spring, when a new apartment house would be built on the vacant lot.

Tom loaned me the equipment I would need: sleeping bag, an ax, a Coleman lantern that burned unleaded gas, and snowshoes, because I had never used cross-country skis.

I left on a Sunday afternoon, a clear cold day with bright sunshine. In addition to what I had borrowed from Tom, I brought a box of food and the boots and parka I was wearing. That was all. I brought no books, no magazines, no beer or wine or brandy; no cigarettes. I wasn't even carrying a watch. I wanted three days and three nights of unbroken contact with the winter environment. Total solitude. No escapes of any kind. I would be alone, in a cabin, at the edge of a frozen lake, surrounded by mountains. The cabin had a wood-burning stove. I had my food, but I would have to cut my own firewood to stay warm. After three days, the chartered plane would come back.

In a single-engine Super Cub, it was a fifty-five-minute flight to Crescent Lake. Across Turnagain Arm and then over the snow-covered, uninhabited mountains of the Kenai Peninsula. Turnagain Arm was a body of water that branched off from Cook Inlet. In 1780, Captain Cook thought it might be the Northwest Passage for which he was searching. But then, after fifty miles, it narrowed and ended, and he had to turn back, not for the first time, which led him to call it Turnagain.

The pilot banked steeply and flew very close to the side of a mountain. Strong winds were making the plane bounce. I could see the pine trees, then the individual branches of the trees. Where there were no trees, I could see, all too clearly, the rocks of which the mountains were composed. A gust of wind hit the plane and it lurched and dipped even closer. I tried looking in the other direction, but there was a mountain out that window, too.

On the first try, only one of the two landing skis locked into place. The pilot picked up a hammer and smacked something. On the second try, both skis came down.

The lake was five miles long, less than one mile across, and curved like a crescent. There were mountains all around it, and mountains rising steeply, to 5,000 feet, from either side. The cabin was at the west end of the lake. The pilot taxied to it and I climbed out and unloaded my gear. The plane took off. In an hour, it would be back in Anchorage. I was here, alone.

The temperature was only a few degrees above zero, and a wind was blowing hard across the lake. In summer, people came here to canoe and to fish and to hike in the mountains. In winter, there was none of that. In winter, there was firewood to cut.

Actually, that afternoon I cut no wood. There was enough for the first night cut already and stacked near the wood stove in the cabin. Each person who used the cabin was supposed to leave behind at least as much wood as had been there when he arrived. That way, if someone wound up at the cabin in an emergency, there could at least be a fire right away.

I put on my snowshoes and walked to the center of the lake. The mountain on the north side rose like a cresting wave. From half a mile out, the cabin seemed just a black dot in the snow. The only sound was the sound of the wind. The sun and snow were bright against the eyes. It was clumsy going in the snowshoes, which I had never worn before. I kept tripping. With each step, the back of one snowshoe would wind up on top of the front of the other. Eventually, I learned to slide my feet forward, and to shuffle, instead of step.

It was staying light now until almost six o'clock. But the mountains were high enough to block the sun from the lake long before that. I went back to the cabin and built a fire. Tom had explained to me how to light the Coleman lamp, but, alone in the cabin, it seemed risky to fool around with matches and unleaded gas. I heated a can of stew on top of the stove and ate by flashlight. I was afraid the lantern might burn the cabin down. After I ate the stew, I went to bed. Solitude was fine, except there was nothing to do.

The thermometer outside the cabin had said zero. Once the fire in the stove had gone out, the temperature inside the cabin could not have been much higher than that. There were spaces between the logs big enough to serve as windows. And enough holes in the roof so that fresh snow fell in with each gust of wind. I wore long underwear, woolen socks, a woolen shirt, and a woolen hat on my head, and I wrapped myself inside the sleeping bag like a mummy. It was a very good sleeping bag, the best that Eddie Bauer made, and I zipped it up to cover my whole head. Even so, it was by far the coldest night I'd ever spent. I would lie awake shivering in the dark, hearing the noise of little animals rustling on the floor by the stove. Each time I fell asleep I dreamed it was morning, that the sun was shining and I was warm. Then I would wake up in the dark. Having no way to tell time, not knowing how much of the night still remained. It was not only the coldest but the longest night I'd ever spent.

Until I'd come to Alaska, I had never even used a sleeping bag. What was I doing here at Crescent Lake? And why had I decided to stay for three nights? I felt an overwhelming urge to call the flying service in the morning and to tell them to come and get me right away. Except, of course, there was no phone. In Alaska, when you went out of a city, you stuck to the plan you had made. Three days was three days. Which would mean two more nights after this. Then the wind blew harder and I heard a rumbling noise from somewhere and I began to imagine how easy it would be for the cabin to be buried in an avalanche.

I dreamed again it was morning and when I woke up it really was. I was shivering inside the sleeping bag, but I unzipped and dressed quickly and started a fire in the stove. This morning, I would have to cut wood. There was a saw in the cabin, and I had Tom's ax. I had never cut firewood before, but if it stayed this cold I was sure I'd be able to learn.

Outside, the temperature was 10 above and the sky gray. Sure signs of snow. I walked, on my snowshoes, into the woods. The idea was to find trees already down. Deadwood. I would saw limbs off and drag them back to the cabin through the snow. Then I would saw them into pieces small enough to fit in the stove. Then split them with the ax, so they would be easier to burn.

I spent the whole morning doing this. I became obsessed with firewood. I wanted a stack big enough to go from floor to ceiling, around all four walls. I worked until my arms were so weary that I could no longer raise the ax above my head. I sweated so much, cutting wood, that I had to take off my parka and my wool shirt and work in only my undershirt.

Then the snow began to fall. Lightly at first, small flakes, with no wind. I ate some cheese and a can of sardines for lunch. After lunch, I shuffled back out on the lake. Even in light snow, the tops of the mountains were obscured. Before long, it was hard to see the cabin. I walked back. I could see how easy it would be to get turned around in a storm and to walk for hours searching for your cabin, while being only a quarter mile from it all the time. I had heard many stories through the winter of people found frozen to death after storms, sometimes within fifty yards of their homes.

I spent the rest of the afternoon cutting wood. Not so much because I needed more, but because there was nothing else to do. I was developing a desperate craving for a book.

A pilot had told me about a young woman named Charlotte who had come into a village in interior Alaska, at the beginning of winter, and had asked him to fly her to a cabin about fifty miles up a river tributary. She had met a man in Fairbanks and now she was going there to live with him. The pilot took her. About six weeks later he decided to fly up and see how she was doing. He found out even before he landed his plane. She had laid pine boughs in the snow, to make a big sign, visible to any plane flying low: CHAR WANTS OUT. CAN YOU TAKE?

I was starting to understand how she felt, and I had only been here for a day. The idea of stripping all vicariousness from your life, of immersing yourself totally in where you were and what you did, would not be easily mastered by someone from the urban Northeast, where one grew addicted to vicarious experience, and where one became as dependent upon outside stimulus as upon food and drink every day.

Toward dusk, on the second day, the wind began to blow. The snow, which had been falling lightly but steadily since midmorning, now came down thick and hard. I ate the second half of my stew, surrendered to a surge of self-pity, and crawled into my sleeping bag while the wood fire was still burning hard.

I felt quite small, with much that was big all around me. But on the state of Alaska highway map, Crescent Lake was considered so insignificant as to be not even listed by name. And these mountains above it were so ordinary—by Alaskan standards—that they, too, were without names.

What was it? Tuesday? Light out? Hard to tell. *Jesus Christ*, the wind was blowing. As I woke more fully, I looked around the cabin and saw that everything inside, even my sleeping bag, was covered with snow. The wind had blown so hard overnight that in the corners of the cabin the snow was almost two feet deep.

It was good I had cut so much wood the day before, because now I was stuck in a blizzard. The temperature had risen to the mid-20s, but the wind had risen far more than that. The snow was blowing so hard I could not see past the cabin porch. I opened the door and the snow was waist-high outside. I had to climb a snowdrift in my snowshoes in order to make my way to the outhouse. And when I got there I saw that only the roof was sticking up above the snow.

The wind blew all day. The snow fell. It was as dark gray as in Barrow at noon. There was nothing to do, no place to go, no way to mark the passage of time.

I had brought a section of the Sunday Anchorage *Times*, to use in getting fires started. And so I cheated, even though I had told myself I would not read. It was the real estate section. I studied every house that was for sale, every apartment that was for rent. And imagined what it would be like to be in each. With electricity, running water, and heat. With magazines and books. And a refrigerator full of meat and fish and beer. And a big double bed with clean sheets, and with a lovely woman to share it all. With even radio and television, which I had never before felt dependent upon. Television, in fact, was something to which I had a powerful aversion. But now I craved it. Just for the noise. Just for the sound of human voices. Just for sound other than this wind.

The blizzard lasted for two days. On the second day, I had to go out and cut more wood. At some point during the two days I saw a moose. Moving slowly through the snow near the edge of the lake. I wished that he would not go away. The sight of another living creature proved to be a great boost for my morale. Other than the voles that scrabbled around the cabin floor at night, I'd had no contact with anything animate for seventy-two hours. By far the longest such stretch of my life, and unrelieved by even the temporary distraction of a book.

What the hell time was it? It seemed to take forever to get light, and then it seemed to take forever to get dark. Did this have something to do with relativity? No, it probably just had to do with being alone. In a cabin. In a blizzard. At the edge of a snow-covered lake. In Alaska. At the end of February. Char Wants Out. Can You Take? And at least Char had been living with a friend.

The pilot had been due back on Wednesday, but Wednesday had been a blizzard day, so I'd cut my firewood and eaten my cheese and wished that the moose would return.

On Thursday it was bright and clear and I woke up filled with joy. I could see across the lake again, could see the tops of the mountains, and the sky. The wind had subsided and all was quiet once more. The first noise I would hear would be the noise of the plane. Then I would see it in the sky. I figured the pilot would be there about noon. Whenever noon was. It did not matter. Having endured four days, including two and a half in a blizzard, I could certainly handle an hour or two in the sun. Knowing that so soon I would be out. Climbing into the plane, putting my sleeping bag and food box and snowshoes and unused Coleman lantern in the back, and then bumping along the lake surface through the snow. Then taking off. And rising above the tops of the mountains that had been looming above me for what had come to seem half my life. I would be heading toward Anchorage. Toward people. Toward life. I didn't think I would be able to explain to anyone exactly how it had felt, being here. I didn't think I'd even want to try. I just wanted to go to a movie, and to a place that served pizza, and I wanted to drink beer and play songs on a jukebox and take a hot shower and make love in the bed in my apartment.

But the pilot didn't come. All day, there was nothing in the sky but the sun. All day, not a sound around the lake. I could tell when it was about midday, and then I watched, disbelieving, as the afternoon shadows slowly started to rise up the sides of the mountains and to cover the surface of the lake. I didn't cut wood. I didn't take a walk. I just sat on my fully packed duffel bag, in front of the cabin, and watched the sky.

It got dark. There was no plane. I went to bed, filled with bitterness and rage. In the morning, I said, I would walk out. From the far end of the lake there was supposed to be a trail that led, eventually, to a road at a place called Moose Pass. I would get out that way on my snowshoes, dragging my duffel bag through the snow, carrying the lantern and the ax. And I would find some-one, somewhere, maybe in this place called Moose Pass, and I would get myself back to Anchorage. And when I reached An-chorage I would go out to the office of the flying service, and I would start swinging the ax. And I would chop the wings off all their planes. Rotten bastards. Sons of bitches. Suppose I had chopped a toe off cutting firewood? Suppose I'd accidentally sawed through my wrist? I could be lying on the cabin floor bleed-ing to death and these bastards hadn't even come to pick me up. This was the worst moment I'd had in Alaska, by far. I even began to feel anger toward Tom, for loaning me all this crap that had enabled me to come here in the first place, and toward the U.S. Forest Service, for having even built this goddamned cabin, and toward anyone who had ever lived in a cabin, in the winter, in the woods. Eventually, beneath the sheer weight of so much impotent rage, I fell asleep.

I was awakened by a knock on the cabin door.

"Come on, let's go," the pilot said. "My coffee's already perking in Anchorage."

It was morning. Another clear day. I hadn't even heard the plane come in.

"Hell," the pilot said. "Usually when I'm two days late for someone, they're sitting on top of their duffel bag ready to go. Looks like you might want to stay."

"Oh, no. That's okay. I'm ready to go."

"Well, you know why I didn't get here Wednesday. That was one hell of a storm, turned to freezing rain in Anchorage, ice all over the planes. Then yesterday I climbed up on a wing to try to chip some of the ice off the struts, and I slipped on the goddamn stuff and fell off the wing and busted my ribs. Wound up in the hospital instead of here. Got 'em all taped up now, but they still hurt like hell. I'm just damn glad we ought to have a smooth flight. Doctor told me definitely to take today off. Stay in bed. Which I am gonna do. But I figured I'd better come down here and get you. Figured maybe you'd been here long enough."

And we climbed into the plane, and bumped along the lake surface through the snow, and took off, and rose above the tops of the mountains, and on a gorgeous, sunny, cold morning—the first of March—we flew smoothly back to Anchorage.

2 Summer

11 Bethel

The ravens are gone, replaced by sea gulls. The snow is gone and I find that I live on a dirt road. The darkness is going, replaced by light. By the first week of May in Anchorage there is light until 10:30 p.m. and again by 4:30 in the morning. The air is thick with dust and with the fumes of motor vehicles and with construction noise, as new apartment houses and office buildings rise. This will be the last year of the boom. Of this boom. Others are expected, but the pressure to cash in immediately is intense.

I have dinner one night with Duane Archer, my friend from the ferry. Afterwards, he takes me to a house on Barrow Street. A small white house, just across the street from the Denali Elementary School. Inside, it is a gambling casino, with crap table, black-jack tables, and a room in the back for high-stakes poker. A croupier and dealer have been imported from Nevada. Duane Archer says he is a one-third partner in the house. Just another of the little deals he has going on the side. Taking advantage of the boom while it lasts.

The surest sign of the end of winter was, I suppose, the Bethel flood. Some years it was bad and some years it wasn't, but every spring, like a crocus, it arrived. The river ice broke up, and then jammed, and the water rushed behind it and spilled over the banks of the Kuskokwim and poured through the streets of the town.

The flood was a social occasion: Bethel's spring carnival. A welcome event. The mayor believed that the flood waters washed disease-causing germs from the town.

Tom Brennan had a secretary who had grown up in Bethel and whose sister, after several years in the Lower Forty-eight, had recently returned there to live. The sister's name was Beverly Hoffman. The Hoffmans were one of Bethel's first families, and it had, apparently, caused quite an uproar the previous summer when Beverly and her hippie friends from San Francisco arrived on Ole Sumstad's barge, the S.S. *Husky*, pitched tents on the riverbank three miles from town, and announced that they intended to make Bethel their permanent home.

I flew to Bethel to visit Beverly Hoffman on the second day of the flood, when the waters were just beginning to recede. The consensus was that the flood had been worse than usual, though not nearly as bad as the year the water had reached the cemetery. That year, for days afterward, arms and legs had floated through the streets.

I took a taxi from the airfield to the edge of town. From there, I traveled to Beverly Hoffman's house in a boat. It was a wooden shack, built up on pilings, on the riverbank, twenty feet above the normal level of the water. The boat dropped me at the front door.

The house had no toilet, but it did have electricity, except during periods of power failure, which made it, by Bethel standards, an upper-middle-class home. In Bethel, many people did not even live in houses, but in 12-by-7-foot insulated boxes that originally had been used to ship refrigerated goods to Bethel on a barge. The rent for such a box had recently gone from $150 to $200 per month.

There were two numbers painted on the outside of Beverly

Hoffman's house. Souvenirs of a recent attempt at progress. It had been decided during the winter that all houses in the town should be numbered. This was Bethel's equivalent of Barrow's $12 million town hall. The city workers, however, had started drinking on the job, and, as a result, had numbered many of the houses out of order. The second time around, they had neglected to paint over their mistakes. Thus, every house in Bethel was numbered twice. Nobody knew which was the right number, and nobody paid attention to either.

The riverbank below the house, which became visible as the water continued to recede, was studded with old oil drums and wrecked automobiles. These were thought to protect the bank from erosion, an engineering concept which seemed unique to western Alaska, and which added substantially to the impression that Bethel had been officially designated as the junkyard of the state.

TAKE OFF YOUR GODDAMNED BOOTS said a sign tacked to the door of the house. Inside, pasted to the refrigerator door, were other stickers and signs:

CALIFORNIA MARIJUANA INITIATIVE—VOTE YES ON 19—
LIFE, LIBERTY, AND THE PURSUIT OF HAPPINESS

PREPARE FOR WORLD FLIP-OUT

ASK US—WE'VE BEEN TO ALASKA

HAPPINESS IS HAWAII

BIG 'N' BOLD—49ER GOLD

LIBRARIANS ARE SOMETHING ELSE

ALASKA OR BUST

ALASKA HIGH

WE CAN HANDLE IT—THE UNION PACIFIC RAILROAD

REEFER MADNESS

MARIJUANA—WEED FROM THE DEVIL'S GARDEN

Beverly Hoffman was twenty-five years old and 25 percent Eskimo. She lived in the house with John McDonald, a tall, quiet man with a red beard, with whom she had formerly lived in San Francisco, and by whom she was now pregnant. Their friend Tom Foote, from San Francisco, also lived there. His girlfriend had recently moved to a different house, a few blocks away, due to personal differences with Tom Foote.

One of Beverly Hoffman's grandfathers, an Englishman, had established a trading post on the Kuskokwim River and married four Eskimo women, each of whom died of tuberculosis. Her other grandfather had come from Norway, looking for gold. Having found some, he sent home for his family, intending to take them on a trip around the world. By the time they arrived, however, he had gambled his fortune away, and did not even have enough money left to send them back. That was how the Hoffman dynasty had begun.

There were now more than two hundred Hoffmans in Bethel, including the mayor of the town, the owner of the fuel company, and Beverly's father, who ran the biggest shipping company in western Alaska. One uncle, the president of the local Native association, had traveled to the White House a few years earlier and had presented a box of dried fish to President Ford. Beverly had five brothers and two sisters, and so many first cousins that there were some she did not recognize when she passed them on the street.

She had gone to high school in Anchorage. It had been expected that she would then return to Bethel. Instead, over her father's strenuous objections, she went to Palm Beach Junior College in Florida. "I needed to find out who I was," she said. "At home, I was just a baby-sitter and a maid."

In Florida, for the first time, she became involved with marijuana, with the peace movement, and with men. After two years, she moved to El Paso, Texas, to live near a friend who was stationed at an army base there. Soon she wound up in San Francisco, where she met John McDonald, who had recently been discharged from the Army after a tour of duty that had involved electronic reconnaissance in Vietnam. They moved into a house on Frederick Street, living with a dozen other people. Tom Foote soon joined them there. He had been hitchhiking through Florida, vaguely planning to go to Australia someday, and had been picked up by a friend of Beverly's who was on her way to San Francisco for a visit. Tom Foote had come with her, and they eventually got married and moved to a farm in Illinois. The marriage failed, however, and Tom Foote returned to San Francisco by himself.

The group earned money by painting and renovating Victorian houses. There were ten bedrooms in the Frederick Street house and all of them were always full. The residents tried to pattern their lives after the philosophy of the rock group the Grateful Dead.

"Basically," said John McDonald, "as we perceived it, this meant doing things you really enjoyed with people you liked." They held frequent garage sales to raise money for tickets to Grateful Dead concerts. Once, everyone in the house saw the Grateful Dead perform for five nights in a row. In addition, Grateful Dead records and tapes were played in the house almost twenty-four hours a day.

After two years of this, Beverly and John, and Tom and his girlfriend, and one other couple, decided to go to Alaska for the summer. Their plan was to utilize Beverly's status as an Eskimo to obtain land under provisions of the Alaska Native Claims Settlement Act. A dentist from Bethel, who was hitchhiking back to Alaska following a vacation in Mexico, stopped off to see Beverly in San Francisco. He told them that if they reached Seattle by the middle of May, they might get a ride up on Ole Sumstad's barge, which was preparing for its annual trip.

They arrived, the six of them: Beverly, who was well known in the town, and her five non-Eskimo friends, who became instantly notorious as the first hippies ever to visit Bethel.

"Those first few weeks," Beverly said, "it seemed like we were all anybody could talk about. 'Hey, have you seen the hippies who came in with Bev Hoffman on the *Husky*?' "

Her father had not even wanted her to leave for college. He wanted even less for her to have returned in the sort of company she had chosen. He told everyone in Bethel not to give them jobs if they should ask, and he told Beverly, the first time he saw her, that he would make certain that they would never be able to find a place to live.

All summer long, they stayed in a tent on the riverbank, three miles from town. It rained every day for the first three weeks. They had no food, except what they fished from the river. During the day they were devoured by mosquitoes. At night they lived in fear that a vigilante group would attack. The third couple left quickly, on a Wien flight. But Beverly and John and Tom and his girlfriend remained. They were still in their tent as summer ended. Beverly told her father they would stay there through the winter if need be. She had come home, she told him, at the age of twenty-five, and it was none of his business who had accompanied her. Besides, she said, if he would just calm down long enough to get to know them, he would discover that her friends were not hippies at all, but energetic and intelligent individuals who, despite their fondness for long hair and old clothes and rock music and marijuana, wanted to make a commitment to Alaska.

Through the first snowfall, Beverly's father held firm. But when the river froze up, he relented to an extent. He still would not help them find jobs, but he did let them know that there was an old house available at the edge of the river downtown. He was, of course, convinced that winter would drive the "hippies" away. But figured he would just as soon see it happen without also seeing his daughter freeze to death.

Beverly's father, however, had miscalculated. John and Tom and his girlfriend did not depart. For, already, they had discovered the one great truth about Bethel, the hidden attribute that more than compensated for the otherwise intolerable things about the place: in Bethel, if you had any resources at all, you could live out almost any fantasy you'd ever had.

"There's no question," said Tom Foote, "that this place is outrageous. It's an insult to nature. The secret is, it's so bad that it's good. If you can put up with the living conditions, you get maximum personal freedom in return. And if you've got any talent at all, in any direction, you can use it to an almost unlimited extent. If there is anything you ever wanted to do but figured you would never get the chance, Bethel is the place to come to do it."

Tom Foote, for example, had always liked books. Within six months—his lack of academic background notwithstanding—he was hired as the Bethel librarian, and was discovering federal grant programs that enabled him to order hundreds of new titles every month. Giving Bethel one of the finest libraries, for a community of its size, anywhere in America.

John McDonald had brought all of his Grateful Dead records north. In San Francisco, when he played them, he sometimes imagined he was producing his own radio show. In Bethel, within six months, he got a job as the morning disc jockey on a real radio station, beaming four hours of Grateful Dead out across the tundra every day. Except for the educational jingles on "Sesame Street," the Grateful Dead were just about the only music the Eskimos of western Alaska got to hear. In addition, because he owned a few good cameras, John McDonald became staff photographer for Bethel's weekly newspaper. He was planning, next year, to make a film of the sled dog race between Anchorage and Nome, and to develop a dog team himself. All of which seemed a considerably more interesting way to spend his life than repainting old houses in San Francisco.

Beverly Hoffman, as a Native, was appointed curator of Eskimo artifacts at the Kuskokwim Community College regional museum. She occasionally filled in on the morning radio show, slipping a little Jimmy Buffet in between tracks of the Dead. Having made peace with her father, she was planning to operate a forklift for his shipping company in the summer, for as long as her pregnancy would permit.

Tom Foote's girlfriend was helping to administer a federally funded program to aid children with learning disabilities. In San Francisco, she had not even been able to find work as a substitute teacher.

"It's amazing," said John McDonald. "It's almost like we staged a coup. Where else could you come to by barge, sleep in a tent, and six months later be controlling the media and reshaping the culture of the town?"

"The thing is," said Tom Foote, "in Bethel, whatever particular talent or ambition you may have, you can be pretty sure that you're the only person in town who has it."

"Once we made it through the winter," Beverly Hoffman said, "people in town came to accept the fact that we were serious. Even my father. He still doesn't actually approve of us, but he has come to respect what we are doing. Even a few months ago he kept asking me when these bums were going home. Now he's screaming at me to get married."

The only problem, Beverly said, was the speed with which Bethel was growing. The eagerness for development. The desire for progress of any sort.

"I really want my baby to grow up in Alaska," she said, "having the feelings I had. Maybe we can do it in Bethel. Or maybe we'll have to move out of town. It was neat here when I was growing up. There were less than one thousand people living here and you really did know everyone in town. Now, with the Land Claims Act, there are all these government agencies and people coming and going all the time and I think it's really trying to turn into a city.

"Right now we're working on developing skills. Hunting and

trapping and fishing. And, next year, mushing dogs. Once we know we can be self-sufficient, if Bethel gets too crowded we can move. As a Native, I'll be able to get some land. We can homestead it. Build a cabin. Go back to living the old way."

"You see," Tom Foote said, "in relation to the people around here, we're at a crossroads. We've already been through the development thing. They're phasing in just as we're starting to phase out."

Then Tom Foote excused himself. He put on his hip boots and sloshed down the front steps of the house, to a boat with a small outboard motor. The sun was shining. The air was warm. It was spring. He was doing a special broadcast on the radio station that afternoon. With Bethel still under six feet of water, he was going to read from *Twenty Thousand Leagues Under the Sea*. It was the sort of thing he would never have been able to do in San Francisco.

12 The Road South

Duane Archer helped me buy a used car. He took me to his friend
Bernie Segal, the owner of Benevolent Bernie's Used Cars, on the
Old Seward Highway. Bernie Segal was a stout man who wore a
cowboy hat and a string tie, and had even more rings on his fingers
than Duane Archer did.

The cars all looked terrible; dented and smashed and covered
with dust. Duane Archer, however, explained that I was a trusted
friend, and Bernie Segal said in that case he had just the thing. It
was a year-old Ford, previously owned by a serviceman who had
suddenly been transferred overseas. The body damage, he said,
was nothing to worry about. Somebody had backed into the car in
a parking lot. It looked to me more like the Army had thrown the
car out of an airplane during paratroop training at Fort Richardson, but the point proved moot. The car would not start. Bernie
Segal cursed it and smacked the hood with his fist. The door on
the passenger side sprang open. This seemed like a television skit.
Finally, for $1,200, I bought a four-year-old Pontiac station wagon

that had no dents. The odometer read 78,000 miles, but that might
have been the second time around. The muffler was loose, so the
engine was noisy, and the exhaust fumes seemed a little too dark,
but both Duane Archer and Bernie Segal assured me that I had
gotten the best buy on the lot. Except, of course, for the Ford that
would not start.

On a warm, sunny day, I drove down the Seward Highway to
Bird Creek, about twenty-five miles south of town. The ice had
gone out of the inlet and flowers were starting to bloom. The snow
had retreated up the sides of the mountains, leaving the lower
slopes green. I hiked up from Bird Creek to Bird Creek Ridge, a
steep, three-hour climb, from sea level to 3,500 feet. I soon passed
above tree line and then the path was rock and dirt and loose rock
called scree. On the shaded parts of the trail, there was still snow.
At the top of the ridge I walked back about a quarter mile. There
was a high rock with a sort of saddle on top. I climbed onto this
and sat down.

The sun was warm but the air, at this altitude, was still cold;
the wind strong, and the snow still a foot deep. I wore a down
jacket zipped up tight, a woolen hat, and gloves. From the top I
had a 360-degree view. Of sharp drops down either side, and the
ridge continuing back, dropping, then rising to almost 5,000 feet
above the headwaters of Ship Creek, seven miles away.

Looking south, into the warming spring sun, I could see the
waters of Turnagain Arm and the steep snow-covered mountains
that rose up the other side. There was no evidence, in any direction, of human habitation. From this angle the road was not in
sight. The only living things were the ravens, which had moved up
from the city for the summer, and furry little mountain squirrels
called marmots. Even with the boom, Anchorage remained close
to the edge.

A bit further south, I stopped at Portage Glacier, which I had
visited with Tom on Thanksgiving weekend. We had been the
only people there on a dark and bitter day. The face of the glacier
was about four miles away, across a lake, but pieces had broken
from the face and floated much closer to the shore. These small
icebergs had been locked in place when the lake froze in the fall.
We had walked to the nearest, which was about ten feet high and

twice as big around. The ice was turquoise: like a large stone from which precious gems could be cut. Glowing so brightly on that dark gray day, it seemed almost radioactive.

Now, at the verge of summer, chunks of glacial ice floated freely in the unfrozen lake. Soon, tourist buses with tinted windows would race down every day from the Anchorage Westward Hotel. Gray-haired women with tour buttons pinned to the lapels of their coats would clamber out and take pictures and talk about how cold the breeze was. The next day, the bus would take them to McKinley Park and then to Fairbanks. From where the unlucky, or unsuspecting, ones would sign up for the optional side trip to Barrow or Nome.

Beyond the Portage Glacier was Mount Alyeska, which was Alaska's one big ski resort. Actually, it was not a resort; just someplace to ski. A few clusters of Swiss-style condominiums had been built, but there were no lodges or hotels to stay in overnight. The nearest hotel was in Anchorage.

Below Alyeska, the mountains pressed closer to the road, Turnagain Arm narrowed, and soon mountains loomed straight ahead. This was the lower end of the arm, where Captain Cook had had to turn again.

The road went southwest, through low mountains, for about fifty miles until it divided, at a point only about ten miles north of Crescent Lake. One fork went south to Seward. The other, which I took, cut west, out of the mountains and across the peninsula, toward Kenai, a little oil and fishing town on Cook Inlet. I drove into Kenai to see Jeff the Cop, another person whom I had met on the ferry, back in November.

Jeff had left the Denver, Colorado, police force the previous fall to take a job in Kenai, where he had been hired as one of the seven policemen in the town. He was twenty-five years old, and was, basically, in search of freedom and adventure and whatever the future might bring. He had been seasick on the ferry, so no one had seen much of him there, but he had followed Duane Archer and me from Haines to Anchorage, driving his four-wheel-drive Jeep pickup and carrying, in the back, a case of Coors beer for which the Kenai police chief had paid him twenty-five dollars. The cans had split open in the cold, and frozen beer had oozed across the back of the truck, giving Jeff his first practical lesson about Alaska.

At first, Jeff lived in a room over the firehouse. Then his wife, with whom he was having a troubled relationship, decided to come to Alaska after all, and the two of them bought a new house. The marriage did not survive the winter, but Jeff's wife did, discovering in the process that, though she might not love Jeff any more, she did love Alaska. She discovered also that, as a hairdresser on the Kenai Peninsula, she could earn twice what she had been making in Denver. She stayed in Kenai—in the new house, in fact—even after the marriage came apart, while Jeff bought another home, in the same development where his first house was. He was living, in fact, just around the corner from his wife.

Kenai had been the first oil boom town in Alaska. Offshore drilling had started in the early 1960s, and, at one point, construction was proceeding so fast that carpenters commuted from Anchorage by airplane every day. But then the much bigger discovery had been made at Prudhoe Bay and Kenai had gone into eclipse. There were six thousand people in the town now, most of them working for oil companies, but it was not in the mainstream of the pipeline boom.

Jeff the Cop had the night off. The evening before, he had investigated a murder. A fifteen-year-old boy had shot and killed his stepfather because the man had been beating the boy's mother. It had been the first fatal shooting in Kenai since Jeff had arrived. There had been, however, ten suicides, nine of which had involved Natives and all of which had involved alcohol.

The evening was cloudy and windy, with occasional sprinkles of rain. We rode around town in Jeff's four-wheel-drive pickup; the same one he had driven from the ferry. Since coming to Kenai, Jeff had bought a camper and a snow machine and a stock car and a motorcycle, to go along with the truck, and was temporarily frustrated only because he could not think of any other kind of motor vehicle he might buy.

Jeff's new girlfriend was Bonnie, twenty-three, divorced, and the mother of a nine-month-old baby. She worked as a secretary for Phillips Petroleum. She was an angular, attractive redhead who chain-smoked and wore a Phillips 76 windbreaker with her name— "Bonnie"— written over the left breast in script. She said she did not take naturally to being a mother and employed baby-sitters whenever she could. She had lived in Alaska all her life but had never been to any part of the state that was not reached by a road.

Fairbanks, Homer, Valdez, yes, she knew these places; had lived in all three of them, in fact. But if you could not drive there, Bonnie did not want to go. Where she really wanted to go was California. She had been to Disneyland and to Las Vegas, and she thought those were the two greatest places she'd ever seen. Besides, in California, there were a lot more places you could drive.

We stopped at a Tesoro gas station where Jeff had heard there might be a rebuilt engine he could put in his stock car. No luck. But we stayed for half an hour anyway, listening to the owner describe how his wife had just taken off with their three children. He didn't know where she was, and the note she had left him said she would never be back. There was, apparently, another man involved, but the gas station owner was not giving up. "I don't believe in divorce," the man said. "The Bible's against it. She'll be married to me for the rest of her life no matter what any judge says. What God has joined together, the Bible says, no man can put in sunder."

We ate dinner at Fresh Frieda's Mexican restaurant. Frieda was a heavy young woman with a loud voice. "You're in luck," she called out as we entered. "I'm using new grease tonight."

Three months earlier, Frieda's twenty-year-old brother, just out of the Army, had been killed in a head-on automobile accident on the highway in front of the restaurant. The other car had swerved across the center of the road. The driver had been drunk at the time. "Around here," Jeff said, "they take drunken driving so much for granted he probably won't even lose his license."

After dinner, we went to the Rainbow Bar, where the weekly "Gong Show" was held. This was a local talent contest for people who did not have any talent. Frieda closed up the restaurant and she and her sister came with us. There was live music, of a sort: a loud and incompetent country and western band. Jeff began to drink Kahlúa and cream. I drank Prinz Brau, the new Alaskan beer brewed in Anchorage. Bonnie drank some V.O. and water and went home. A lady at the next table, who was even heavier than Frieda, was celebrating her birthday. A cake was brought to the table and everyone sang "Happy Birthday," though Frieda sang loudest of all. Jeff was trying to talk her into entering the "Gong Show," which was about to begin. Each week, he served as a judge for the show. I asked him if he could drive me back to his house before it started. He agreed, though he could not understand why

153

someone would want to go to bed just when the fun was beginning.

"I'm so happy up here," he told me in the truck. "I have loved this place from day one, and it just keeps getting better and better."

It was raining the next morning. Jeff was asleep. He had not come in until 3 a.m. I ate some Sugar Pops, which was all he had for breakfast. There were fresh bulldozer tracks in the mud around his house, where the evergreens had been knocked down to make room for it. The smell of fresh paint was heavy in the air. I got in the car and drove on.

Past Anchor Point the road swung east and began a long, gradual descent into Homer, the town at the edge of Kachemak Bay. These were the final miles of the road system of North America. If you got in your car in New York City and started to drive, Homer would be as far as you could go. An eight-hundred-foot bluff rose behind the town, and across the bay the Kenai Mountains climbed, snow-covered, to 4,000 feet. A long, narrow strip of land —four miles long and in places less than a quarter mile wide— reached from the edge of the town into the bay. This was the Homer Spit. It contained eighty acres of usable land, valued at $100,000 an acre. For years, the Spit, which was part beach, had been used as a campground. Now the Homer city council wanted to toss out the campers, close up the little shops, and lease the whole thing to the oil companies, which wanted to use the Spit as a staging area for exploratory drilling in Kachemak Bay.

There were about fifteen hundred people in Homer in the summer, and, unlike the population of the towns which could not be reached by road, almost all of them were white. Homer's population was expected to double in five years. Not only because of the increased oil company activity, but also because people from Anchorage were starting to discover that it was worth their while to drive four hours to escape the city for the weekend. As Anchorage grew, the people who had originally moved there to get away from it all now found themselves needing to get away *from* the place that they had come so far to get away *to*. The weekend procession of campers and pickup trucks down the highway to Homer in summer was beginning to resemble the traffic patterns on Long Island parkways in the vicinity of Jones Beach. Many

Homer residents welcomed this growth because it would bring them more money, but others believed it was destroying the essence of what had drawn them to Alaska, and to Homer, in the first place.

I parked on Main Street, which had been a dirt road for seventy-five years, until this summer, when it had been paved. There was a rifle in the window of the Rexall drugstore, a Bushnell Space Master 11, with telescopic sight, on sale for $159. In Alaska, even the drugstores sold guns.

I walked across the street to the office of the Homer *News*, the local weekly paper. A recent survey had showed that 93 percent of the adult population of Homer read the paper every week. The survey had been taken in the most scientific of all possible ways: by asking the one thousand adults in town. Nine hundred and thirty had said yes. This was, of course, in a town without much other entertainment. There was a movie theater, but the projectionist was a right-wing political extremist and a member of a fundamentalist religious sect. Acting on his moral and political convictions, he spliced out any portions of films which he considered to be objectionable. Sometimes, in Homer, the feature films were not much longer than the cartoons.

The owner of the Homer *News* was a thin, intense thirty-one-year-old man named Gary Williams, who was also mayor of the town. He had little in common with Arthur MacIntosh, the editor of the paper in Nome. Gary Williams had grown up in Homer, on land that his father had homesteaded, in a cabin that his father had built. He had not enjoyed the experience. Like Olive Cook and Beverly Hoffman, he had been eager to get out.

"In the Lower Forty-eight, I suppose kids grow up dreaming of wilderness and open spaces. Well, I had bears in my backyard from the time I could walk, and I didn't find that a particularly rewarding situation. I would have fantasies about libraries and concert halls. I would lie awake at night, in that cabin, imagining what it would be like to live in a city, where I could see the reflections of streetlights on wet pavement when it rained."

He had gone to college in California and then lived in Mexico and Oregon. He came back to Homer "for six months" when his father, who owned the local hardware store, had gotten sick. That was four years ago. His father died, he inherited the store, and, on the day he sold it, he learned that the local paper was for sale.

Now, as both publisher and politician, he was deeply involved in Homer's period of transition.

"Most people's conception of Alaska," he said, "is no bigger than the size of their own lot. Economics defines their morality. A lot of folks in town were watching others cash in, and it was getting to be like the smell of blood to a shark. There's no question that we're going to have development in Homer. We've already had a substantial amount. But what I tried to say was, gee whiz, for once let's not be selfish. Let's do it right. Let's not lose all control. Let's remember who we are, where our center is, philosophically. The tendency, you know, is to go with your programming, and I could see these people being programmed to start thinking of Homer as an oil town." He spoke in the soothing, well-modulated voice of an all-night disc jockey on an FM radio station. His political style, he said, was patterned after that of California governor Jerry Brown: to pose existential questions in as vague a form as possible, rather than trying to mold public opinion directly.

He had become mayor, in a close election, by defeating a member of the old guard, Hazel Heath. She owned a gift shop for tourists, at which she sold a thick and syrupy rhubarb-juice concoction called Homer Spit. There was a certain amount of resentment toward this young man who took both himself and the future of Homer so very seriously, and who had, within three years of breezing in from Oregon, wound up as both the political leader and the media baron of the town.

"In Oregon," he said, "I did some heavy training as a runner. In the company of Dyrol Burleson, who, in the early 1960s, was one of the leading middle-distance runners in the country. Training with him, training so intensively, I learned to think in images. I had no choice: the entire experience was beyond words. It was just too profound. I can't even begin to describe what it was like. But I can say that it enabled me to get out of the rational trip I had been into for so long, and to begin to function on a subconscious, visceral level.

"Applying that to politics, I began to approach problems the way my father approached a job as a carpenter. He would build an entire house without blueprints. He would 'see' the finished building as he worked. In running, when I felt pain, I learned to 'see' the pain and then to send energy to it. Here, politically, I try to 'see' Homer as it should be. To 'see' in images, what solving a problem successfully should feel like. Then I try to communicate that vision. It's more complicated in politics, though, because you are not just dealing with yourself or with an inanimate object. In politics you're dealing with mass psychology and ·that's an area where I've still got a lot of learning to do."

I read the lead paragraph of the editorial that Gary Williams had written for that week's Homer *News*.

There is a "price" involved in any human activity. For the athlete it is the discipline of enduring physical pain to increase his stamina. For the poet, concentrating his descriptive powers, and hours of writing and re-writing his work. For the Alaskan, his "price" seems the simple act of living in an area made dynamic by the interface of an idle frontier and the clashing philosophies of construction and conservation.

Then, as if on cue, an old man walked into the Homer *News* office. A man who had lived in Homer for twenty years. He wanted to place an ad in the paper to announce the sale by auction of his land. He was leaving, moving to Oregon. Not to get away from progress, but because progress was proving so difficult to achieve.

"I've been trying to subdivide part of my place," he said. "But the government keeps getting in my way. They don't like my septic-system plans. I could live on half my land and cut the other half up into forty half-acre lots, every one of them with a view of the bay. But I'm fed up with all red tape. So I'm going to sell the place outright. The whole place. Maybe some Anchorage developers will buy it. Some people who know how to fight the government."

The man left. "See what I mean?" said Gary Williams. Then he put on a pair of shorts and running shoes. At his peak, he had run a mile in 4:06, and, at a slower pace, in Oregon, had run up to seventy miles per week. Now, with his new responsibilities, he'd had to cut back to five miles in the morning and three in the afternoon. On occasions when he found internal pressures and angers building to an intolerable level, he would run, as fast as he could, up the 2.2 miles of dirt-road switchbacks that led from the bay to the top of the bluff eight hundred feet above the town.

I ran with him along the beach. He slowed his pace for my sake. The temperature was in the 50s, it was cloudy, and a strong breeze was blowing off the bay. We could see glaciers and snow-covered mountains as we ran, and the purple fireweed bright and high in the fields above the beach. In the distance we could see also an ARCO oil-drilling platform.

That evening we went to the Club Bar, which had been the cause of the most passionate confrontation of Gary Williams's tenure as mayor and newspaper publisher, bringing what he called "fear and loathing" to Homer.

There had been a big fire in the Club Bar the previous fall. Rebuilt, it had opened on New Year's Day. To celebrate its rebirth from the ashes, so to speak, the owners unveiled a surrealistic mural, painted on the front outer wall, facing Main Street. Amid a number of abstract symbols, the painting portrayed nude male and female figures, genitalia included. A number of the more conservative members of the community were offended. In fact, outraged. Phone calls were made to Gary Williams, demanding that, in his capacity as mayor, he order that the painting be covered.

"You see," he said, "people smoke dope in the Club Bar. People make noise. People get drunk. So it had always seemed a disreputable place to those who did not participate in, or approve of, that life style. The nude figures in the painting were seen by these people as a deliberate attempt to offend. A thumbing of the nose at decency. Whereas the owners and the artist claimed they were simply symbols of regeneration. All I could tell people when they called was that to the best of my knowledge there were no laws, either local or state, that prohibited the use of nudity in art forms. I told them this was a problem they would have to mediate with the owners. I said I had no reason to get involved. Some of these people were extremely upset. They seemed to think that their wives and daughters would be forever damned to hell if they happened to look the wrong way while walking down Main Street. I said, well, maybe you'll have to expand your consciousness a bit. However unhappy it may make you at first, maybe you'll just have to accept this as a new part of your lives."

A week later, paint was splattered on the mural, by persons unknown, in an attempt to cover the parts considered lewd and offensive. The next day, the dispute took on an uglier dimension, when a newsletter entitled "The Club Bar Episode" was sent to all Homer residents by the minister of a fundamentalist church. Five pages long, it said, in part:

The criminal antichrist immoral filth just spewed out upon the wall of the saloon in our town was put there for the purpose of further tearing down the moral strength of the town. . . . This outburst of perversion in downtown Homer incites lust in the heart of the unsaved heathen, militates against and nullifies the power of the Gospel of Jesus Christ. . . . What is in the heart and mind and soul of [the Club Bar owner] and his co-conspirators against Christ is not just sex perversion but MURDER! . . .

Certain poor non-Christians in the community who do not have Christian understanding, stand by bewildered and ask: "Why, when already the bars in the town are a constant trouble to the community, does this Club Bar want to come forth with this picture on its walls and antagonize further the good people of the community? Do they not realize they are making trouble for themselves?" The answer is not difficult when one understands the antichrist Jewish purpose of breaking down the morals of the communities and the nation, so they can later bring the nation under red bolshevism.

The riffraff that has poured into Homer in the last several years, which is supported by taxpayers' dollars in the form of welfare checks, is cryptically the same element precisely which took over Russia in 1917. And what this INSANE crypto-Jewish riffraff has planned for Homer and its citizens is no less than what the same antichrist Jewish riffraff did to Russia, and now has done to Poland, East Germany, China, Cuba, Vietnam and other nations of the world. . . .

This picture, taken by itself, and considered alone in the entire global conspiratorial effort, is but a tiny thing. But, considered by the antichrist enemies of God and man in the community of Homer, it is a GIGANTIC achievement toward the final destruction of the Christian people here. . . .

The minister added that the mayor, Gary Williams, "obviously favors the Club Bar, its lewdness and the local Jewish revolutionary element." And there was more, much more, most of it an even more frenzied, crazed tirade against Jews, of whom, in fact, there probably were not more than a dozen on the entire Kenai Peninsula.

The letter quickly became even more of an issue than the painting itself. "People were stunned," Gary Williams said. "Dazed. That this sort of thing could have been spawned in this community. One of the things of which we'd always been most proud was the atmosphere of tolerance that had prevailed among people of widely differing life styles and beliefs. The painting definitely became subsidiary to this kind of Nazism, which just shocked and sickened so many people."

Three nights later there was a city council meeting, at which the question of the painting was to be discussed. In the wake of the hate letter, more than three hundred people attended, by far the biggest crowd at a city council meeting in Homer's history. The owners of the Club Bar were there, as well as many of their customers. Also in attendance was the minister, surrounded by a small group of followers, including two Homer policemen in plain clothes.

"The tension, the volatility, was incredible," Gary Williams said. "I felt it had to be released. So I did something very risky. I opened up the meeting to everyone, to speak not just on the specific issue of the painting, but to say whatever was in their hearts. To speak on what was pressing from within. I could sense this desperate need for catharsis. The minister spoke first and launched into a long, inflammatory tirade, and I finally had to rule him out of order and gavel him down.

"But then the next speaker got up. A man named Cliff Culkins. A welder. He'd been around town a long time and everyone knew him and respected him as a man who had plenty of common sense, even though he generally didn't have much to say.

"He was brief. He just said, 'I would rather that my wife and my children were exposed to the Club Bar sign a dozen times a day than to be exposed once to the things I have heard and read from the Reverend.' Then he sat down.

"For a moment, there was silence. Then it was like the Holy Spirit descending: a sudden wind; the rush of catharsis. The whole room erupted. Everyone jumped up and began applauding wildly. The minister and his people left, and, in a spirit of accommodation, for the good of the community, the artist and the owners of the bar agreed to paint towels over the genitals in the picture.

"I went out to see the minister the next day and told him I felt he was counterproductive and hurting the community. After that meeting, he was finished in this town, anyway. He's leaving, as a matter of fact, leaving Alaska. In fact, he may already be gone."

Gary Williams paused and then smiled. "Now it's summer, and we're back to reality. That other business, I think, was just a form of cabin fever. We always fight about our moral issues in the winter. In summer, we're too busy fighting about big things, like money and development. For instance, how upset can you get about an abstract painting when you see that ARCO oil rig in the bay? That thing is real; that's not abstract. And it's really here now. In our town. And we can't just paint a towel across it to make it go away."

The next morning I met Clem Tillion down by the harbor and rode in one of his boats seven miles across the bay to Halibut Cove. An early mist was burning away and it looked as if a sunny, breezy day was taking shape.

Clem Tillion was in his middle fifties. He had red hair, a long face, big teeth, a wide smile, and a voice that cut through salt air like a knife a man would use for cleaning fish. He both looked and talked as if he might originally have been from Maine, but actually it was Northport, Long Island. He had come from there, thirty years earlier, right after World War II, when it was still possible for a man to arrive in Alaska with nothing and wind up with whatever he wanted just by combining intelligence, a willingness to take a chance, and a capacity to work all day and half the night, almost every day of the year.

For fifteen years his business had been ferrying harbor pilots out to boats that were waiting to enter Kachemak Bay. He also ran the tourist boats out of Homer in the summer. These boats, which were operated by his daughters, brought the tourists to his wife's art studio at Halibut Cove, where they had an hour to admire the wildlife pictures and landscapes that she had painted with octopus ink. They were also given an opportunity to buy the pictures. In addition, Clem Tillion owned some fishing boats, and in addition to that, he owned about half the land around Halibut Cove, and in addition to that, he had served for more than a decade in the Alaska state legislature, was currently Republican leader in the state senate, and would, at the next election, become lieutenant governor of the state.

We docked below his house, which sat on a bluff overlooking a protected corner of the bay. He made tea and we sat on a sun porch. This was a full-sized house, with electricity, running water, and toilets that flushed.

"I joined the Marines, under age," he said, "at the start of World War II. When I was seventeen, I fought at Guadalcanal. I liked it. I liked the shooting. I liked the war. When the shooting stopped, things got dull, and that's when I got in trouble. One night I lit six sticks of dynamite in an incinerator outside an officers' and nurses' dance. The entire damn officers corps messed their drawers. I was given solitary, bread and water, the whole bit. After that, I went AWOL for forty days. Spent even more time locked up after that. Still, it was the best investment I ever made. I learned about girls in those forty days. Learned all I needed to know. Made all the mistakes a young man could make. As a result, I avoided a lot of the same mistakes in later life.

"I liked the war so much that when I got out of the Marines I thought of hiring myself out to the Chinese Nationalists. My family had a long history of fighting overseas. My grandfather was in Venezuela, Colombia, Uruguay, went to the Panama Canal Zone to put down an insurrection, finally got killed in the Philippines. He was a half-breed Mohawk Indian, a steelworker, one of those guys with no fear of heights. Huguenot, on the other side. Ancestors helped settle New Rochelle. My father was an architect. Helped design Manhattan Towers. He was shot twenty times in World War I. He was one of only three surviving officers from the Twenty-third New York Regiment. They suffered almost total casualties. Started with nine hundred men and ended with thirty. My father got a Silver Star.

"I suppose I should've been an architect, too. Instead, I was a high school dropout, and so, after the war, I was back East smuggling black-market cattle by truck from Teaneck, New Jersey, to Suffolk County, to get around some slaughterhouse requirements. Figured there wasn't much of a future in that, so I came West.

"Came up to Alaska in 1946. Wound up in Fairbanks for a while, delivering drinking water during the week and dealing cards in a gambling house on the weekends. Then I came down to Anchorage. Slept under a skiff on the beach because I didn't want to pay two bucks a night for a canvas cot indoors. What the hell, I was a kid who had just finished fighting a war.

"I picked up a pamphlet one day that talked about homesteading opportunities on the Kenai Peninsula. I hopped a freight down to Moose Pass, then rode part of the way down the Kenai River on a raft, and wound up walking the rest of the way. Walked into town in 1947 with long hair and a beard and not a penny to my name. My wife says I was the first hippie in town.

"Her family had just come down from Anchorage the year before. Her father jumped off a Danish ship in San Francisco in 1912 and came up here. Didn't speak any English. Managed to join the

Army anyway. He was stationed at the Chilkoot Barracks in Haines and he homesteaded some land there. Later, he went to work as a powder man in the Independence mine, up in the Matanuska Valley. Then he got a railroad job and worked out of Cantwell, stringing telegraph poles through McKinley Park. He was living in Anchorage during World War II and when they shut down the red-light district at the end of the war he moved the family down here. He said a town without a whorehouse is no place to try to raise a daughter."

A retired naval officer named Squeaky Anderson was operating a fish cannery at Seldovia, on the other side of Kachemak Bay, and Clem Tillion went to work for him. Then he had a chance to buy his own fishing boat for $1,400, which was, at that time, a year's pay. Squeaky Anderson gave him a letter and sent him to Anchorage to see Elmer Rasmussen, the biggest banker in Alaska, and the man whose daughter had married Robert Atwood. The letter said simply: "The kid catches fish." Rasmussen loaned Clem Tillion the money.

"Most people will tell you Elmer Rasmussen is an egotistical and arrogant old man. But I'll tell you this: he's the only banker in the state who backs the fishermen. He must have financed two-thirds of the crab fleet in Kodiak. He was always willing to take a risk on a young Alaskan who looked like he wanted to work.

"Old Squeaky was a hell of a man, too. He was Norwegian. The first foreign-born commodore the U.S. Navy ever had. When Squeaky died, Elmer took him back to Anchorage and buried him with all those snobs. He should've left him right there in Seldovia. Buried him between a couple of his squaws."

It was midday and Clem Tillion had some things to do. He was not a man who remained idle for very long. When one owned as many boats as Clem Tillion did, and kept them operating in as many different capacities as he did, with, it seemed, a family member or in-law at the helm of every one, there were always several tasks to be performed. Especially when a man had to spend almost six months a year in Juneau, immersed in politics, away from all this.

"I always wanted to live on an island," he said, walking down a series of planks toward his dock. "I always wanted water at my back. For security. I was a product of the Depression. I saw my father turned out on the street. I learned the hard way that, in really bad times, city people, and city skills, aren't worth a damn. The only real security a man has is his own piece of land and the knowledge of how to live off it. All I've cared about my whole life has been providing security for my wife and my children and myself. And I have been ruthless in doing it. I have literally ripped the guts out of the earth around here in order to get what I have today. Ripped the guts out of more than a few fish, too. And I still don't relax. We buy a year's worth of groceries at a time and ship them down from Anchorage ourselves. Save forty percent doing that. Hell, I got back from Juneau this year and found that coffee had doubled in price. Well, we're still drinking last year's coffee, at last year's price. We keep a two-year supply of fuel on hand, too. And plenty of lumber. By the time one of the kids around here is eight years old he can handle the wheel of a boat offshore. By the time he's eleven, he can run the forty-footer over to Homer by himself. It not only gives the kid a sense of his own value, it frees an adult for something else. I've been very fortunate, so I don't think the day will ever come, but if it ever did happen that suddenly we had no money any more, we would have shelter and food, which is something city people could not be sure of. And I guarantee you this: if that day ever did come, every member of my family—sons, daughters, sons-in-law, and grandchildren— would know enough about the land and the water so that they'd be able to survive."

Clem Tillion was not only the entrepreneur but also the patriarch of Halibut Cove. There were, however, tucked away, out of sight, at various points around the cove, a few non-Tillions who had been there for a while. It was one of these I went to see, by small boat, in early afternoon.

His name was Tom Larsen. He was seventy-seven years old, a Norwegian who had been in Alaska for fifty years. He lived in a little wooden cabin without electricity or running water. He lived alone, except for a goose which he kept as a pet.

He had come first to Juneau in 1925 and worked in a sawmill. Then he prospected for gold and worked in a mine. Then he drove a gravel truck out of Chitina when the Richardson Highway was being built. Then, at the start of World War II, he did construction work for the Army Corps of Engineers at Yakutat. After the war he had came through Anchorage, and down the peninsula, and started his own sawmill in Homer, cutting planks for the fish traps used by Squeaky Anderson's cannery at Seldovia. But when Alaska became a state in 1959, the use of such fish traps became illegal, so Tom Larsen moved across to Halibut Cove, where he fished on a small scale, grew his own crops, and worked in his own carpentry shop in the winter.

"I did everything you could do in Alaska. I did what I wanted to do and consequently I enjoyed Alaska very much. That's what I came for: to see how many things I could do. Not to get rich. I liked it here from the first day I saw it. This was a free country. You could build anywhere you wanted to, do anything you damned pleased. Now these people who have been out here only fifteen or twenty years are crying because they say it's getting too crowded. Well, what the hell did *they* come for? They crowd me. But that's understandable. That's progress. That's the game. We can't all eat the cake and make it last forever. The party's over. Too damn many roads, if you ask me. That's what spoils it. But some of them ne'er-do-wells over in Homer—they can't get enough. They homestead some land and get rich. Now they're in a hurry to get richer. What the hell for? Brains don't come with it, that's for sure."

Tom Larsen had white hair and very red cheeks. He was wearing high rubber boots, an old cap, an old blue jacket, blue shirt, suspenders, and baggy black pants. In his carpentry shop, he made doors and window frames. "I'm using this Philippine mahogany now. It's piss poor." There were feathers mixed with sawdust on the floor. "Used to have chickens," he said. "Goddamn feathers everywhere."

Behind the shop was his garden and a greenhouse with a tin roof. He grew brussels sprouts and lettuce and carrots, using chopped kelp as fertilizer. Further out, he grew potatoes. "I ought to get two hundred pounds of potatoes out of that little patch if it turns out right this year."

His cabin was just one room with a wood stove. Food, clothing, and books were piled high. There was a bed, a table, and other than that, everything else was cardboard boxes. For food he had honey, condensed milk, Tang, Kava instant coffee, Hungry Jack pancake mix, and artificially flavored mashed-potato mix. Also an onion, an orange, a jar of lemon juice, some vitamin C pills, and a

CB radio near his bed. The microphone within arm's reach, in case some night he might need medical help.

There was a calendar on a wall that showed a picture of his home town in Norway. He had left there at the age of twenty-one. He'd not been back. He'd never married. "When I came to Juneau," he said, "I used to dance to beat hell—still do for that matter. But I'd tell the women I'm not the marrying kind. I came to Alaska to be a prospector and prospectors are always broke. What the hell, I was only telling them the truth. You see, if you marry, then you got to worry all the time about supporting other people, and you can't do what you want any more. And I didn't come to Alaska to be told I couldn't do what I want. Besides, you might wind up with a shrew for a wife and then your days are living hell."

His only living relative was a half brother in Norway whom he had not seen for fifty years, and now Tom Larsen wasn't even sure about him. "He's four years older, and this year when I sent him a letter at Christmas, I didn't get a reply. I don't know. He might be dead. What the hell. I've seen all that I want to see, and this is where I want to die. I'd like to be buried right here. Unless I drown someplace, and that can't be helped.

"This is a good harbor. The bay only freezes over once in a while. I'm just glad I came down here in time. No, it's not too isolated. You can call a plane and have one here in twenty minutes. Hell, I'd say it's not isolated enough. With all that progress over in Homer, we're hanging on for dear life.

"Lonesome? No, I don't get lonesome. It's in the big towns that you're lonesome. Not the small towns. I'll bet, for instance, that New York has a lot more lonesome people per capita than Homer does. And I can't think of *any* lonesome people on Halibut Cove."

Tom Larsen took me around the cove in his boat. It was a classic afternoon: the sky blue, the water green, the sun warm, the breeze cool, the snow-covered mountains in the distance. The air was a lyric blend of the smell of salt water and the smell of the pine trees that came down to water's edge. Tom Larsen told me about some of the other people around the cove. Like Roland Lee, a consumptive who had come there to die. He put a tent up on a bluff, and even though the ground was not his to live on, everyone left him alone, respecting a man's right to have whatever last glimpse of earth's beauty pleased him most. Then Roland Lee built a cabin next to his tent. Then he built a house behind his cabin. And when finally approached on the matter, he was found to be living in one of the most comfortable dwellings on the cove. "I don't know what I had," he said, "but I got over it."

Not far away, tucked back in the woods, was the cabin of Jack Swank, who had been a professor of mathematics at Georgetown University in Washington, D.C., but who had, some forty years earlier, left wife and children and built himself a little trapper's cabin on the cove. "He was just a dirty old man," Tom Larsen said. "Chewed snuff and Beech-Nut tobacco at the same time. But he corresponded about mathematical problems with professors all over the world."

We passed a wooden raft with a little shack built on top. A sign on the shack said: FEDERAL BUILDING—U.S. POST OFFICE—HALIBUT COVE. The mail was brought out by boat from Homer, and left inside the shack every day. We put ashore by a little wooden building that had been, for a couple of years, the Halibut Cove school. Children in the lower grades had attended. But there had been some trouble with the teacher, who apparently had much preferred to fish rather than teach. Now the children of Halibut Cove—most of whom were one sort of Tillion or another—traveled seven miles by boat to the Homer school every day.

Tom Larsen came to dinner at the Tillions'. Afterwards, he told stories of the old days. Of prospectors he had known in Juneau, men who had gone over the Chilkoot Pass and into the Klondike in 1898; who had gone out to Nome in 1900. These had been, except for the Russians, the first white men ever in Alaska. Tom Larsen had known them before they had been transformed into myth.

Then Clem Tillion told some stories of fishing, and of boats, and of his early days in Alaska, including the story of a man named Hilmer Olsen, a fisherman and carpenter who had been living in Halibut Cove when the Tillions first arrived. They became good friends: Hilmer Olsen, in fact, carved the first bedstead on which the Tillions slept as man and wife. Eventually, Hilmer Olsen's wife died, and then Olsen himself developed cancer. It was incurable, and quickly grew painful. The last task Hilmer Olsen performed as a carpenter was to build his own coffin. When he was finished, he put it up on sawhorses in his workshop. Then he sat at a desk and wrote a letter. He put the letter in an envelope and addressed it to

Clem Tillion. Then he took it, by boat, to the Halibut Cove post office, out on the raft. When he came back, he spread a tarpaulin on the floor of his workshop, next to the coffin. Then he lay down on the tarpaulin, and shot himself through the head.

The next day, as he did every day, Clem Tillion went to the post office on the raft to pick up his mail. He found the letter from Hilmer Olsen and opened it. The letter said: "Come over tomorrow. I've got a dirty job for you. Don't bring your wife."

It was 9:30 p.m., still light out. Tom Larsen said goodbye and went to his boat. Clem Tillion took a walk through the woods. The wind had shifted; it was blowing from the southeast. That meant rain, Clem Tillion said, in the Gulf of Alaska, and poor weather in Homer by tomorrow.

We walked half a mile through the woods to a house that one of Clem Tillion's daughters and her husband were building. Then we passed another cleared area where one of Clem Tillion's sons would build a house. There were houses, and house sites, for Tillion children tucked away like hidden Easter eggs all through the woods of Halibut Cove. And there would be plenty more land available for houses for Clem Tillion's grandchildren. He had come to the right place at the right time. He had known what he wanted and he had known how to go about getting it. And had known how to protect it once he had it. In Juneau, for instance, in the legislature, while others debauched, Clem Tillion had quietly arranged for the designation of tens of thousands of acres on the south side of Kachemak Bay as the Kachemak Bay State Park; a wilderness area that would forever be protected from development. It was, indeed, a noble conservationist measure. And it was indeed no accident that the Kachemak Bay State Park surrounded, on three sides—with the waters of the bay on the fourth—the land that Clem Tillion owned on Halibut Cove. Thus assuring that the only bulldozers that Tillions of future generations would ever see approaching the perimeter of their rustic wilderness would be bulldozers that they had summoned themselves.

We kept on walking until 10:45. It was still light but the sky was gray now, and the wind could be heard, and the tops of the evergreens were starting to sway.

"It's been a good life," Clem Tillion said as we walked back toward his house. "I can't see any reason to have lived it differently. And I suppose, if a man can say that, when he gets to be my age, it means that somewhere along the line he must have done something right."

13 The Road North

A few days later I drove north, to Palmer, in the Matanuska Valley. It was a town I had passed through in November, in Duane Archer's truck, at the end of the trip in from the ferry. Palmer was the farm town of Alaska, a quiet little place for forty years, but now, being only forty miles from Anchorage, it, too, was starting to boom.

Palmer was the seat of government for the Matanuska-Susitna Borough, referred to in Alaska as Mat-Su. The other town in the borough was Wasilla, twelve miles to the west. Wasilla was the fastest-growing town in the state. It was on the main railroad line, while Palmer was off on a spur, with no passenger service any more. And Wasilla was on the Parks Highway, which, since it had been paved three years earlier, had become the main road to Fairbanks, cutting more than a hundred miles off the trip. Palmer was on the Glenn Highway, which was part of the old road to Fairbanks.

In the three years since the Parks Highway had been paved, Wasilla had gone from being a railroad stop with just an airstrip and one general store to being an extension of urban Anchorage. One new shopping mall had already been built and another was under construction. Subdivision houses were being put up as fast as lumber was obtained. Dow Chemical had purchased a 250-acre site at the north end of town.

The population of the Mat-Su Borough as a whole had increased by more than one-third in the past year. And there were sixty different real estate agencies at work in the borough, to make sure that the pace did not slacken. Were the new state capital actually to be constructed at Willow, twenty miles up the highway from Wasilla, the rate of growth would go off the top of the chart. Even without it, projections called for the borough population, which had been 6,500 in 1971, to be almost 40,000 ten years later.

Wasilla, it seemed, would be riding the crest of the wave. But Wasilla was all growth; it was all new; at the start of the decade there had hardly even been a Wasilla. Palmer was the town with a past, with character, with dimension, and the change that was coming to it interested me more.

I crossed the Knik River on a road that was flat, paved, and two lanes wide. Steeply rising mountains had been nearby to the east, but now, as I drove over the river, I moved away from them, toward the center of the valley.

It was a cool morning with low gray clouds and a rising wind. There were occasional patches of blue sky to the east, over the mountains, which remained snow-covered near the peaks. There were few other cars on the road but those that were out were moving fast.

Near the road, a bulldozer had made a clearing in the woods. There was a sign stuck into the ground at the front of the clearing, and strings of little colored plastic flags stretching from the sign to the trees on either side. The sign said: WINDSONG. OUTSTANDING HOMESITES. 90% FINANCING.

A bit further up the road I passed the Pioneer Peak Baptist Church, a trailer park, a lumber mill, an auto junkyard, then Triple-A Wrecking, which was a bigger auto junkyard, then the Butte Body Shop—Radiator Repair, and, closer to town, an industrial park, the state fairgrounds, and the Alaska Transportation Museum, with an old locomotive in front of it.

The main street of Palmer contained a liquor store, a bar, a

171

liquor store, a café, a bar, a liquor store, and a small, uninviting hotel. There was an old railroad station, painted bright green, with signs that said: PALMER—ELEVATION 241 FT. and TO SEWARD, 156.8 MILES and TO FAIRBANKS, 325.7 MILES, but the train didn't stop here any more.

Besides the liquor stores and bars, there were two banks, a Rexall, a ladies' apparel store, a variety store, a barbershop, and Pippel Insurance. The grocery store and most of the gas stations were a couple of blocks away. The north-south streets were paved, but the east-west connecting streets were not. The tallest structure in town was the tower of the Matanuska Maid dairy cooperative, which supplied milk and eggs to stores in Anchorage and Fairbanks. At one time, the cooperative had sold fresh milk and eggs and butter produced by Matanuska Valley farms, but now, because so many of the local farms had shut down, and so much of the land had been sold to real estate developers, Matanuska Maid imported more than half of its dairy products from Seattle.

I stopped for coffee at the Frontier Restaurant. There was a sign in front of the large dining room which said: THE COLONY ROOM WELCOMES THE GREATER PALMER CHAMBER OF COMMERCE EVERY WEDNESDAY AT 12 NOON. Except someone had crossed out the word "Commerce" and had printed the word "Comics" above it. And although the Matanuska Valley did contain eleven of the twelve remaining dairy farms in Alaska, the Frontier Restaurant, like every other restaurant in the state, served only non-dairy creamer with its coffee.

I drove to the east edge of town, past a collection of trailers and modular homes, to the farm of Rowland Snodgrass, who was seventy-five years old and had first come to Palmer in 1915, which was twenty years before the arrival of the colonists from the Midwest who were generally considered to have settled the town.

From the fields, there was a good view of the Matanuska Glacier, and of Lazy Mountain, and of Matanuska Peak, which was snow-covered and more than 6,000 feet high. There were two International Harvester Farmall tractors at the edge of the driveway, an unpainted barn, and a modern split-level house with freshly cut grass around it and a flower garden being watered by a sprinkler.

Rowland Snodgrass was a tall, slender, extremely literate man, with the strong hands and good color that a lifetime of farming can produce.

"My folks came to Kodiak first," he said. "That was in 1907. They came out from Kansas. My dad opened an experimental station for the Department of Agriculture on Kodiak. I was actually born in Oregon, though. The only doctor on Kodiak was a drunk, and he had bungled things terribly when my older sister was born, and, as a result, she had died. So, for me, my mother went to Oregon, which was the nearest place where she could find a sober doctor.

"We lived in different parts of the state. The year after Dad set up the experimental station here, we moved down to Seward. Then for seven years we were in Fairbanks. We bought this farm in 1932. It was three hundred and twelve acres originally. Forty acres got taken for the Palmer townsite when the colonists came out in 1935. Now there are only fifty-five acres left, and it's half owned by my son. I didn't want him to farm, but, at a hundred thirty-five pounds, he turned out to be the best hired man I ever had. He went to the University of Alaska, majored in economics, then did graduate work at the University of Oregon, and went on to law school at the University of Washington. He's come back to Palmer by his own choice. He's building a house right over there, across the field. He's going to help me farm this land and he's going to open a law office in town. For a fellow with his background and ability, it's not where the money is, but, even with all the changes, Palmer is still the place he likes best.

"When we first came here, there wasn't really any farming going on. The last of the gold stampedes had occurred up at Nilchink, about sixty or seventy miles northeast of here. Actually, it wasn't all that great a stampede. I don't think anyone found very much gold. But some of those fellows had been tramping around for twenty years and most of them were pretty tired. A lot of them wound up settling here. There was hay for their horses and they could raise potatoes, that was simple enough, and shoot rabbits whenever they wanted meat. Eventually it sort of grew into a retired miner's community. They were nice old fellows, almost all of them bachelors. Some of them might farm a few acres, but mostly they just liked to sit on their front porches, like southern gentlemen, and contemplate life. Just plain nice people, really, scattered all over the valley in small, modest, rather clean cabins. They made it a very enjoyable place to grow up in. It was a lot of fun for a bunch of little kids to gather around and listen to stories. All summer long we pulled potatoes out of the fields and ran around barefooted. We'd stop on our way back from fishing and trade the old fellows some trout for some eggs.

"This place, and Fairbanks, too, reminded me of Tom Sawyer and Huckleberry Finn. Fairbanks especially, because of the river bending right through the town.

"Eight years ago, I visited upstate New York in the fall, and I said to myself, you know, three hundred years ago this must have been fine country to live in. Well, Palmer was like that when we first arrived.

"I guess the only thing that Palmer was really famous for was that Matanuska Valley colony the government started. Actually, it was my dad who really got the thing going. He had become colonization agent for the railroad, and they were trying to increase their volume of traffic by attracting more settlement to the areas along the railroad line. Dad traveled down in the States, trying to persuade farmers to come up here. The deal was, at first, that the railroad would transport your car free, as well as any household effects you could pack in the car, but other than that you were on your own. I guess Dad got about a hundred and twenty-five families to come up. He was pretty well sold on the valley by that time and I think he did a good job of selling it to others. The following year, Colonel Ohlson, who was the head of the railroad, made a deal with the government and they shipped up all these chronic reliefers at government expense. The whole thing was set up like a socialist state.

"It was kind of exciting, in the summer of 1935, to sit there and see a bunch of them get off the train, not having any idea, really, what they were in for. Some of them made it and some of them didn't. Some of them were the kind that just couldn't make it anywhere. The government shipped up new ones to replace the ones who went back. There were about a hundred and seventy families involved, but after five or six years there were more of my dad's people left, even without any subsidies, than there were of the government colonists.

"Our own farm was doing really well. By 1940, we had fifty or sixty milking cows. We were the biggest dairy farm in the valley. Then the war came, and to save money the Department of the Army decided that all the troops down at Fort Richardson would get recombined and powdered milk instead of fresh milk from the valley. Ernest Gruening, who later became governor and senator, went to Washington and fought like hell about that, and in the end, the Army backed down. I think, until Vietnam, it was the only defeat the U.S. Army ever suffered.

"At the peak, there were more than seventy dairy farms in the valley, but it's less than a dozen now. There are just too many problems involved in any kind of farming in Alaska. The short growing season, obviously, and then the higher cost of everything. Equipment, feed, labor, whatever it is, it just costs too damned much to get it up here.

"I've tried to stay ahead of the game through education. I went to Alaska Agricultural College—that's the University of Alaska now—from 1928 to 1932, and I taught there for three years after that. Then I went down to the University of Southern California to take some courses in agriculture and chemistry. A few years later, I went to the University of Colorado for work in animal husbandry and range management. There's always something new you can learn. In 1954, I went to the University of Wisconsin and worked toward a doctorate in agricultural economics, with a minor in geography. These are just things you do to avoid getting too isolated up here. I never did get the Ph.D. I never got around to the language requirements and I never got around to writing my thesis. I was just too busy doing other things. You always are if you're a farmer. I may still do it. I could probably find some time over the next ten years. But I don't know—I suppose by now it's sort of lost its value.

"Around here, you just go along solidly and quietly, and maybe you don't really amount to a great deal, but that's the kind of life that some of us sort of enjoy. Having seen California, Colorado, Wisconsin, and even other parts of Alaska, I must say: none of them ever seemed quite as nice to live in as this place."

That afternoon, I went to the office of Pete Green, one of the town's leading real estate developers. He was a heavy, dark-haired man wearing a western-style suit and cowboy boots. There was a sign on his desk that said: I SPEAK REAL ESTATE-EZE. He had come to Alaska five and a half years earlier, from Hobbs, New Mexico, hoping to cash in on the oil boom. "I knew," he said, "that there were going to be big doings happening up here."

In New Mexico, he had been employed by a firm that sold land throughout the Southwest, often through advertisements in magazines. "The company had to shut down for a little while." Pete Green explained, "while it was getting itself straightened out with the federal government. Just one of those situations where you have to lay back a little bit until you get your affairs back in order. I figured I'd use the free time to come up to Anchorage for a look-see.

"I came into town on a Saturday night. Sunday morning I went out for breakfast to the Black Angus Restaurant on I Street. I had my western clothes on, of course, and this other fellow who was also wearing western clothes comes up to me and says right away that he can see we're kindred spirits. Turns out he just sold his cattle ranch on Kodiak Island. He was raising his own beef out there, growing his own feed, and even owned a slaughterhouse. He said the state had just hired him as an expert, and he was flying that night up to Nome to show them how to set up a slaughterhouse for reindeer.

"Well, we both had a little time to kill, so he took me around to the Elks Club. I'd been an Elk myself for a long time. Let me tell you something—here's a little tip for you—if you ever want to get ahead in real estate, join the Elks.

"Anyway, I got into a poker game down there that afternoon and then a little dice game called four-five-six. My buddy took off for Nome, but I stuck around and by the end of that first night I'd turned a twenty-dollar bill into three thousand dollars. I said, man, this is the place for me.

"A few nights later, I was back playing poker again. There was a real estate man from Anchorage in the game. Real big-time operator. Everybody was afraid of him. Now, I've been a poker player, been playing cards, all my life. To make a long story short, there was one particular hand where he opened and I raised him and then he raised me and everybody else dropped out, and I called him. And, as it turned out, I won the hand. Holding only two pair. Hell of a big pot, too. First time all night anybody had called this fellow's bluff. He said, I like you—I like the way you play poker. What's your line of work? Real estate, I told him, and he said come on down to the office in the morning, you're hired. Just as soon as I can get you a license, I'll turn you loose. So the next morning I go down there and meet his secretary and the two of us fall madly in love. The boss got me a job with the state

Division of Lands for nine months, until I was issued my license—
it took a little extra time because of that fuss back in New Mexico
—and by the time I got the license the girl and I had split up, and
believe me, the split was none too amicable, so there was no way I
could work in that office. Instead, the boss set me up in business
up here, and I've done so well so fast that now I'm completely
independent. And let me tell you something: I'm still taxiing down
the runway, buddy. I haven't even started to fly.

"Palmer has a great future. We're going to put in a two-
hundred-forty-acre industrial park—the only one in the state. On
the smaller scale, we've got builders crying out for lots to build on.
But we're just plumb out of lots. Don't have any lots. Can't find a
building lot in this town. You got some time this afternoon, take
a walk around. Look for a lot. You find one, you come back here
and see me, and I tell you what I'll do. I'll give it to you as a gift.
That's 'cause there ain't none. So what's the answer? Expansion.
Start building out of town. Up the road and down the road, build
on both sides of the road. And on the side roads and on the back
roads. And then you build some new roads and build along them.
The only problem is, we've got to lick this notion that somehow
there's something wrong with development. Look, it goes right
back to the Bible: What is the purpose of land? What is its greatest potential that the good Lord wants to see fulfilled? The greatest potential is for human habitat. Everybody's bitching about this
wilderness; about wild-animal habitat. I say, first things first: What
about human habitat?"

Later in the afternoon, I went to see Pippel of Pippel Insurance.
He was bald, except for bushy gray sideburns. He wore rimless
glasses, pale green trousers, and a shiny black shirt with an over-
lay of large, bright green leaves. His manner was brisk. A Kiwanis
luncheon had already interrupted his day, and people were lined
up in an outer office, waiting to see him. When an area is in the
process of doubling in population within two or three years, there
are a lot of people, apparently, who need insurance.

Pippel's father had been among the most successful of the original Matanuska Valley colonists. He had, in fact, caused consider-
able turmoil by breaking away from the co-op and setting up an
independent dairy business.

"My father had an advantage," Pippel said, "in that he knew agriculture before he came up here, so he knew what had to be done. A lot of the others, that first summer, just got off the train and began to live like pioneers. Shooting bears, catching salmon. Meanwhile, Dad was out there clearing land. As a result, he got a year ahead of them, and then he saw no damned reason to sit around in that co-op situation, waiting for them to catch up.

"I remember my first moments in Alaska. May of 1935. The boat docked at Seward, and us kids ran down the gangplank toward that mountain that's right there overlooking the harbor. My mother was yelling, 'Don't climb the mountain! Don't climb the mountain!' She'd never seen a mountain before and she was terrified that we'd fall off. But we were just like iron filings drawn to a magnet. We must have run halfway up before we even stopped to take a breath. I remember looking down and seeing our ship—it had seemed like such a big ship when we'd got on it, but now it was just a little boat way down in the harbor. I never got over that feeling. We were from the flatlands of the Midwest, and I had never before looked down on anything from higher than I could climb up a tree. I fell in love with the mountains that day and that's a love affair that's never ended.

"Up here, we're so close to the mountains—they're right there, within arm's reach, every day—that after a while you get used to them. They just become part of your life. Then you travel some-where else, and you find yourself looking around trying to find them. You keep on wondering: What is wrong? Where are the mountains? And you always wind up feeling kind of lost.

"We stayed up here from 1935 to 1939, then my dad moved back to Wisconsin and ran a dairy farm for a year and a half, then we moved back to Anchorage. Dad went out to Eagle River, above Anchorage, and started a hog ranch just after World War II. I married a Palmer girl in 1949 and moved back here and I've lived here ever since.

"Sure it's changing, but what the hell? Palmer sat here with a population of twelve hundred and eighty people for thirty years. In the 1940 census, 1950, 1960, and 1970, the size of the town didn't vary twenty people. So now we've doubled and everybody says it happened overnight, but really it's taken forty years.

"What's happened is that a lot of the original colonists are reaching, or have reached, retirement age. And when they go to sell their land to get some money to live on in their old age, they find a choice: they can sell to a farmer for five hundred dollars an acre, or they can sell to a developer for three thousand. What would you do? Sure, it's always nice to say, let's retain this land for agriculture—as long as its someone else's land.

"On the other hand, maybe it is too sudden after all. At least, I know I'm working too damn hard. I've been getting up at five o'clock in the morning just to play tennis, because I don't have any other time. And that's not right. What good does it do you to make all this money if you can't take the time off to spend it? That's a question that people everywhere else have probably been asking themselves all their lives. But up here it's something that's just beginning to confront us."

There were dark clouds in the sky and a cold wind off the glacier when I left Palmer at quarter past four. I drove west, then turned onto the Fishhook-Willow road, a dirt-and-gravel road open only in summer. It crossed the green and foaming Little Susitna River, and then began to climb, in a series of steep switchbacks, toward Hatcher Pass, an old gold-mining area, four thousand feet above Palmer and fifty road miles to the west.

Fireweed lent the only touch of brightness to the afternoon, and soon, above timberline, even that was left behind. At the pass, wisps of chilly cloud blew across the road, and patches of last winter's snow were visible in shaded areas. Coming down from the pass, on the west side, below timberline, there were thick rows of evergreens lining both sides of the narrow, bumpy road. Rain began. There were occasional clearings in the woods, where people had bulldozed building sites, but not many of these. The air was cold and damp, but sweet with the heavy scent of pine. In another twenty miles, pavement began, and a bit further on, at Willow, eighty road miles west of Palmer, the Fishhook-Willow road ended at a stop sign; at the Parks Highway, running north and south, between Anchorage and Fairbanks.

This was the area where, according to current plans, the new state capital would be built. It would eventually become a city with a population of 30,000. Assuming, of course, that the voters of Alaska, in future referendums and through future votes of their representatives in the state legislature, continued to approve the expenditure of perhaps two billion dollars for the project. Now, however, at six o'clock on a chilly, rainy summer evening, the only species in the area represented by 30,000 members was the mosquito.

I turned north on the Parks Highway and drove twenty-five miles until I came to the turnoff for Talkeetna. Twelve miles in, at the end of one of North America's longer dead-end streets, was Talkeetna itself, population approximately one hundred; an Alaskan settlement which, unlike Palmer or Homer, seemed determined not to allow its population ever to rise to even one hundred and one.

Talkeetna had one main street, three blocks long, which was not paved. It ended at the Talkeetna River on the west, and on the east, at the Alaska Railroad tracks. The houses were wooden frame, of simple construction. The post office was housed in a trailer. Talkeetna seemed a quintessential Alaskan settlement, in this respect: it had more pool tables (three) and more airfields (two) than it had gasoline stations (one). There were also a hardware store, a grocery store, a combination grocery-hardware store, and the Fairview Inn, the oldest building in town, circa 1927, which was a bar. In addition, there was the Talkeetna Roadhouse, which served meals and offered overnight accommodations, but which, despite its name, was most emphatically not a bar. Operated —it seemed, sometimes, against their will—by a taciturn and dour old couple named Close, who had been in Talkeetna for thirty years, the Roadhouse had a 10:30 p.m. curfew, enforced by locking both the front and back doors, and signs posted on the walls warning that the use of profanity would not be tolerated. Dinner was served at 6 p.m. sharp and don't come in at 6:05 and expect to be fed. Likewise for breakfast, which was served at 8 a.m. only.

Talkeetna had been, originally, with its access to the railroad, a staging depot for gold-mining operations. These had pretty well disappeared, however, and the only noticeable signs of an economy in the town—actually it had taken great pains not to incorporate itself as a "town"—were related to its proximity to Mount McKinley. Talkeetna was the settlement in Alaska that was closest to the south wall of the mountain, up which the majority of ascents were made. It was the last place that climbers saw before beginning their ascent, and except for those who died on the mountain or who had to be evacuated by aircraft directly to an Anchorage hospital, it was the first place they saw when they came down. A member of the first climbing team ever to make a successful ascent of the mountain in winter ran guided expeditions up McKinley from a base on Talkeetna's main street. There were three air taxi services which specialized in flying climbers and their supplies to the most widely used base camp, which was 7,200 feet up the mountain, on the surface of the Kahiltna Glacier.

In search of an atmosphere more convivial than that offered by the Talkeetna Roadhouse, I took a room at a place called the Rainbow, which was off by itself, up another dirt road, on what was, distinctly, the wrong side of the railroad tracks.

The Rainbow, if not precisely convivial, was at least more typically Alaskan: I was kept awake half the night by hollering from the bar, by the barking and howling of dogs which were kept chained to the trees outside my window, and by the clicking of billiard balls, a sound which traveled surprisingly well down the length of the corridor that separated my room from the Rainbow's licensed premises. Eventually, the rain became heavier, drowning out all other sounds, and I slept until 9 a.m.

It was cloudy again in the morning, by my calculations the seventh consecutive cloudy day of summer. I re-entered Beautiful Downtown Talkeetna, which was marked by a sign that so proclaimed it. The words were painted on the insides of split logs which had been nailed together to form the sign, at the end of Main Street closest to the railroad tracks.

Two young men with beards and long hair and one young woman with long hair were sitting on the front steps of the B & K Trading Post, smoking cigarettes. A car moved slowly up the street and pulled into the Phillips 76 station to get gas. A green Jeep was in front of the Fairview Inn, the driver at the wheel, and a man was leaning against the window of the Jeep, talking to the driver. Four small children were walking up the middle of the street, in front of the Talkeetna Leather Works, which was located in a log cabin, and in front of the office of Mac. A. Stevens, registered surveyor, and then past the Quonset hut that was the home of Cliff Hudson, the pilot, who specialized in flying climbing parties to Mount McKinley. A Dodge pickup truck stopped in front of the grocery store. A girl came out of the trading post, carrying a large box, and disappeared around a corner, in the direction of the post office. That was it: half the population of Talkeetna, present and accounted for.

The sun found a crack between thick, almost muscular gray clouds, and shafts of light reached tentatively toward the ground. Then the clouds reconverged and the sunlight was squeezed out again.

The two young men with long hair and the young woman with long hair finished their cigarettes and stood up and walked slowly toward the river, which marked the western edge of town. The car from the gas station pulled up a few yards and the driver went into the grocery store. The gas station attendant went back inside his garage. The green Jeep moved away from the Fairview and the man who had been leaning against the window went into the inn. The four small children were no longer in sight. There was, in fact, no one in sight. At 10:30 in the morning, in the middle of summer, in the middle of the week, the main street of Talkeetna was deserted.

I knocked on the front door of a small house on Main Street, across from the Fairview Inn. It was the home of Roberta Sheldon, who was the daughter of Bob Reeve, and who had been, until he died, Don Sheldon's wife.

Bob Reeve and Don Sheldon were not names that meant much outside of Alaska, but within the state they were at least the equivalent of Roy Rogers and Gene Autry, or possibly Neil Armstrong and John Glenn. Bob Reeve had been one of the most famous of Alaska's aviation pioneers. He had been, in fact, the first man ever to land an airplane on the surface of a glacier. Don Sheldon had been of the second generation. Until his death, which came, not in an air crash, but from cancer, he had been the most renowned of Alaska's contemporary pilots. The man who had done the most flying, and the most spectacular flying, in the vicinity of—sometimes in the very, very immediate vicinity of—Mount McKinley.

In a state whose nature had been changed so drastically by aviation; where the theory of relativity had been put into practice by the original bush pilots, and the dimensions of time and space forever altered; where the air taxi and its operator had become an integral part not only of the mythology but of the economy and of

182

the social fabric, men such as Bob Reeve and Don Sheldon had acquired legendary dimension. To have been the daughter of one of these men, and then the wife of another, had bestowed upon Roberta Sheldon uncommon status.

She was thirty-seven years old, dark-haired, attractive, a mother of three. She had chosen to remain in Talkeetna following the death of her husband, and now she was committed to seeing that Talkeetna itself remained. That it did not become another Wasilla.

The two major threats were, first, the proposed capital move; and, second, the plan, strongly supported by Alaska's senior United States senator, Mike Gravel, to build a dam across the wild and scenic Susitna River north of Talkeetna, in order to provide additional electric power for the development that was spreading north from Anchorage. But even besides the big threats, there seemed to be a steady flow of little annoyances, as bureaucracy, and modern times, nibbled away at the essence of Talkeetna.

"A week ago," Roberta Sheldon said, "a man from Juneau came in on the train. He was from the Department of Highways. He had plans with him to show where fifty-six stop signs and yield signs should go. He said the state had been given a federal grant as part of a program to improve traffic safety, and now we were going to have these signs stuck on corners all over town. Except we don't have fifty-six corners in town. We've barely got five or six. Anyway, the man said he wanted to talk to someone in the local government. I told him there wasn't any local government. I told him we didn't want any local government, we didn't need any, and—even though I was trying to be polite—I told him we didn't want his stop signs either.

"I think that was a little too much for him to handle. I think he'd expected Talkeetna to be like Juneau. That he'd step off the train and be taken to lunch by the mayor at some fancy hotel. Now he finds out that, first, we don't have a fancy hotel, and second, we don't even have a mayor.

"He asked me if I would call a town meeting, so he could at least explain to the people about his signs. I said, sure, I'd call a town meeting, but I didn't think anybody would come. I told him people around here don't like to go to meetings much, and they weren't going to like hearing about his signs much either. He just couldn't seem to understand it. He was, you know, a real government type.

"Well, only about fifteen people showed up at the meeting, and that was just as well, since they all started shouting at him at once. Finally, I got afraid that someone was going to hurt him, so I suggested that, instead, everybody just sit down and write out their opinions. They wrote things like: 'We do not need signs to tell us what to do or where to go' and 'Give them to Wasilla.' Those were some of the polite ones. And that got him kind of upset. He was back on the train to Anchorage the next day, with his plans rolled up under his arm, but he said we hadn't heard the last of this, and I'm afraid he's probably right.

"It's really got us kind of buffaloed. All these things do. The capital, the dam, we just don't want them, because they're going to destroy our way of life. A couple of weeks ago, Carr's, the big supermarket chain from Anchorage, tried to buy out the D & A, which is our little grocery store. And Sheffield, the hotel man, has been trying to buy the Fairview Inn. I think maybe things around here are just a little too perfect, and the commercial interests have begun to recognize that. I'd say those folks have picked up the scent of money, and that scares me. It seems as if the wolf is at the door."

A record played in the background as she spoke: *Diamonds and Rust*, by Joan Baez. Other records lay on a table near the phonograph: Jackson Brown, Vivaldi, Sibelius, a recording of the Brandenburg Concertos, an album of Gregorian chants, Phoebe Snow. There were photographs on the wall of mountains and of airplanes and of her husband, Don Sheldon. Some Lego pieces, with which her youngest child had been playing, lay on the floor.

Roberta Sheldon had been born in Seward and grown up in Anchorage. She worked as an airline stewardess, starting with Reeve Aleutian, her father's company. Next she worked for Flying Tiger, on flights that took military dependents from San Francisco to the Orient, and then, for six months, she flew between New York and Europe. "It was living in New York that really did it," she said. "That's when I decided, for sure, that Alaska was for me."

She had attended the University of Alaska for two years before deciding that "I just wasn't a scholar. I was wasting my time and Dad's money." Then she worked as a Kelly Girl in Anchorage, doing secretarial chores on a temporary basis. Dissatisfied with her life and her work, and not knowing what to do next, she met Don

Sheldon, who had paused, while in Anchorage, to visit her father.

"For the next year," she said, "he seemed to be dropping by my folks' house an awful lot, and I just happened to be there every time. I'd keep track of when he was coming by. Of course, when he got there I'd just sit still and not say anything while the two of them talked. We finally went out on a date. On April 1. On May 16, we got married. It only took a month and a half once things got rolling."

After a three-day honeymoon, they returned to Talkeetna, and she helped him run the flying service for fifteen years. It had been two and a half years since he died.

"It's been difficult," she said. "I'm only now starting to realize that I've been quietly hysterical all that time. I'm only now starting to feel normal again. Starting to think reasonable thoughts.

"At first, a lot of people encouraged me to get out. To leave Talkeetna. They said there would be too many memories here. And I was tempted. It might have been easier. But I just couldn't sell out and leave it flat. The business had too much meaning to Don, and to me. So I tried running it with other pilots. Last summer, though, I sold the air taxi certificate. I had to. I couldn't run an air service and raise kids and do justice to both, because they're both twenty-four-hour-a-day jobs.

"I still don't want to leave Talkeetna, though. There are too many things I would miss. The river, the sound of the trains going through every night, and, of course, the Mountain."

Unlike Palmer, where the mountains are spoken of with a small *m*, in Talkeetna, when people say mountain they mean McKinley, and it is referred to always with a captial *M*. This comes from living only forty miles from its base. And in the flying business, from contending every day with both the Mountain and the weather it produces.

"Now," Roberta Sheldon said, "I can't imagine living anyplace else. I feel my destiny is right here. Maybe next year, when my youngest child starts at school, I'll get back into the air taxi business. I love it; I just love it; and it's been such a big part of my life.

"Also," she said, "I'm thinking of writing. I would like to try to get what this town is down on paper. I'd like to capture the humor of the town, the independence, the way the land has shaped the people, and just the fine values of living here. Right now, of course, I'm not working at all. I still feel it's important for the kids to have their mother at home." Then she laughed. "Besides, there aren't any jobs in Talkeetna anyway."

From a corner of the room, a CB radio began to make noise. Roberta Sheldon went to it and picked up the microphone. A party of Japanese climbers, descending from the summit of McKinley, had reached their base camp on the Kahiltna Glacier and were calling for their pilot to pick them up.

"Are you calling Hudson Air Service?" Roberta Sheldon asked.

There was a great deal of static, and a muffled, heavily accented voice. But Roberta Sheldon's ear, apparently, was better attuned to this sort of communication than was mine.

"Roger, Roger," she said, "I will get him on the radio. Please stand by. Please wait."

Then she spoke to the Hudson Air Service. "Ollie? This is Roberta. I've got your Japanese climbers on B-411. They want a pickup." She put down the microphone. "Ollie is Cliff's wife," she said. "She's covering for him. He's off on a trip somewhere. I think he had a charter with some fishermen. He probably didn't expect the Japanese to be down this soon. Ollie will make up some excuse about the weather." She shook her head, and laughed softly. "God," she said, "I never thought I'd see the day when I was passing messages to Cliff Hudson."

It had not been a very friendly rivalry. Don Sheldon had been in Talkeetna first, and when Cliff Hudson and his brother Glenn arrived and set up a new flying service, the town suddenly began to seem too small. "This was a very hungry country," Roberta Sheldon said. "It was really a struggle, after you put gasoline in the plane, to find money left over for groceries. There was one terrible fistfight that people still talk about, in the early days. Not Don, but a partner Don had at the time got into a fight with Cliff's brother Glenn, right out there in the middle of the street. Right in front of the Fairview. I don't remember what it was about, specifically. Everything was really about fighting over the small amount of business that there was. It was really about fighting to survive.

"Cliff's brother was killed in a crash. Then Don's partner pulled out, and so it was just Don and Cliff. And now, of course, it's just Cliff, and a couple of newer fellows who've come along, but with the climbing so popular, there's plenty of business to go around.

"It's so ironic that Don isn't here. He felt indestructible. He felt that nothing could hurt him. He talked so much about that that I think he got a reputation for being reckless as a pilot, but actually he wasn't all that reckless. Around here, of course, it's a risk every time you get off the ground, and especially every time you fly toward the Mountain, but Don was always very much aware of his margins. He spent his whole life fighting the elements, and he won. That's the ironic thing about it. After all that, it wasn't the flying that got him, it was cancer."

There was a short silence in the room. "That's what I put on his gravestone," Roberta Sheldon said. " 'He wagered with the wind, and won.' " There was a slightly longer silence. The record was over. The radio quiet. Outside, the street was still empty.

14 Kahiltna Glacier

In the afternoon, five National Park Service rangers arrived in Talkeetna. They had driven down from McKinley Park, where they were stationed, in order to climb Mount McKinley.

It had not been a good year on the mountain. Already, since spring, three climbers had died, while sixteen others, suffering from altitude sickness or frostbite, or having been injured in falls, had required rescue by air. Now the Park Service, which had responsibility for the mountain, had decided to take a closer look.

Only two of the rangers were full-time employees of the Park Service. The others were hired for the summer season. Of these, one worked on a cattle ranch in Texas the rest of the year, one attended college in California, and one, Jack Hebert, twenty-six years old, lived with his wife in a cabin they had built themselves, on the Ambler River in the western Brooks Range.

In summer, Jack and Beth Hebert were backcountry rangers, hiking together through the more remote sections of McKinley Park. For most people, such a summer would have been the essence of wilderness adventure, but for Jack and Beth it seemed almost an urban experience in comparison to the way they lived the rest of the year.

"We thought at first," Jack Hebert said, "that Alaska would be exciting country to visit. It had never occurred to either of us that we could live here."

Jack had grown up in Washington, just outside Mount Rainier National Park. His father had operated a guest ranch and motel, and, as a boy, Jack had spent almost as much time mountain climbing, skiing, and riding horses as he had walking. As far as he knew, there were only two occupations in the world: logging and being a park ranger. Not sure which he would choose, he majored in forestry at the University of Washington, and worked, in summer, as a seasonal ranger at Mount Rainier National Park. Whenever he could, he climbed a mountain, even after a fall that tore apart the calf muscles of one leg and opened a cut that required more than a hundred stitches to close.

Beth Hebert, a year younger than her husband, gentle and slender, with long blond hair, had been raised in Indiana, but she had always wanted to go West. While attending Indiana University, she worked, one summer, as an unpaid volunteer at Mount Rainier Park. Jack Hebert was there, but Beth was going with someone else at the time. That fall, however, her boyfriend was killed in a hiking accident in the Grand Canyon. Beth returned to Washington and she and Jack got married. The following summer, they came to Alaska to work as seasonal rangers in McKinley Park.

That had been the summer of 1973, the last year that Alaska's open-to-entry land program had been in effect. Certain lands, divided into five-acre sections, had been made available for settlement. Anyone who wanted to could claim five acres at no cost, simply by staking it out. Actually, it was not so simple, since most of the land was hundreds of miles from any road, and besides, once you had it, what could you possibly do with it?

Two couples from McKinley Park, however, had decided to stake out land on the Ambler River, which flowed into the Kobuk River, in the southwestern Brooks Range. It was the farthest-north, most remote land available. The two couples had chartered a plane to fly them up when the park season ended in September, and there had been one extra seat on the plane. Jack had gone with them for the ride, but when he got there and saw the beauty and isolation and perfection of it all, he developed a new vision of the life which he and Beth might someday lead.

"I was twenty-two years old," he said, "and I had always been a really restless person, and I had always hoped to find a way of life that might satisfy that restlessness. When I saw that country around the Ambler, that was it. The restlessness just vanished, and I felt instead a really deep inner peace. I knew right away what I wanted to do. I wanted to come back the next summer and build a cabin on the land and live there with Beth all winter long."

That first winter, Jack and Beth left Alaska. They went to the Tetons, in Wyoming, where Jack worked for a ski touring guide service. They returned to McKinley Park in the spring and worked again, as backcountry rangers, through the summer. "All summer long," Jack said, "we made food lists and materials lists and we would order stuff from Fairbanks, and I would make plans for the cabin."

They chartered a plane and, with the two other couples, flew back to the Ambler River on September 1, 1974. It was a clear day in the Arctic, and the fall colors had spread across the tundra. The blueberries, Jack said, were big as apples. "I was pretty amazed at how beautiful it was. Also, pretty intimidated. September first is kind of late in the year that far north, and not only didn't I have a single log cut for our cabin, I had never built a cabin before. I got a real deep chill down my spine when I saw that plane take off and leave us there. But then I just got out the chain saw and went to work. You never saw a cabin go up so fast. We were running on sheer paranoia. We didn't get the floor down—in the beginning we had a dirt floor—but other than that, we were finished by the end of September."

They were half a mile from each of the other couples. They would meet occasionally for meals, but other than that, it was solitude. The plane that had flown them up returned in late September, bringing mail for all, and dog food for the one couple that had assembled a dog team. On October 7, a friend flew in with some fish, and after that they didn't see anyone until the end of November.

"It was just so intense. Watching the river freeze. We could hardly stand it, it was so beautiful. Once we got the cabin built, we made a fish camp, about eighteen miles up the river. We built a cache and stored all the fish we caught and when freeze-up came we hauled the fish back to our cabin with the dogs. We also shot a caribou for meat. We were really lucky in that respect. We had been thinking only about scenery, not about resources, but the river was so full of fish and the caribou migration came so close to our camp that we wound up with plenty of both.

"God, it was amazing. I can still feel it so strongly. The intensity, up at the fish camp, just before freeze-up. The tundra was deep red from autumn, the caribou were in their fall coats, and the herd, as it migrated, was passing so close to us that we could hear the noises of two bulls sparring. *Clack-clack.* The sound of their antlers as they hit, just floating across the fall air.

"In four days at that fish camp, we caught eight hundred fish with a net. Whitefish. Just dipping in one little spot. It was really cold, about ten above, and the fish would freeze as soon as we pulled them out of the water. God, it seemed like there was no richer place on the earth. Then we started thinking. Imagine: it all used to be like this. Two hundred, three hundred years ago, which isn't really so far back when you think of it in evolutionary terms. I mean, even New Jersey, where you come from. Can you imagine how rich and wonderful New Jersey must have been three hundred years ago? See, we were in the Arctic, feeling this richness, and the Arctic, in terms of resources, is really not that rich at all.

"We didn't have five acres, we had a million. We were thirty-five miles from the village of Kobuk and forty-five miles from Ambler village. We went into Kobuk at Christmastime, a two-day ski trip down the river, and we met an old white man who had lived there for many years and who told us to come back in spring and he'd teach us some of the traditional Eskimo skills. We did go back, and spent about two weeks in the village, living with him. He taught us about toolmaking and how to tan caribou and moose hides, and how to dry meat and how to make the baskets that the Natives of Kobuk are known for.

"I think we really changed during that winter. For one thing we became very shy. Like, when we got to the village in the spring, we found that we were not looking anyone directly in the eye. We were just so unused to other people. You see, things didn't work out so well for our friends. The other two women were gone by December. It just wasn't a kind of life that they could live. Then the two guys would come over to visit and wind up staying for two weeks. It was pretty heavy there for a while.

"Those two left in March and then we were all by ourselves. That was, I think, the only time when we started to get lonely or depressed. Usually, when one of us was in that kind of mood, the other one would compensate. But there are little things that make you sad: like, you spend a week making something and when you're done there's no one to show it to."

The strangest part, Beth Hebert said, was coming back into the city after eight months of isolation. "Up on the river," she said, "we had gotten so tuned in to picking up every little subtle change around us, it was like our pupils had really opened wide. And then Fairbanks, wow, that was too much all at once. It was like we were being assaulted. By impressions. By stimulation. I remember I was standing on the street talking to this person and a woman walked by and she was wearing perfume and I stopped what I was saying and just stared after the woman, and then I said, 'Oh, it's perfume. That woman is wearing perfume.' And this person I was talking to just said, 'Huh?' Now we're more used to the transition, but that first year was really weird."

They worked in the park again for the summer, and that fall returned to their cabin by canoe. Down the Yukon and then up the Kobuk and then just a left turn at the Ambler and they were home. But already they found that the neighborhood was changing.

"Two other couples and one single guy had gone up that summer and had built cabins on land that we used to go to. That sort of bothered us for a while. They had as much right to do it as we did, of course, but when you're the only ones there, and you think all of this will always be here, just like it is, and it will always be just for us and our friends, and then you go back four months later and see cabins, well, it just took a little bit away. Then the other thing was, it didn't really seem so wild the second year. Because we knew what was in the next valley and the valley beyond. We spent a lot more time out of doors the second winter. A lot more time away from the cabin. We had our own dogs that year and we'd take trips when it was sixty-five below just for the experience. Running along twenty feet ahead of the dog team, breaking trail, and the ice fog so thick you couldn't even see the dogs behind you. It was exciting, because everything relating to traveling like that is also relating directly to your own survival.

"We got back last fall and found that there were seven cabins in the valley. One guy even had a CB radio. It had been so wild and exciting for that first year. But by last year it seemed almost routine. Actually, in the middle of winter, we went to Hawaii for six weeks. We figured by then our sourdough image was well enough established.

"Now, I think that phase of our life is pretty much over. We've got the cabin and we've got the land and I'm sure we'll always keep going up there, but I don't think we'll really live there any more. This winter, I'm planning to stay around the park. I'm building a couple of cabins for some people. Beth is going to Fairbanks for the fall, to take some art courses at the university. Then we'll have to see what happens next. We just sort of fall into things, like we did with the cabin in the first place, and I think that's the best way for us to live. When we start trying too hard it seems like we block too much out. We stop letting things happen to us. We've always had an adventure to look forward to, and I think probably we always will. But right now we don't know what to do next. I mean, in a way it's kind of scary. How something that is so wild and exciting can so quickly become almost routine. If going up to a mountain range in the Arctic and building your own cabin and living in it through the winter stops being an adventure, what is it going to take to turn you on?"

Well, climbing the highest mountain in North America, for one thing. The sky had cleared, for the first time in a week, and the afternoon had turned warm, and everything in and around Talkeetna seemed colored a fresh summer green. Beth Hebert had ridden down to Talkeetna with the group, in order to drive their car back to the park. In the high sun of late afternoon Jack and Beth could be seen together, walking by the river, holding hands. They seemed the most joyful, contented couple in Alaska. They had each other, they had their youth, and they had the wilderness of Alaska to work and play in.

There was dinner—six o'clock sharp—at the Talkeetna Roadhouse. Then Beth Hebert drove back to the park. The rangers walked slowly along the dusty main street, stopped at the Fairview Inn for a couple of beers, then went to sleep at the Talkeetna Motel, with daylight still strong in the sky.

In the morning, they would fly to the Kahiltna Glacier, 7,200 feet up the mountain, and from there, after a couple of days of acclimatization, which I had arranged to spend with them, they

would begin their ascent. The climb was expected to take about a
month.

A bright, sunny morning, which was good, because Cliff Hudson
did not fly to the Kahiltna Glacier in bad weather. Which was one
of the reasons he had survived almost thirty years as a bush pilot
in Talkeetna. "Always gonna be another day," he had said the
night before, over beer. "Just gotta make sure you're here to see it.
Heh-heh-heh."

At least that's what I think he said. With Cliff Hudson it was
hard to be sure. Where airplanes were involved, he was a perfec-
tionist of the highest order; a man obsessed with precision. In such
non-life-and-death matters as use of the English language, however, he was considerably more lax. Especially after he'd had a few
beers. Heh-heh-heh. The little laugh was always there. It seemed
unconscious, a nervous tic. The least that could be expected after
thirty years of the sort of flying that Cliff Hudson had done around
Talkeetna. With his old foe and neighbor, Don Sheldon, dead,
Cliff Hudson was the premier glacier pilot of Alaska; the living
pilot who had made the most landings on McKinley; the man to talk
to, the man to go with, if landing on the surface of a glacier, in a
single-engine plane, at an altitude of 7,200 feet, was something
that you really had to do. Heh-heh-heh.

This summer there had been so much traffic on the mountain
that Cliff Hudson had taken on an assistant, a young pilot named
Doug, from Los Angeles. Doug was only twenty years old, but he
had worked as a flight instructor in Los Angeles. He had been
flying climbers to the glacier all spring and summer, and taking
fishermen and hunters to the rivers and the lakes, and flying anyone and everyone wherever it was that they happened to want to
go, working the sixteen-hour days that were standard for bush
pilots in the summer, when every hour of daylight had to be utilized
to offset the short, dark winter days when no one went anywhere.

Everyone in Talkeetna said that Doug was very good. This
meant, at least, that he had not yet cracked up any planes and that
he had shown no overt signs of lunacy, above and beyond those
that were considered normal for Talkeetna. Nonetheless, when it
was explained that both Cliff Hudson and Doug would be flying
members of the National Park Service Mount McKinley Expedi-

tion to the Kahiltna Glacier in the morning, every member of the expedition immediately volunteered to fly with Cliff. Heh-heh-heh.

Cliff Hudson had shaved off half his beard. The right side of his face was bearded; the left side bare. He had done this, he said, to demonstrate to his two teen-aged sons how foolish they looked in long hair. So far it had not worked. "The dumb shits," he said. They still had long hair, and Cliff Hudson was stuck with half a beard.

His appearance sometimes proved disconcerting to clients. Especially to those who were, perhaps, already a wee bit squeamish about flying through, around, or onto the surface of the continent's most massive mountain range. The one man in whom they needed to have absolute, unquestioning confidence was their pilot. They wanted a man with a keen eye, rugged features, and perhaps just a trace of insouciance. A man with style, with flair, a man obviously brimming with confidence in his equipment, and in his own skills, and in his mastery over the forces of nature. A man, in fact, very much like Don Sheldon. Instead, now, with Sheldon gone, they found themselves confronted with Cliff Hudson: the poor posture; the squint; the nervous little laugh; the ratty old shirt that he seemed to change no more often than he changed his engine oil; and now, to make matters worse, there was this situation with the beard.

Even with a full beard, Cliff Hudson looked much more like a man who might approach you on Fourth Avenue in Anchorage seeking a quarter that might help him buy a bottle of wine, than he did a skilled and seasoned glacier pilot—a man to whom you were about to entrust your life, as you witnessed firsthand the classic duel between the laws of gravity and the laws of aerodynamics.

A team of Japanese climbers, in fact, upon disembarking recently from the train, and upon being met by this shuffling, inarticulate man with half a beard, claiming to be the renowned pilot Cliff Hudson who would fly them to the glacier the next morning, had very nearly stopped right there; had balked at the prospect; had decided, unanimously, to take the next train back to Anchorage and to postpone their climb until this business with the pilot was straightened out.

Finally, Cliff Hudson explained to the Japanese that he had

shaved half his beard off for religious reasons. Ah, a religious gesture. The Japanese understood. They were mollified; even cheered.
A man of God would be their pilot. A holy man. An ascetic. What
good fortune. What a splendid omen for their climb. There was
much bowing and smiling and many expressions of trust and affection. All of which gave enormous pleasure to Cliff Hudson, and to
those who heard him tell the story, in his mumbly, inarticulate
way, as he shot pool and drank beer late into the night at the
Talkeetna Motel. He figured now that they thought he was a mys-
tic, he could probably add 20 percent to their bill.

"What's the weather going to be like on the mountain?"
     "Mumblemumbmlmm."
     "What was that, Cliff?"
     "Oh, mumblemembummbulmumblem. Heh-heh-heh."
There were no seats, except the pilot's seat, in Cliff Hudson's
plane, which was a Cessna 185. He had removed the seats in order
to fit in as many climbers and as much gear as possible on each
trip, so as to require as few trips, for each expedition, as possible.
     The plane had not been painted since its purchase years be-
fore. There were dents and nicks and scrapes all over, and it would
make a horrible racket and would bounce crazily as it sped down
the gravel airstrip in front of Cliff Hudson's hangar, right behind
Main Street in Talkeetna, but he would get it up in the air, by
God, even with the weight of the climbers and their gear, the way
he'd been doing for almost thirty years, and in forty-five minutes
or so, having left behind the green land of rivers and lakes and
trees in summer bloom, and having flown through the pass that led
to the frozen, unchanging kingdom of ice and rock that was the
interior of the Alaska Range, he would lean forward a bit, squint a
little harder at the surface of the glacier below, begin to move the
control stick slightly forward, and ease down to it just as loose and
free and natural as a small boy starting down a snowy hillside on a
sled. And he knew where the crevasses were, so the plane would
not disappear into one of those. And he knew the angle at which
the glacier sloped upward, and the angle at which his skis should
first make contact with the ice. And later on, when it was time for
engine maintenance to be performed, Cliff Hudson would fly the
plane to Anchorage and would stay there with it until all the

mechanical work was done; inspecting every part, and overseeing every hour of the labor; sometimes even sleeping beside the airplane on the floor. It was true that Cliff Hudson's planes did not look like much from the outside, but you could be as sure as it was humanly possible to be that there would be no surprises from the engine. It was not the paint job that you had to worry about when the winds of the Alaska Range began to bounce you toward a jagged wall of rock and ice, 10,000 feet above the ground.

"Sheldon always walked away from them," said a man who had been in Talkeetna for a while, "but over the years he must've cracked up thirty-five planes. Cliff, in thirty years, hasn't hurt one."

"No big deal," Cliff Hudson said. Then he mumbled a sentence which seemed to contain the words "careful" and "judgment," which, given the topic of conversation, seemed reassuring. But Cliff Hudson did not want to talk about flying. Flying was something he did, not something he tried to explain.

He looked up at the clear sky and at the mountain. "Well," he said, "guess we better rattle on up. Heh-heh-heh."

I spent three days and two nights on the glacier. It was hot in the daytime with the sun up and the sky clear. So hot, so bright, in fact, and the sun so strong in the clear air at that altitude that after an hour or so of sunbathing, the people on the glacier had to retreat inside their tents.

In the evening, however, in the first hour after the sun had passed to the west of Mount Foraker, and shadow covered the glacier's surface, the temperature dropped 30 degrees. I had worn a wool shirt and down jacket, but I had brought only hiking boots, no winter boots, on this trip, and my feet grew painfully cold. At night, inside my sleeping bag, in the tent that Cliff Hudson had loaned me, I was torn between a desire to keep the front flap open so I could lie awake gazing at the face of Mount Hunter, just two miles east of the glacier—a face that glowed like the face of a deity through the blue twilight of the northern summer night—and a desire to seal the flap as tightly as possible, in order to keep out the cold air.

The section of the glacier that was used as a landing strip, and as a base camp by McKinley expeditions, was a tributary of the main Kahiltna. We had flown north above the main glacier coming in, and then had turned right at a break in McKinley's southern ridge, and had landed about two miles up the side glacier. Mount Foraker, 17,000 feet high and only three miles to the west, was in full view, looming like a tidal wave above us. To the east, Mount Hunter, though 2,000 feet lower, was even closer, and thus an even more startling apparition. A ridge rose above the landing area to the north, obstructing the view of the summit of McKinley, but that was a loss which seemed not to matter in the midst of such sudden magnificence. This did not seem part of Alaska; not even part of the planet Earth. I felt that I had been swallowed up by mountains; that I had gone inside the belly of the whale.

I had hiked in mountains before, and had, in fact, grown deeply attached to the slow and gradual pleasures that a long mountain trek could produce. But McKinley was an entirely different kind of experience. Both physically and in terms of emotional and psychological reaction, it went way beyond hiking. There was no way for a hiker to get here; once here, there would be nowhere for a hiker to go.

Having seen McKinley from a distance of 170 miles, in Anchorage; and from 60 miles, in Talkeetna; and from an altitude of several thousand feet above its summit, when flying past it in an airplane; to be, now, actually on the mountain, one-third of the way to its summit, surrounded, consumed by immensity and splendor beyond anything I had ever imagined—this was as dramatic as new life; or sudden death.

One had to be careful on the glacier. It was not an environment designed for casual human habitation. First, one had to wear sunglasses at all times. As the unobstructed sun reflected off the snow that covered the glacier's surface and mountain walls, the brightness was dangerously intense. Snow blindness would quickly result if one tried to absorb the beauty unfiltered. Also, one had to be careful where one walked. Beyond the immediate base camp area, there was the danger of falling into a crevasse. More than one climber had died that way, right here, at the very beginning of the ascent.

So, really, all there was for me to do—since I was not involved in the packing of food and the loading of sleds and the other preparations for the climb—was eat and sleep and look around. The eating and sleeping did not amount to much: it was the looking that filled my days and nights.

After a short while, it became almost painful—the inability to look in all directions at once. To know, for example, that as I was gazing at Mount Hunter in the bright light of late afternoon, Mount Foraker, in the other direction, was there to be seen also, as the shadows of evening slid slowly up its icy walls. And an even more intense pain, a peculiar, almost delirious feeling, a sort of sweet agony, from knowing that my time here would, of necessity, be so brief. That in one day, or two, the climbers would move on, would move up, and I would fly back to green Talkeetna, to the ordinary world of Alaska in summer, which, until now, had seemed so extraordinary.

15   Valdez

The first oil reached Valdez at 11:02 on a Thursday night. By coming closest to guessing the amount of time required for the oil to travel through the pipeline from Prudhoe Bay—38 days, 12 hours, 56 minutes—a crippled widow from Anchorage won the $30,000 grand prize in the building-fund lottery conducted by St. Patrick's Catholic Church.

It had been more than nine years since the original discovery of oil at Prudhoe Bay, and, as these things went, it seemed a significant moment in Alaska's history. The state, and the way of life of its people, had been transformed. Not just by the pipeline and by the population increase and economic boom which the pipeline had brought, but by the related events. The Native Claims Act, which had so drastically altered life for the Eskimo and Indian, and which might never have been enacted had it not been for the desire of the Congress to see pipeline construction begin. And now, as a result of that provision of the Native Claims Act which required that Congress set aside a portion of the federally owned land in Alaska as parkland and wilderness, there was the controversial Udall bill—officially designated as H. R. 39—which would preserve more than 100 million acres; a proposal considered a great blessing by some, but viewed by many Alaskans as nearly sufficient grounds for secession. The arrival of the oil in Valdez, then, appeared to mark more than just the completion of a multi-billion-dollar circuit: it symbolized the Americanization of Alaska.

Valdez was only about a hundred miles east of Anchorage. The cities were separated, however, by the Chugach Mountains, with peaks as high as 13,000 feet, and by the Columbia Glacier, which was itself a bit larger than Rhode Island. To drive, therefore, one first had to travel northeast, almost two hundred miles, to Glennallen, and then south, parallel to the pipeline, on the Richardson Highway, through Thompson Pass, a distance of more than three hundred miles. It was an all-day drive from Anchorage, but I could fly in less than an hour, which I did, the day after the oil had arrived.

The afternoon was sunny and breezy, the temperature 65 degrees. I flew on Polar Airlines, in a plane with eight seats, seven of which were occupied by businessmen in suits and ties. These were men connected, I gathered, with the oil. Most of them had just flown up from Texas; some had not been to Alaska before. The day was so sunny, so clear, and the view, as we flew over the mountains, so spectacular, that they soon stopped talking business, and fell silent, and simply stared.

Valdez (pronounced Val-deez) was located at the end of Valdez Arm, a long, narrow, curving fjord that reached in from Prince William Sound. The fjord had been named first, in the 1700s, by a Spanish explorer, in honor of a Spanish naval minister. The town had begun as a mining camp but had grown considerably in size and importance in the 1920s when the road had been cut through from Fairbanks. Valdez was the northernmost ice-free port in North America, a quality that had played the major role in its selection as southern terminus of the pipeline.

Valdez had, perhaps, the most beautiful natural setting of any town in Alaska. Mountains—higher and more rugged mountains than in Juneau—curved around it on three sides, broken only by the waters of the fjord. In its pre-pipeline days, Valdez had billed itself as "the Switzerland of Alaska," though one would have been hard-pressed in Switzerland to find its equal.

Three events stood out in the pre-pipeline history of Valdez. There had been, most tragically, the earthquake on Good Friday of 1964. The quake's damage in Anchorage was nothing to what took place in Valdez. The entire town, in fact, had been destroyed. Hit first by the earthquake, then by the resulting tidal wave, Valdez had ceased to exist. More than forty people had died, and a new town had to be built, three miles up the shore from the old. This was done quickly, from necessity, without thought to charm or scenic value. The new Valdez, even before the pipeline, was a harsh, tinny hodgepodge of prefab homes and trailer camps. The barracks-style housing erected by pipeline contractors had not improved things. There were 8,000 people now, where a decade before there had been 800. And, in addition, there were 4,000 oil workers housed at the terminal, which had been built across the water from the town.

Before the earthquake, the main event in the history of Valdez had been the fire, in 1915, which had completely eradicated the business district. Before the fire, Valdez's chief notoriety had come from the fact that it had been the site, in 1898, of the first hanging ever to take place in Alaska. The victim had been one "Doc" Tanner, a prospector, who had murdered two of his partners the day before. His final words, uttered with the noose already around his neck, were reported to be: "Gentlemen, you're hanging the best man with a six-shooter that ever came to Alaska." He might have rested more easily if he'd known that, someday, so many of his spiritual descendants would come to inhabit the town.

All the motel rooms in Valdez were taken, but a pipeline public relations man let me sleep in a spare room in his home. It was a modern, prefabricated house, with thick, shaggy carpeting on the floor. There was plenty of hot water, and electricity, and a Farrah Fawcett poster over my bed.

There were hard-cover books in the living room, which was not a common sight in Alaska. Works by Solzhenitsyn, and Albert Speer, and Wilhelm Reich, and Arthur Schlesinger, and David Halberstam. Also biographies of Einstein and Franklin D. Roosevelt and Golda Meir. There were also a number of newspapers and magazines: *Rolling Stone, The New York Times Magazine, The New York Times Book Review,* two copies of the Valdez *Vanguard,* eight issues of the *New York Review of Books,* and one copy of *The Sporting News.* Also current issues of *Time, Harper's, Newsweek, People, Us, Gourmet, Gentleman's Quarterly, Playboy, National Lampoon, Car and Driver, Road and Track, Atlas: The World Press Review, New Times, Alaska, Aviation Week & Space Technology, Sports Illustrated,* and *Airline Quarterly.* There was also a record player with more than a hundred albums, a chess set, a game of Risk, and a three-track tournament cribbage board. It did not appear so much that the public relations man worked and lived here as it did that he was under house arrest.

"Well," he said, "there's no radio in Valdez, very little TV, and last winter we had three hundred and seventy inches of snow. I mean, how much can you drink?"

I looked at the Valdez *Vanguard.* A front-page story reported the results of a recent study which showed that 90 percent of adult Native males in Alaska suffered from hearing deficiency. Ten years earlier, the problem had not existed. The blame was attached to the fact that, on the average, an adult male Eskimo or Indian in Alaska spent from four to six hours a day using noisy equipment: snow machines, chain saws, motorcycles, or high-powered rifles.

There also was a front-page announcement that, within the month, Valdez' first coin-operated car wash would open.

I turned to the police report:

Police received a report that the wing of a float plane at Robe River had been burned with cigarettes.

A resident of Robe River subdivision reported that someone had stolen a marijuana plant from inside a trailer. The case was closed due to lack of investigative leads.

Police received a report at 1:40 a.m. that bears were tearing up the city campground. Officer Vera went to the scene and chased the bears away.

The owner of a taco wagon reported that someone had broken into it. A window with an approximate value of $15 was broken and two bags of potato chips were stolen.

There was also coverage of the city council meeting, at which, by a five-to-two vote, a proposed ordinance—requested by the Valdez police chief—that would have prohibited the possession of machine guns in the town, was rejected. Opposition had been led by Red St. Pierre, owner of Mel's Sporting Goods, who said the ordinance was a violation of the constitutional right to bear arms. Mayor Lynn Chrystal also had voiced opposition, saying he was against gun control of any kind.

One final item in the police report caught my eye: "CB operator Sweater Girl reported a person lying on the side of a road. Upon investigation, it was found that the person was sunbathing." Normally, in Valdez, where the sun seldom shone, a person lying by the side of the road was presumed to be either wounded, dead, or passed-out drunk.

Even now, in fact, at 6:30 p.m., new clouds were moving in and beginning to blanket the high, sharp mountains that rose above the oil tanks around the harbor. I accompanied the public relations man to the Sheffield House for dinner. We had a drink in the dark, carpeted bar, looking out upon the small boat harbor, through tinted glass. In many Alaskan bars, the stuffed heads of wild animals decorated the walls, but in Valdez, at the Sheffield House, the area over the bar was lined with hard hats.

The clouds grew thicker and darker after dinner. Sometime in the night, rain began. By 7:15 the next morning the highest visible point in all of Valdez was the upper floor of the split-level house across the street.

I borrowed a car and took a tour of the town, passing one home whose owners, instead of sending out birth announcements, had simply painted the news, in large black letters, across the front of the house: IT'S A GIRL. BORN 12/31/76. 8 LB. 3 OZ. By now the paint was faded, and somewhat washed away, from 370 inches of snow in the winter and an equivalent amount of rain all summer long.

The ARCO *Juneau*, which would carry the oil from Valdez to a refinery in the state of Washington, had pulled in and docked by the oil tanks. It was the length of six football fields, weighed, when empty, 120,000 tons, and the sides of it were so high that they disappeared into the clouds that hung low over the water.

A plane managed to penetrate the overcast, delivering copies of the Anchorage *Times*. After having ballyhooed the pipeline for a decade, and having proclaimed the arrival of the oil in Valdez to be the greatest event since statehood, the *Times* had not bothered to send any of its reporters to Valdez to cover the event and was relying upon wire service stories instead.

One such story reported that oil from the first barrel would be added, drop by drop, to several thousand ball-point pens, which would then be sold as souvenirs. Proceeds from the sale would go to a lobbying group that was urging the construction of a new pipeline from Prudhoe Bay to Valdez—this one for natural gas. The *Times* also urged, editorially, that the main street of Valdez be renamed "11:02 Boulevard" to commemorate the moment when the oil had arrived.

That afternoon, I visited the Valdez Travel Service, which was the busiest travel agency in the state.

The manager was thin, intense, and thirty years old, with a week's growth of beard on his face, a shirt opened halfway to his waist, and a gold chain and medallion around his neck. He answered the telephone and wrote out tickets as he spoke. There were four other people behind the counter, equally busy.

"Last year," he said, "we sent three hundred people just to Hawaii. Second-busiest spot was Tulsa, Oklahoma. I guess people were just going home. We're the only travel service in town and we've got seven thousand construction workers here doing eight weeks on and two off. And they sure as hell don't want to spend those two weeks here."

His two partners in the agency were leaders in the Native business and political community in Anchorage. Through them—because they were Natives—the partnership qualified for a low-interest loan from the Bureau of Indian Affairs. Also through them, and their power in the Native community, the new corporation qualified for a large bank loan in Anchorage. The two sums together had been enough to buy the Valdez Travel Service, and the non-Native had come down to run it.

"Insane, man. It has been totally insane. For the first six months I was too busy to even find a place to live. I slept in the back of the office. No running water. I couldn't have made money any faster if I'd been minting it. We did two million dollars' worth of business the first six months. The same pace this year, too, but now with the line finished, this thing is really going to fade. And, man, I'm fading, too. Fading fast. I'm burned out. And getting out. The place is for sale, and I've got a new manager coming in tomorrow. Some out-of-work actor from L.A. I forget his name, I've got it written down here somewhere. Some guy who was in a movie with Anne Bancroft. I'll be out of here within two weeks. I'm going to Columbia, Maryland. Our little corporation just did a deal with Morrison Knudsen, the big international construction firm. They've got this mammoth job in Saudi Arabia, building dams, highways, bridges, the whole schmeer. We're going to handle their traffic management. Shipping their people in and out. Man, it's going to make this thing look like nothing but the corner candy store. So much money involved there I'm not even allowed to talk about it. We got it through my same two partners, too. See, these guys are really heavies when it comes to that Native political shit. They told Morrison Knudsen, if you want to get any work on this big natural gas pipeline that's going to come, then maybe you ought to let us work for you in Saudi Arabia. The old quid pro quo, man, know what I mean? Hey, if I'm not making much sense, don't be alarmed. I mean, I've been partying, partying, *partying*. But that's the whole thing out here these days. If you can latch on to a Native with some clout as a partner, that's just like having your own little oil well all to yourself."

A young woman in a tight dress came into the travel agency. She had two deep scars across her face. Her hands were trembling and there was a look of extreme tension in her eyes.

"I got to see you," she said to the manager. "Right now."

"I'm busy, sweetheart. Can't talk."

"I said I got to see you." It was not just her hands; it was her whole body that was trembling.

"Lunch tomorrow. Meet me at the Sheffield. One o'clock." A phone rang and he answered it. "Oh, hi. Yes, listen, you're all set. Well, almost all set. The good news is, I've got you confirmed out of Seattle. The bad news is, the plane from Anchorage is full. You're on standby. What? No, no, don't worry. You'll get on. Just have faith. Well, no, I can't *guarantee* it, but you'll get on. There. Does that make you feel better? Does that sound like a guarantee?"

The woman in the tight dress had not moved. She was carrying a large handbag. She reached into the bag and took out a gun. She did not point it at anyone, and she did not say anything. She just stood there, holding it, as if it were a travel brochure, with her whole body trembling.

The manager spotted the gun. "Got to run," he said, over the telephone. "Have a great trip. Bye." He hung up. "Now, Mickey," he said soothingly. "Put that away."

"Lunch tomorrow, bullshit," she said. "I'm really upset. I need to talk to you right now."

"Sure, baby, sure. But not in the office. Remember what I told you about guns in the office? Let's just go outside for a minute or two."

The manager excused himself and stepped out from behind the counter. He put an arm around the woman's shoulders and guided her carefully toward the door. She put the gun back inside her bag. It was a .357 Magnum, the kind which, if handled correctly, could kill a bear.

The manager was gone for fifteen minutes. When he returned there was perspiration on his forehead and his week's growth of beard seemed shiny with sweat. A phone was ringing. He answered it. "Oh, hi, Joan. Yeah. What you do is, if it's not confirmed— Hey, can you give me a call back? I've got about six people in the office right now. And a lady with a loaded .357 Magnum sitting in my car, waiting for me to buy her a drink."

He hung up. He took a couple of blank ticket forms from a locked metal box that was inside a safe behind the counter. He explained that he was going to have to be out of the office for a while.

"When I first got here," he said, "Mickey was the number-one hooker in town. Then she had a real bad car accident. Got those scars. After that, she wasn't number one. Except with a few of the sickies. So she started running coke, from New York. A thousand per trip she got paid. Once a month. I handle her airline and hotels. She flies to New York with the money and the next day she flies back with the stuff. Except last week something got a little messed up. She left here with twenty thousand in cash, and yesterday she came back empty. Said she lost her purse. In the ladies' room at La Guardia. Hell of an excuse, right? The man she's working for is less than happy. Told her she had three days to come up with the twenty thou. Or else those scars would be the least of her worries. So what does she do? She comes to me. Wants five hundred cash and a one-way ticket to San Francisco. Says she knows a plastic surgeon down there who will fix up her face. With a new face and some phony IDs, she figures no one from here can ever trace her. I think she's got a boyfriend waiting down there with the money, but who knows? She is not, by any means, one of the more stable ladies in Valdez. What I really think is that she's going to kill herself. I think she's going to blow her brains out with that three fifty-seven sometime in the next twenty-four hours. But at least if I give her the ticket and the money I won't have it on my conscience."

He walked toward the door, shaking his head. Three phones were ringing, and there were five customers lined up, waiting, at the counter.

"Wow," he said. "I bet this kind of shit doesn't happen in Saudi Arabia."

I drove out of Valdez and up the highway to Thompson Pass. A low sky; a steady drizzle. Woods, thick with evergreens, lined both sides of the road. In the harbor, the tanker slowly was filling with oil and, gradually, riding lower in the water. It would take two days for the tanker to be filled. I drove past occasional cabins, and trailers, in little clearings in the woods: the suburbs, as it were, of Valdez.

The road climbed past Keystone Canyon to Bridal Veil Falls. The thin streams of water came down the hillside like strands of white ribbon, or lace. The waterfall was active, from all the rain, and spray from it soaked the surface of the road.

Past Sheep Creek, where there was a pipeline camp, the road began to climb steeply. Up 2,000 feet in six miles to Thompson Pass. Twenty-five miles from Valdez and more than 2,700 feet above sea level. The pass was hidden by low clouds. There was still snow at the sides of the road, and reflectors, twelve feet high, on either side, so in winter, with snow everywhere, you would not drive off the side of the mountain. There had been, at one time, a stone cabin at the pass, used as a shelter by early travelers. Because the snow was so deep every winter, the door to the cabin had been built not in a wall but in the roof. I got out of the car and walked through the snow up the side of the pass. A cold, wet breeze blew. There was mist and fog everywhere. There were no sounds, except for the breeze.

Back in Valdez, it was 20 degrees warmer than at the pass, but the overcast was heavy, and now, in drizzle, toward midnight, it was dark. Across the harbor, the pipeline terminal and the oil storage tanks were brightly lit. From a distance, in the darkness, they looked benign. Almost cheerful. As if they were the lights of an amusement park.

The social highlight on Sunday, to commemorate the arrival of the oil, was the Oily T-Shirt Contest, the idea of which was to get the biggest-busted women in Valdez up on a platform in the tightest possible T-shirts, and then to spray the T-shirts with oil. With pipeline oil so messy and expensive, Wesson oil was used instead.

Many of the contestants wore shirts that had slogans printed across the front. "Oil Filter." "Holding Tanks." "Ms. Unrefined Crude." Skies were gray, and the temperature was in the 50s. A noisy, beery crowd of several hundred had gathered in a parking lot. Audience applause would determine the winner. Most of the crowd seemed made up of men whose stomachs stuck out considerably farther than did the women's busts.

The contestants paraded up and down on the platform for a while, as the men grew drunker and shouted vulgar remarks. A winner finally was chosen. Number Eleven. She had a 39-inch bust, but she appeared to be a stranger in town. An outsider. *A ringer!* She was from Seattle, she said, and she had driven to Valdez in her van, on a business trip. There was no doubt about what kind of business she was in, and as the winner of the Oily T-Shirt Contest she might be able to double her price.

At the conclusion of the contest, a couple of the drunker, fatter, grosser members of the audience climbed clumsily up onto the platform and began trying to pull the T-shirts off the women. A great deal of screaming and pushing and shoving ensued, until the Valdez fire department turned on the hose and knocked everyone to the ground and swept the platform clean. Screaming, raving, obese, drunken men poured out of the parking lot where the contest had been held and into the streets of Valdez. A large bonfire was started. Fights broke out: first with fists, and then with bottles and rocks. The winner of the contest, Number Eleven, retired to the privacy of her van. A line soon formed outside it. The first annual Valdez Oily T-Shirt Contest was deemed by all a great success.

The post-pipeline era, whatever it would bring, had begun. The occupying army had taken control. And, in Valdez at least, the triumph of the irresistible force seemed complete.

16 Anchorage

The Glacier Pilots were in first place. They were way ahead, eight games in front of the Fairbanks Goldpanners, their archrivals, while the Kenai Oilers and the Valley Green Giants from Palmer lagged further behind.

The Alaska League played the best amateur baseball in the country. The teams were composed of college players from the Lower Forty-eight, many of whom would eventually turn pro. Tom Seaver had played in the Alaska League, as had Dave Kingman and Chris Chambliss and Rick Monday and Randy Jones.

The star of this year's Glacier Pilot team was a teen-aged outfielder named Mickey Hatcher, who would wind up with the Los Angeles Dodgers. The stadium, Mulcahy Park, was just outside the door of my apartment. I would walk over, many evenings, and sit along the third-base line, with the wind from the Chugach Mountains at my back. The temperature was usually in the 50s. The lights were not turned on until the seventh or eighth inning.

In Fairbanks, farther north, they didn't need lights for night games at all. On July 4, in Fairbanks, the Goldpanners played a night game that started at midnight, without lights.

Even at midnight, after an extra-innings Glacier Pilot game, there would still be a flat, dry light in the sky, with a full moon bright overhead. And, to the north, 175 miles, the orange glow of Mount McKinley still visible.

Bush Pipeline on the radio: a way to make contact when you were out in the backcountry without a telephone, or when you were trying to reach someone who was.

"For Mom at Shell Lake. I had my physical yesterday and it was all right, except it cost fifty-one dollars. Gordon."

"To Julie at Chase. Ellen will be at Talkeetna Saturday. Would like you to come down."

"To Mom and Sparky at Peter's Creek. Come into town as soon as possible. Might have a job lined up for Sparky."

"For David Burns at Gakona, or on the Gulkana River. Call your attorney at 274–7522 at once. From Geri, your attorney's secretary."

"For Boulder Creek Lodge. The transmission won't be finished until tomorrow. I'll be out with fresh supplies if the weather holds and I'm able to make it through the pass."

Also on the radio, a commercial for Rustic Wilderness, a new development of weekend and vacation homes, north of Anchorage.

"It's no fun driving through the crowded streets of Anchorage all week and having nothing to look forward to on the weekend. After putting in a hectic week in the city, don't you think you deserve a little peace and quiet?"

Rustic Wilderness could provide it, starting at $49,900 for a prefabricated cottage on a quarter-acre lot at the edge of a lake. Singers in the background crooned the chorus: "It's the reason you're in Alaska."

The new McDonald's, on Fourth Avenue, had become the second-busiest McDonald's in the world. A few doors down, a Jewish delicatessen had opened. Pastrami, lox and bagels, matzoh-ball soup. They even had the Sunday *New York Times* delivered; it arrived by noon Monday and cost $4.50 a copy. But McDonald's still did the volume business.

There were a couple of Natives leaning against a wall outside McDonald's, drinking something straight from the bottle. Not the first morning, obviously, that they had spent in this way. Behind them, I could see the steel girders rising for what would become a new Sheraton Hotel. A Sheraton owned by the Calista Corporation, which was one of those created by the Native Claims Settlement Act.

That was the way it went for Natives in Anchorage: either attaché cases and consultants flying up from San Francisco or else swigging straight from the bottle. A hand-lettered sign in the liquor store window across the street gave a clue to what they might have been drinking: SPECIAL. 190 PROOF. GRAIN ALCOHOL. $1.95 PINT. 2 FOR $3.75.

I walked past Sunshine Plaza, which was a new shopping center owned by the Natives. They had apparently told the builder to paint the exterior the color of the sun, but it had come out, instead, looking like a fluorescent tennis ball. I walked up Fifth Avenue, past Grubstake Loans, and the 5th Avenue Washeteria, and the Anchorage Fur Factory, and past the Bonfire and the Embers, two sexually oriented bars between which one chose, apparently, depending on the degree of one's fervor. Then Muffler City, with oversized truck tires displayed on the sidewalk in front, and United Auto Supply and Alaska 4-Wheel Drive, and the Mexican Kitchen food wagon, and the Pagoda Restaurant, featuring American and Oriental food.

Then I found what I was looking for: the office of the Alaska *Advocate*, which was the new statewide weekly paper. Howard Weaver, co-founder, part owner, and editor-in-chief, was on the telephone, canceling his libel insurance.

"What I need," he explained, "is a bodyguard, not libel insurance. Out here, they're more likely to shoot you than sue."

Howard Weaver was a rarity: an Anchorage resident who had actually been born in Anchorage. His parents had arrived from Texas in the early 1950s and had built a wooden frame house in a section called Muldoon, which even today was on the outskirts of the city, but which twenty-five years earlier could very nearly have been classified as wilderness.

It was an Okie sort of neighborhood. People raising chickens and pigs and putting old Ford automobiles up on blocks. *Grapes of Wrath* goes to Alaska. Howard loved it. He grew up in Anchorage watching the city grow all around him. One of his most vivid childhood memories was of the weekend that Walter Hickel opened the first shopping center in Alaska, on Northern Lights Boulevard. Howard and his friends hitchhiked in and spent the whole day just riding the escalators up and down.

When Howard was fourteen, his father was killed in an automobile accident. His mother began to drink heavily. Within four years, she, too, was dead. Howard went to Johns Hopkins University in Baltimore. After his sophomore year, he got married to a Mormon, which, considering the life style he was developing, was a mistake. He dropped out of Johns Hopkins and came back to Alaska and moved into his old house in Muldoon. The marriage dragged on for four years, mostly because Howard was a stubborn sort; not overly quick to admit a mistake.

By the time he was divorced, at twenty-three, he was well embarked upon his career—as a rough-and-tumble newspaper reporter. The kind with poetry oozing from his soul. He was built like a young Jimmy Breslin. He had a red beard and limitless energy and a profound respect for the language. Every evening he drank whiskey until midnight, the way he imagined Breslin must have been doing in New York. During working hours, however, he wrote as well as anyone on an Alaskan newspaper had ever written.

The *Daily News* was the scrappy little morning paper, the one which always seemed in danger of going under. It had been taken over in the late 1960s by a man named Larry Fanning, who had been managing editor of the Chicago *Sun-Times* until he found himself romantically involved with the wife of the newspaper's owner, Marshall Field. Following a divorce and remarriage, Larry and Kay Fanning came to Alaska with the dream of running a tough, small, liberal newspaper at which the highest standards of journalism would be maintained. Toward that end, they purchased the Anchorage *Daily News*. Two years later, Larry Fanning dropped dead of a heart attack. Kay Fanning was still struggling to keep the dream alive, in a city where the priority placed on good journalism was not very high. The Anchorage *Times*, the afternoon paper, the Atwood paper, with its pro-development, boomtown slant, and its subservience to the will of the big business interests, seemed the sort of newspaper with which more residents of Anchorage felt comfortable.

At the *Daily News*, Howard Weaver had been one of three reporters whose series about the statewide influence of the Teamsters Union had won a Pulitzer Prize: the first ever awarded to an Alaskan newspaper.

Figuring that, at twenty-five, he was "entitled to one big mistake," Howard had raised $100,000 and had added several thousand dollars of his own and, with two partners, had launched the Alaska *Advocate*, which he envisioned as sort of the *Village Voice* of Alaska, except that the "village" was two and a half times the size of Texas.

The paper had been in operation for six months. The paid circulation was 1,850. There were just not enough people in Alaska; particularly, not enough who liked to read.

"Next," he said, "we might try a sale of unregistered stock. Can you believe it? Twenty-five years old, with a Pulitzer Prize in my pocket, and I'm going to wind up in prison for stock fraud.

"Actually, this month we're almost breaking even. Of course, that's without anybody getting paid. Once in a while we give a little money to one guy who's got child-support problems, just so we can keep him out of jail. The others understand. We'll pay salaries as soon as we're able. In the meantime, they have the excitement of knowing that they're working for a cause. Although, what the cause is, I'm afraid I can't remember any more.

"I'll tell you what this has become for me. This is a classic example of the Peter Principle in operation. Here I am, the best fucking reporter in the state, and I'm too busy to cover stories any more. I sit here all day in this diddly-shit office, in a building that's about to be condemned, doing arithmetic and trying to play businessman, about which I know nothing and care less. And I go home so tired at night that I can't even make love any more. Now, that's not supposed to happen when you're only twenty-five.

"I've run through my savings, mortgaged my house, and I've even had to cut back on beer consumption. And what the hell for? To keep a weekly newspaper alive in Anchorage, Alaska. In the clear light of day, you know, it doesn't seem an especially noble ambition. It's cold, it's dark, and we're losing every battle that we fight. And this town is turning into shit. You've got to be crazy to live here any more without an airplane. With your own plane you can still get to Alaska in half an hour. You know: 'Alaska,' in quotes. You can still find the good things that are left. In my Volkswagen, I go half an hour and I can't even get home from work any more, with all the traffic.

"I've had offers from Outside, some damned good offers. But this is my home town, and there aren't many people who can say that. Maybe I wish it wasn't, but it is. And goddamn it all, I still care about the place. A lot's going to happen in the next few years, just like a lot already has. I wouldn't feel right about leaving.

"Besides, there are parts that are fun. I just made a deal with Jimmy Breslin's syndicate to pick up his columns for seven dollars a week. They said it would be twenty a week and I told them we couldn't afford that, which was true, and then I told them we could only use one of the three every week anyway, so we should only have to pay one-third the rate. Then I gave them some shit about how people in Alaska really loved Breslin and how this was his only chance for an outlet on the Last Frontier, and goddamn, they bought it. Actually, I don't think there are a hundred people in Anchorage who have even heard of Jimmy Breslin, but for me it's the greatest thing that ever happened. Imagine, sitting in this office in Anchorage, Alaska, with three Jimmy Breslin columns in front of me, deciding which one I'm going to use. It's the most fun you can have in Alaska for seven dollars. I'd pay that much just to read them myself, even if we didn't put them in the paper."

All of the 375 million acres of land in Alaska had, at one time, been owned by the federal government. When Alaska became a state, in 1959, 104 million acres were given to it. When the Native Claims Act was passed in 1971, 44 million acres were given to the Eskimos and Indians and Aleuts. That still left the federal government owning more than half of Alaska, and left the United States Congress with the task of deciding how much, and which, of this federal land should be protected from development.

Morris Udall, the congressman from Arizona, working with environmental groups, had sponsored a bill that would preserve 114 million acres as wilderness, national monument, and national park, leaving the remainder open for development, for mineral exploration, for motorized recreational use, for logging and fishing and farming, and, possibly, for private purchase. This was in addition to the 104 million acres of state land that could be opened for development, and the 44 million acres that were available to the Natives.

Even so, there was passionate opposition to the Udall bill among Alaskans, many of whom believed—a belief fostered by the Anchorage *Times*, the Teamsters Union, the big oil and mining companies, and the political establishment—that the federal government was, in fact, trying to take away, or "lock up," land that rightfully should belong to Alaska.

Hearings on the bill had been held in a number of cities across the Lower Forty-eight. Now a hearing was scheduled for Anchorage, with Morris Udall himself to be present, as well as John Seiberling, the congressman from Ohio who was chairman of the House subcommittee which had primary responsibility for the bill. More than a thousand people had signed up to testify at the meeting which was expected to be somewhat acrimonious. There had even been published suggestions that the personal safety of representatives Udall and Seiberling could not be guaranteed.

On the afternoon before the hearing, I talked to Tony Motley at the Petroleum Club. The club was private, on the top floor of the Anchorage Westward Hotel, with membership restricted to people in the oil industry and to people with whom they did business. Tony Motley, who had been Alaska's secretary of commerce at one time, was director of a group called Citizens for Management of Alaskan Lands—a businessmen's group that had been formed to fight against the Udall bill.

"We started a day late and a dollar short," he said. "I've got to take my hat off to that conservation lobby: it really is well organized. At Chicago, the testimony went against us, thirty-three to one. That was not a public hearing; that was an environmental rally. Atlanta was pretty rough, too. But the further west we came, the more empathy we found with our cause. Denver was better, and in Seattle, which is, as you know, the gateway to Alaska, and where people understand a little more about the issue, the testimony was almost even, for and against.

"Then, of course, we had the hearings in Southeast. In Ketchikan and Sitka. There it was thirty-three to one the other way. For our side. Because there the people had something at stake. Like a whole way of life. They want to fish and cut timber and be able to enjoy themselves, in their free time, in whatever way appeals to them. They don't want to be told by Washington that from now on they're going to be nothing but curators in a museum.

"Not that it's going to do any good. Seiberling has already stated that nothing he hears up here is going to cause him to change his mind. He's got this guilt thing about messing up the rest of the country. You know, he comes from Akron, Ohio, which is not exactly a very pretty place, and now he wants to make us in Alaska atone for every environmental desecration that's ever been committed anywhere else.

"What we're really up against, you see, is a small band of people who want to change the recreational patterns of most Americans. They're telling us that we've got to wear a backpack and a pair of waffle stompers or else we're not even going to be allowed to see the most beautiful areas of our own state. Damnit, I've got a camper and a trailer and I know how to fly a plane, and on weekends I like to lease a float plane, and I want to be able to go wherever I please, and not be told I've got to walk a hundred miles to get there.

"Let's face it: wilderness is not recreation to most Americans. That's just a fact. That's the American way of life. And what this state needs is not more wilderness; it is more recreational facilities that the majority of the population—and not just a bunch of college kids—can enjoy. I mean, if you have the determination and the desire to get out there on your own where nobody else goes, fine, that's great, that's super. Do it, by all means. But goddamnit, you don't need more than one hundred million acres, at the expense of other forms of recreation."

He paused for a sip of Scotch on the rocks. He was wearing a white button-down shirt and sunglasses. He had a tennis racket in his car. He was quite at home in the Petroleum Club, and I could see that he would be quite at home, too, in Washington, D.C., where the final decision would be made. The citizens for Management of Alaskan Lands, he said, had already committed $900,000 to the fight.

At the hearing, the next day, arguments against the bill seemed to be primarily of two kinds. One was the economic argument: the nation needs the resources that might be lying under these lands, and the people of Alaska need the jobs that would be created by exploitation of these resources. The other argument had to do with recreational use of the land, and basically, it was Tony Motley's argument: by classifying so much acreage as national park and wilderness, you are making it the private preserve of a few rich college kids who have the time and energy to go backpacking. Why not open it up? Build roads to it, and hotels on it, so all of us can enjoy it, and can enjoy a few creature comforts as well.

The arguments in favor of preservation tended to be idealistic and vague. Those supporting the bill were, in fact, supporting the concept of doing nothing. Of leaving things as they were. Of leaving things as they had been, in most cases, since the last Ice Age. This was a hard argument to make in the waning days of the oil boom, when so many people were so worried that the momentum of growth and development would soon diminish.

A civil engineer from Anchorage: "It is a common feeling among Alaskans that the level of development here was okay when they came, but they wish they were the last person allowed in the state. This, of course, is a very selfish attitude, but it does point up the fact that many people feel the social cost of a more dynamic economy is greater than the material and financial benefits that accrue. I, for one, see little that is better and much that is worse in the quality of life here in Anchorage as the population has doubled since my arrival.

"These lands in question are federal lands, not state or private lands. Despite loud cries to the contrary by the local news media, they never have belonged exclusively to the people who migrated here recently. I hope that my generation is not the last generation of Americans to be able to experience true wilderness."

On the other hand, there was the point of view of a man who had lived in Anchorage since 1961: "I would like to say that half of the population of the state of Alaska lives in the Anchorage area. We have two places to recreate and enjoy the wilderness. One is the road north, and one is the road south. I suggest you look at streams near Kenai, or lakes or campgrounds, and try to find one that is not overly populated, that does not have a person on every rock, or a lake with at least ten boats on it. The recreational facilities in the Anchorage area are overloaded. Because, if you look at Mount Susitna and you point your finger to the left of it, from that mountain all the way west to Russia there is not a road. If you take the lands within the United States and you tie them up to where only the people that can afford to fly there can get there, you are making a serious mistake that your son will be sorry for. Some people can afford to fly to different areas, but ninety percent of the population cannot. If you take all the land in our state and you make it a park that nobody can come to, you will defeat the purpose that your committee was formed for, and the purpose for which you are here today."

The six congressmen moved into separate rooms, to allow more Alaskans a chance to testify.

"I am not a member of the physically elite," one woman said, "as I am forty-six years old and I have a ruptured disc in my back. Spending time in the wilds is sufficiently important to me that I exercise enough to overcome these handicaps. It is not necessary that all of America be easily accessible to all Americans at all points in their lives. A balance is needed. Most of America is accessible, including some pretty fantastic mountain scenery. We need some places that are hard to get to, that cost us something in effort and sacrifice. They mean more if we have to work for them. Alaska is our last chance to insure that a balance is retained."

W. E. Bradley, a state senator from Anchorage, disagreed: "An untouched wilderness area is not worth a lot to our state and country if its people are unemployed, cold, and hungry. I sincerely believe God gave us the land and waters and all the resources thereon and therein—plant, animal, and mineral—organic and inorganic—for man to use and improve if we can. . . . Why was man put here in the first place, except to use, improve, and enjoy?"

The argument went back and forth, through a long afternoon. It was the only chance that many Alaskans would ever have to speak directly to the men whose decisions would shape the destiny of their state.

"I am an eight-year resident of Alaska. I live in the Alaskan bush by choice, and not by necessity. . . . I came to Alaska not with gold or oil fever in my eye, but to search for a way of life that I found here, and to which I have come to grow deeply attached. I did not come up here with a view to obstructing development but, since living here, I have become aware of the development mentality which appears to operate on the premise that destruction of the natural habitat must be equated with personal gain."

"We need oil. To go to the extreme and say close everything up and leave it for future generations—number one, that's not the

American way. We have to have the right to raise *our* standard of living."

"I have lived in Alaska twenty-nine years, which is almost all of my life, and I fully expect to spend the balance of my life here, and I think that those of us who do choose Alaska do so because we find a way of life here that differs from anything that's available in the rest of the country. And I think in the whole of the United States there should be at least one region that offers an alternative . . . centered on harmony with nature and not exploitation of it. I think Alaska offers the best opportunity for such a life style, and I believe it is in the best interest of Alaska and of the nation as a whole to allow this kind of life style to flourish here."

"Listen. This wilderness image should not be used to lock up our lands. Of course, we are emotional. You are, too, and you show your contempt for us in Alaska in numerous ways. In the roughshod method of riding over our desires, and our needs, and in making development a dirty word, and your partiality to the preservationists that hate mankind. Through their hate and selfishness they would deny the free Americans the right to be ambitious and industrious, to work and earn a livelihood through their own sweat and brains. They would have us become a welfare nation. We Alaskans want to live and work and play in our own backyards."

Toward evening, as the sky turned gray over Anchorage, and a light cool drizzle began to fall, John Seiberling leaned forward to the microphone. He was a thin, balding man in his middle fifties, with a spare, dry, sometimes acerbic manner that caused him to resemble an old-fashioned family physician.

"Let me," he said, "before we officially close this hearing, give you a few statistics. We have made a tentative count, and we find today we have actually heard two hundred seventy-seven people in the various sections we have had here, and it might surprise you to know that of those, one hundred thirty-six expressed support for this legislation, one hundred thirty-one expressed opposition, and ten gave us a general position or neutral position. So, that's a rather interesting outcome, and, frankly, I am rather surprised by it because I thought there would be an overwhelming amount of opposition.

"I thought one of the interesting points that was brought out here was that a lot of people came up here to find an alternate way of life, and that's what they hope to preserve. I can certainly say this: in terms of seeing nature without any disturbance by man, there is only one place in North America that I have been in—and I haven't been through all of Canada—and that's Alaska.

"For years I have been asking myself, what is it about the Alaska landscape that is so unique? It isn't just the wilderness. It's the undisturbed wilderness. Ohio is beautiful, and while I fly over it, the patterns are fascinating, but those patterns are shaped by man to the point where they are unrecognizable, in terms of the original architecture of the land, even though 'Ohio' in Chippewa means 'beautiful land.'

"Alaska has the opportunity to take some areas that are significant in size, and to keep them the way the Creator fashioned them. And when you fly over this land, or stand on it or look at it from the top of the mountain, the streaks are those of a great artist. The abstract designs are absolutely beyond the wildest imaginings of Picasso.

"The fascination of Alaska, not just from the air but from the ground, is that nowhere else I have ever been can one see so clearly the hand of the Creator. It's important to people to know that there is some place in North America where they can go, or where even if they never go, they know it exists, where there are large stretches of land, at least large enough so that you can stand at some point and there is nowhere in any direction where you will be able to see any of the marks of man.

"It's important not only because it's unique, but to remind man of his place in the scheme of things, and that he is, after all, a temporary occupant of a planet that is unique perhaps not in all of the universe, but in a good part of it, and that he is not the Creator. He is the beneficiary of a system of life that he can destroy, but he did not create it, and to me that is the significance of Alaska and the significance of wild Alaska."

He paused, and looked out over the hearing room, which by now, at 7:30 p.m., was more than half empty.

"You know," John Seiberling said, "one man's freedom is the freedom to mess up another man's freedom. And the only way you can protect and have a rational society is to put some rules down so a guy doesn't build a house and find the next day they put a sewage plant or glue factory or filling station or something right next door. And the same thing is true with wilderness and with resources. You have to stake out the areas where there is going to be one kind of use and the areas where there is going to be another, and that is what we are trying to do." He paused again. And then smiled faintly.

"I am sort of amused by the people who have said that because we want to have some federal control over the development of federal lands, that we are socialistic. My grandfather started the world's largest rubber company, and he did it by borrowing five thousand dollars from his friends and putting up three thousand dollars of his own and his brother's money. They were broke and they bought a factory, and they decided what they were going to do with it, and they took a chance, and they ended up creating the Goodyear Tire and Rubber Company, and if he had taken a small view of things, you know, this never would have happened, and Akron, Ohio, would still be a small town.

"But I was thinking of his later years when he became more and more interested in the environment and he gave some land to a park, and—I have told this before and I apologize to my staff because they have heard this, but I think there is some meaning that it ought to have for the people in Alaska.

"He gave some land to start a park system in and around Akron, and in his old age he used to like to ride through the park, and one day a woman who took care of me passed him and asked, 'Mr. Seiberling, you always want to go through this park, but this land is very valuable today. Don't you miss all of the dividends that you could have gotten if you had sold this land and invested the money?'

"And he said, 'You see those children playing over there? You see that family having a picnic, enjoying these beautiful trees and ravines? Those are my dividends.'

"And that's the kind of dividends that I hope we can leave for the people of Alaska."

17 Bettles

A few days later, I took the train north to McKinley Park. The morning was sunny, but puffy clouds covered the tops of the mountains to the east. There were Boy Scouts, and some hikers, and a number of older people on the train. I carried a paper bag that contained bread, salami, cheese, an orange, and two bottles of mineral water. A conductor came down the aisle, handing out pieces of paper that gave a history of the railroad, a description of McKinley Park, and that had, on the other side, a map and mile-by-mile description of the route the train followed between Anchorage and Fairbanks.

We left on time, at 9:30 a.m., and moved east, along the edge of Knik Arm, toward the clouds. It was the same route I had taken on the day I had driven to Palmer. Past Fort Richardson, and Elmendorf Air Force base, and over wide, fast-flowing rivers that were thick with glacial silt, and past lakes whose shores were lined with birch and spruce.

The Chugach Mountains were to the right, but I was, by now, past the point of marveling at them; from constant exposure, I had come to take them almost for granted. And I had, after all, seen so much more. The Chugach had become the friendly, local mountains. I had been taking day hikes in them from Anchorage and, on several occasions, overnight hikes to areas such as Williwaw Lakes and Wolverine Peak and the twin peaks of Knoya and Tkishla.

I had bought my own sleeping bag, made by Snow Lion, and some good Danner boots, and even though I was still using Tom and Marnie's tent, I had, at least, learned how to put it up and take it down. I also owned, by now, a Jansport frameless pack, a Gerry rain poncho, and a little butane cartridge portable stove. There were muscles in my legs that had not been there when I had boarded the ferry in November, or even when I had spent my time alone at Crescent Lake.

There was fireweed along the tracks, but much of it had sprouted now and the colors had faded. Birchwood Airport, a hundred small planes, red, blue, yellow, white; this was something else I had come to take for granted. Eighteen hours a day, in the summer, around Anchorage, you could look up and at any given moment count half a dozen small planes in the sky.

We crossed Knik Arm at its eastern end and then the Matanuska River, which emptied into the arm. We were moving away from the cloud-covered mountains now, through bright sunshine, with flawless blue sky overhead.

Wasilla. Wasilla Mall. Wasilla Realty. The Land Company. Space—Rent or Lease. Contractors and Distributors. Tool Rental. Wasilla Realty again. Acreage—Homes-Lots-Waterfront. Mini-Warehouse for Rent. Now Leasing. Wasilla Valley Center. Wasilla Branch of Mat-Su Real Estate. Wasilla Building Supply. Mat-Su Title Insurance. Mobile-Mix Concrete. Boise Cascade, with huge piles of freshly cut lumber. A new thirty-store mall with a gravel airstrip behind it. Selective Realty—New Homes. By the time we were past Wasilla, with open space out the windows again, clouds had moved overhead.

The train reached Talkeetna at 12:30 p.m., thick clouds in the sky, and the other passengers, apparently, in the glass-domed observation car. I was alone in the last car on the train. The air was chilly; some of the clouds were light gray and some dark gray, and wind was beginning to blow through the trees. Talkeetna: Roberta

Sheldon, Cliff Hudson, the cranky old couple at the Roadhouse. Jack and Beth Hebert holding hands by the river in the warm sun of late afternoon.

The Susitna River, north of Talkeetna, was a dull green beneath the gray sky. We began to climb. Talkeetna had been 350 feet above sea level. Curry, which was where passengers had stayed overnight when the Anchorage–Fairbanks rail trip had taken two days, was at 550 feet. Then, in twenty-five miles, we climbed to 1,280 at Chulitna. If it had not been cloudy, there would have been a fine view of Mount McKinley, but in summer the mountain is visible only one day out of three. It just sits there, catching all the wet wind from the Pacific and turning the moisture into clouds and rain, and—at higher altitudes—snow. There were people from Anchorage who had gone to McKinley Park half a dozen times on their vacations and still had not had a glimpse of Mount McKinley.

Ten miles past Chulitna, the track crossed Hurricane Gulch over a steel bridge, 1,000 feet across and 300 feet straight down to the creek bed below. The track climbed steadily and the train slowed as we approached the high point: 2,363 feet, with a broad plain stretching out on both sides. The mountains here—the foothills of the Alaska Range, actually—had a different, more open, western feel than did those around Anchorage. They were colored reddish brown, the tree growth was stunted and sparse, and the valleys between them were wider.

We stopped briefly at Cantwell, an old mining and railroad town. There were only three signs visible: CANTWELL CAFÉ, LONG-HORN BAR, CANTWELL LIQUOR. Back to basics. After Cantwell, on a slight downgrade, we picked up speed, reaching McKinley Park Station at 4:15. Almost everyone except me left the train.

North of the park I saw a bull in a field, and trailers, and a German shepherd by the river. Three bearded men, in old shirts, and one plump young woman, in rimless glasses, were sitting on, and leaning against, a new powder-blue Ford pickup truck. The train stopped, lurched backward, and stopped again. Moved forward for about fifty yards. Stopped. Lurched backward. Stopped. Moved backward again, a hundred yards. Jolted back and forth until 5:45. The woman sitting on the pickup truck put on a checkered flannel shirt as the air cooled. A bearded man in an old soft hat smoked a pipe. There were a few thin, light clouds overhead.

The train moved forward, and this time kept moving. Into Nenana at 7:15. Blue sky, and sunny again. Pioneers of Alaska—Igloo No. 17. It was a gray frame house, boarded up. A Native girl carrying a baby boarded the train. Nenana was where they ran the wire to the tripod on the ice every spring, and when the ice broke up and the wire jerked and stopped the clock in the tower on the shore, then Alaska's winter was officially over, and whoever had come closest to picking the exact minute, hour, and day won the annual Nenana Ice Classic, which was the Alaskan state lottery. The prize, if you won it alone and did not have to share it with others who had picked the exact time, could be more than a hundred thousand dollars.

No ice in the river this evening, though. The land around it was brushy, green and flat. Hills and bluffs rising to the left. Tuyana Barge Company—Absolutely No Trespassing—steel girders stacked into piles; fifty-five-gallon fuel drums piled near a crane at the edge of the river. Now the train crossed the river, making a slow curve, almost 180 degrees, and the tracks wound behind a bluff on the far side, and the low sun streamed directly through the windows, and then we swung, slowly, around another bluff and, across the river now, continued, picking up speed, north to Fairbanks.

The Native girl sings softly to her baby. The glare of the sun is reflected off the river, through the crisscross of the steel girders of the bridge. We pass a sign that says: GOLDEN SPIKE. It is explained on the sign that this was where President Harding hammered the last spike into place to mark the completion of the Alaska Railroad track from Seward to Fairbanks. The sign does not mention—but residents of Talkeetna do—that the President took the train to Talkeetna as soon as the hammering was completed, had numerous drinks in the Fairview Inn, and wound up dying three days later. For a long time, residents of Talkeetna proudly boasted that President Harding had been poisoned at the Fairview Inn.

Oil tanks shining silver by the river. Sound of cards being shuffled in the rear of the car. There are mountains far, far off to the east. The train stops in front of a yellow house and the Native girl and her baby get off. There is an enormous snow machine, called a Playcat, in the front yard. And a huge TV antenna rising from the roof of the house. Two white men in T-shirts come onto the front porch of the house to greet the Native girl. One seems to be about her age; one is older. Her husband and father-in-law?

The train is moving faster now, through tall, thin pines, and all that can be seen, on either side and to the front and to the back, are very low, slightly rolling hills. This is the Interior and it goes on this way for miles, the view out the window not changing, as if the train were not moving at all.

The train was moving, however, and reached Fairbanks at 9 p.m., with plenty of daylight still in the sky. I went to the Traveler's Inn, one of Walter Hickel's motels, where there was a hand-lettered sign in the lobby: ABSOLUTELY NO HOOKERS ALLOWED IN ROOMS AFTER MIDNIGHT.

In the morning, I flew from Fairbanks to Bettles, one hour north. The morning was warm and there was haze over the rolling green hills. Some of this was smoke from forest fires. More than half a million acres of Alaskan land were burning: fires started by lightning, hundreds of miles from any road.

North of the Yukon River, pipeline camps seemed the only signs of human habitation. The pipeline itself, silver-colored, and the unpaved, dirt-colored haul road that ran alongside it, stretched together, like mismatched railroad tracks, toward the northern horizon.

A sign in Bettles said:

WELCOME TO BETTLES FIELD, ALASKA.
35 MILES NORTH OF THE ARCTIC CIRCLE.
POPULATION 51.
ELEVATION 643 FEET.
LOWEST RECORDED TEMPERATURE, 1975, −70.
HIGHEST RECORDED TEMPERATURE, JULY 1955, +92.
HIGHEST RECORDED MONTHLY SNOWFALL,
OCTOBER, 1945, 35 FEET, 4 INCHES.
AVERAGE ANNUAL MEAN TEMPERATURE +21.

Bettles was the place that people passed through on their way into and out of the Brooks Range.

Ray and Barbara Bane lived in a one-room cabin at the edge of a dusty dirt road about a mile from the Bettles airfield. There was no plumbing, but there was electricity, and even—due to Ray's recent affiliation with a bureaucracy—a telephone. After fifteen years in Alaska—most of them lived in the bush—Ray Bane had been hired by the National Park Service to help plan the proposed

Gates of the Arctic National Park, which would, if the Udall bill became law, encompass eight million acres of the central Brooks Range—an area four times larger than any existing national park, and more than half again as big as Massachusetts.

"I was born in Wheeling, West Virginia," Ray Bane said. "We were poor. I was the only one in my family to finish high school. The only reason I finished was so I could keep playing football. I loved football. I'm only five-nine, but in those days I was stocky.

"I met Barbara in seventh grade. Met her at Warwood Junior High. But I got left behind in seventh grade, and it took me years to catch up. Her parents did not approve of me. She was an all-round good girl. An only child. Involved with the church, that sort of thing. And her family was higher-class than mine. Her father was a truck driver, and had worked in a coal mine for a while. She lived in a decent part of town. I lived in the part that had the blacks, and quite a few other minority groups. I was a hell raiser. I drank a lot. I was always in fights. I had a bad reputation. You might say that my education included some things that hers didn't. But I hung in there. We got married in the summer of 1959.

"Barbara had just graduated from West Liberty State College, near Wheeling. She got a job teaching while I finished my last year at Marshall College, in Huntington. She had relatives up in Ohio, and our dream at that point was to both be teachers and to live in a suburb of Cleveland.

"The only exposure I'd ever had to Alaska was a Walt Disney movie—*White Wilderness*—about the wildlife. Then a friend of mine from college went to work in a cannery out there. When he came back—he knew how much I loved the outdoors—he said that Alaska had the most outdoors he'd ever seen.

"I found a map of the place and I put it up on our wall. We were living in a one-room apartment in Huntington, so I spent a lot of time staring at that wall. Barbara came home one day and found me writing letters to dots on the map. I would just pick out any dot that looked interesting and write a letter inquiring about teaching jobs. Every time I got a reply I'd have to go back and look at the map to see where it was from. We heard from a lot of places—Anchorage, Fairbanks, Ruby, Sitka. And we decided, let's just go out for one year. Just for the experience. Then we could come back and live in Cleveland.

"We chose Sitka because it looked good on the map. It was in the southeastern part of the state, and on the water. I think we were a little afraid of the cold. Actually, the big reason we chose Sitka was because the school there was under the auspices of the Presbyterian Church, and the Presbyterians said they would pay our way out. No one else had said that. We were so broke we really didn't have much of a choice.

"We went out in the fall of 1960, Kennedy was running against Nixon and we made sure we got absentee ballots so we could vote for Kennedy. We taught at the Sheldon Jackson High School and Junior College. The Presbyterians were running it for the Bureau of Indian Affairs. It was a big regional school to which kids were sent from villages all over the state. Barbara was the music director and I taught social studies and directed school plays. There wasn't any football at Sheldon Jackson.

"We liked Sitka very much. But we both met a lot of Eskimo kids from the Arctic. They kept telling us we should go north. They said Sitka was nothing. To them, Sitka seemed like California. They said up north was where the real Alaska was. Some of the stories they told of their way of life made it seem really exotic. So we said, gee, before we go back, maybe we should go north for one year.

"I went to Juneau for a teachers' convention in the spring and came back with job offers for both of us from Barrow. We went back to West Virginia for the summer, and up to Barrow in the fall of '61. We figured Cleveland would always be there.

"In those days, Barrow wasn't such a bad town. There was some drinking, but not the open hostility you have now. There wasn't any special housing for teachers, either. We were given a three-room shack to live in. With an outhouse and a honey bucket, which was where you dumped the pail you were using as a toilet. We hadn't had that at Sheldon Jackson. We hadn't even had that in West Virginia. We built shelves all around the walls. Our food for the year had been delivered by barge. That shack looked like a store when you walked in.

"There were seven teachers in town that year, and, except for us, they were really into bridge. Sitting there day after day, playing bridge. They wouldn't even look out the window. From that time on, I have never played cards. I never will. I just became so disgusted with those people who would play cards all the time and ignore their environment.

"We were actively discouraged by the BIA from having social relationships with the Eskimos. We weren't even supposed to use the Eskimo language, or to let them use the language inside the school. But we still managed to go whaling and sealing and caribou hunting. And it was in Barrow that I got interested in dogs.

"Everyone in town had a dog team, and they were always rushing back and forth on the streets. There were only a few early, primitive snow machines. Eventually, I got a dog team of my own. A guide had given it to a dentist as payment for a set of false teeth. I got started because I was desperate for something to do. I couldn't talk to the Eskimos, and all the other white folks were playing bridge.

"I was the biggest joke in town when I started. The first white man they'd ever seen using dogs. Eventually I reached a point where, most of the time, the dogs would stay in front of the sled. So then I decided to take a trip. As soon as the school year ended I took off for Wainwright, the nearest village, which was about a hundred miles away. It took me about ten days to get there, which was probably more time than it would have taken me to walk. But when I did get there, I fell in love with the place. The people in Barrow had always said, if you want to see things done the old way, go to Wainwright. That is where the old ways are still alive. Wainwright was a village of maybe two hundred and fifty people, where Barrow was a city of three thousand. And it turned out that there was a new school in Wainwright. It had just opened up. Before that, the kids had been sent to Barrow to go to school. We went out there in the fall of '62. Stayed for three years. Teaching school, running dog teams, hunting, trapping, fishing from skin boats, really learning the Eskimo way of life. We had some wonderful experiences with those people. They were terrifically proud of the way they lived, and very generous about sharing it with us. By then, of course, Cleveland had become a thing of the past.

"But after the three years, we asked ourselves: Is this what we want for the rest of our lives? We felt frustrated, because there was so much more that we wanted to understand, but we just didn't have sufficient background. Then I met an anthropologist named Dick Nelson, who was writing a book about Wainwright. He persuaded me that I should do graduate work in cultural anthropology. He said the University of Wisconsin was very good.

"We moved to Madison in 1965. I went to graduate school, and

Barbara taught elementary school. We came back to Wainwright in the summer so I could do research on a project I had started with Dick Nelson: studying how the Eskimos utilized the inland environment, as opposed to the coast. Then Dick got a contract from the Air Force to gather data on Eskimo survival techniques. We went out on the sea ice to whaling camps and sealing camps. We subsisted entirely on Eskimo food for six weeks: caribou meat, seal, walrus, whale. I actually got to like it after a while. In the fall we went back to Wisconsin.

"It was tough. I really felt the loss of freedom. And the crowds. Waiting on line for whatever it was you wanted to do. Or waiting for a bus on a corner, and suddenly starting to gag on the fumes. In the Arctic, I had been able to jump on a sled behind a dog team and go forever. Now, I couldn't even go onto the property of the person next door.

"We had brought two huskies with us, and I bought another one, and then I borrowed four pet huskies, and put together a dog team of my own. I used to drive the dogs across campus. Everyone thought I was nuts. Here was a campus where people were making bombs and hoping to blow up the Pentagon, and everyone was marching and singing against the war, and I was on the back of a dog sled, yelling, 'Mush!'

"We had to drive two hundred miles, with seven dogs in a station wagon and the dog sled on top, to find a national forest where we could go mushing and camp out. One day up there I found a new trail and went for miles. Deeper and deeper into the woods. I was starting to feel good for a change. I was finally getting some open space around myself. Then all of a sudden I heard music. It got louder. And even louder as I kept going. And then I burst out of the woods and found myself in the middle of a skiing resort. That was when I knew I had to go back.

"I had gotten an A in every course I took. Well, one B. I had already started writing my dissertation. But toward the end of the second year, I began to realize that this Ph.D. business was really a trap. You spend nine months a year in a little cubicle somewhere, straining to get out to the field for three months. We were both miserable. So I said, the hell with it: let's go back.

"We were afraid that Alaska was changing. We'd been reading *Alaska* magazine, and the *Tundra Times*, which was the weekly Native paper. They'd had stories about how the snow machine was in, and how the old way of life was disappearing from the villages. We felt we wanted to experience a little more of it before it was gone. We applied to the state for teaching jobs. They said we could go to Huslia, which was an Eskimo village on the Koyukuk River, as deep in the Interior as you can get. That was when Barbara encouraged me to learn how to fly. Otherwise, in a place like Huslia, you could feel kind of stuck. I put my dissertation in a drawer and I took flying lessons, and I got my private pilot's license in five weeks. We sold our house and our property in Wisconsin and bought an airplane. We flew it to West Virginia to break it in, and to visit for a while. Then we flew back to Alaska. And I think that was the greatest joy we've ever known. Coming back. God, we were Tom Sawyer and Huck Finn again.

"We taught in Huslia for three years. Then we went to Hughes, the next village upriver, about fifty miles. The school was smaller, with a lighter teaching load. Also, the life style in Hughes seemed more relaxed. Besides, it was closer to the mountains. To the Brooks Range. And we had started to feel that we wanted to be as close to the Brooks Range as we could.

"By '67, when we got back, the snow machine was everywhere. I mean, it was *all* snow machines. There were huskies around, but no one used them. There was not one person in Huslia running dogs. Well, we did not buy a snow machine. Which the Natives thought was really dumb. Instead, we bought a registered female Malamute and started to breed her. We wanted to build up a dog team of our own.

"We taught in Hughes for three years. Then we applied for a leave of absence. Our dog team was in good shape by this point. We wanted to be able to use it. So we started to plan a trip to Barrow. We planned it thoroughly. It was no spur-of-the-moment thing. We built our own sled, we designed our own tent, we trained the animals for long-distance travel, we researched various trails.

"On February 12, 1974, we took off. It was almost sixty below when we left Hughes. The people were taking bets we'd never make it. We traveled twenty-five miles down the river the first day. In ice fog so thick that, standing on the sled, we couldn't even see the dogs. When it gets that cold, you don't even need pollution to make ice fog. The first night out, it was seventy-four below. Well, we really hadn't expected anything like that. It wasn't much fun.

But it was twenty-five miles to a village either way. Twenty-five miles back to Hughes, or twenty-five miles to Huslia. So in the morning we kept going. Figuring it had to warm up. When we got to Huslia there was a radio message telling us that Barbara's father had died. She chartered to Fairbanks and flew home for the funeral. Two nights after seventy-four below, she was sleeping on clean sheets in West Virginia.

"It stayed cold. Fifty below every morning. Later on, out on the coast, I ran into some pretty bad gales. Cape Thompson, Cape Lisburne. I got caught in a gale going across to Kobuk, and I think that was the worst time of all. But I was able to camp at a hot springs below a pass, which might have saved me, or at least saved the dogs.

"I stayed four or five days in Shungnak, trying to fix up the dogs' feet. The weather was moderating by now. Then, when I got to Ambler, I heard that Barbara was up ahead, waiting for me, in Selawik. Oh, boy. I made a hundred and twenty miles in a day and a half. We stayed in Selawik for several days.

"In between villages, we'd camp out and not see anyone. In villages, we'd stay in Native homes. The people were just great everywhere. They'd feed our dogs, send messages for us, help us in any way they could. Without them, we couldn't have made it. In a couple of instances, the supplies we'd shipped ahead had not arrived.

"We went on to Kiana, and Noorvik, and then we stayed in Kotzebue for a week. The idea had never been to set a speed record. We wanted to visit as many villages as possible along the way; to experience as much as we could. Sesolik, Noatak, Kivalina, then out to Cape Thompson. That was rough. Winds forty gusting to sixty, and that was when the wind would die down. We went to Point Hope, to Point Lay—got weathered in there for a week.

"When we reached Wainwright, they were so happy to see us that they put on an Eskimo dance. That was something. We'd been gone from Wainwright for eight years. All the kids' faces had been down here—waist high—when we had left. Now they were up to eye level. Barbara said she felt like a grandmother. We got to Barrow on April twenty-third."

Ray and Barbara Bane lived in Hughes for three more years, in a log cabin they had built themselves. Ray received a contract from the National Park Service to study subsistence living among the Natives of the Kobuk and Koyukuk river areas, people who still hunted and fished for their food. The purpose was to determine how that way of life could be protected if the area were included in a national park in which hunting, fishing, and the use of snow machines would be prohibited. Ideally, an Eskimo would be permitted to shoot the moose he needed for winter food, without allowing planeloads of hunters from Fairbanks to open up a weekend hunting lodge. The issue got trickier, however, when the Eskimo shot ten moose and shipped nine to an Anchorage butcher.

This spring, due to growing racial animosity, Ray and Barbara Bane had had to leave their cabin in Hughes. The Natives—at least a number of the young Native men—did not want white people in the village any longer. There had been incidents of vandalism to the cabin, and there had been threats. Ray Bane, however, expressed no bitterness toward the Natives, only sorrow.

"Those people are in despair," he said. "They see their whole culture disappearing in a matter of five or ten years. And what have they got to replace it? They've got money to buy booze with, and after the booze is gone they've got nothing.

"This forced progress is destroying the people and it's destroying the land. And neither can ever be replaced. The pipeline caused outsiders to suddenly discover what was up here. Now there's this tremendous pressure to cash in. From all these people who have come into the state just in the past couple of years, and who see wilderness not as something sacred, something with an almost spiritual value, but just as another form of merchandise.

"I honestly feel that some of them have a hatred for the land. Or maybe just a general hatred. They come here because of their frustrations elsewhere and they try to take out their frustrations on the land. They want to conquer it. A macho thing. And then, of course, they all want to get rich.

"Oh, don't let me get started. We're so wrapped up now in this question of what's going to happen to the land that I'm afraid we've started thinking of the Brooks Range as the center of the universe."

Ray Bane had already spent fifty-one days in the Brooks Range this summer, on hiking trips and river trips, exploring country that very few people—in some cases, perhaps, no one at all—had ever seen. Now he was about to go again, on a twelve-day hike along what might someday be the eastern edge of the Gates of the Arctic National Park but was now simply uncharted wilderness.

Ray's immediate superior, John Kauffmann, chief planner for the Gates of the Arctic, would be flying up from Anchorage in early afternoon, accompanied by an environmental photographer and writer named Boyd Norton, who was working on a picture book about the National Park Service Alaska proposals, and by a friend named Ogden Williams, who had recently retired from the State Department. I had met John Kauffmann in Anchorage some weeks earlier, and he had invited me to make the trip: almost two weeks on the ground in the wildest, northernmost, most remote, least explored mountain range in North America; a range which, in its entirety, lay above the Arctic Circle.

John Kaufmann was a tall, thin, bald-headed man, fifty-two years of age. He had a neatly trimmed gray beard and smoked a pipe. He was a member of the family that had owned the Washington *Star*, but, out of a deep and abiding commitment to the value of wilderness, he had been in Alaska, with the Park Service, for six years, exploring the Brooks Range in summer—by air, by water, and on foot—and the rest of the year working in Anchorage to create a system that would allow others to experience this country as he had, with its beauty and wildness undiminished.

Boyd Norton was a former nuclear physicist who had worked for several years at an Atomic Energy Commission reactor station in Idaho. He had grown disenchanted with the nuclear age and had, in a sense, reverted to the opposite extreme. For the past ten years he had been a photographer and writer, specializing in books and photographic essays on the outdoors. He lived in Evergreen, Colorado, had arrived in Anchorage only the day before, and had never before been to Alaska. He was forty-two years old and had a gray beard that was not as neatly trimmed as was John Kauffmann's. He appeared to be in less than optimum physical condition, and, in addition to his regular pack, he was going to have to carry a tripod and his cameras and film through the Brooks Range.

Ogden Williams was fifty-eight years old; bald, brisk, and cheerful, in an old-school, hail-fellow way. Jolly good. I say there, old chap, you've got the odd mosquito on your back.

With my own lack of outdoor experience factored in, we seemed a curious group: neither the rugged band of seasoned outdoorsmen—except for Ray Bane—nor, on the other hand, the college-kid jet-set elite, who were—the advocates of development would argue—the only kinds of people who could ever gain access to, or derive enjoyment from, a wilderness area such as the Brooks Range in its present, undisturbed state.

John Kauffmann had packed food for the trip in Ziploc bags. It would be freeze-dried food for breakfast and dinner, but real food —tins of sardines and smoked oysters and clams, bars of cheese, real crackers—for lunch. There were also bags of "gorp"—a combination of peanuts, raisins, and M&Ms—to be used as energy-replenishing snack food between meals.

We stood in the sun outside Ray Bane's cabin and divided the food bags among our packs. Ray Bane talked about the biggest animals he'd ever killed. A walrus once, off the coast of Barrow, that had weighed 3,000 pounds. He said walrus made very good dog food. The previous fall he'd shot a 1,200-pound moose. He had used black powder and a musket, just to make the whole thing more sporting. It had taken eight hours to cut the moose into pieces small enough to bring back to his smokehouse by sled. Then it had taken six days to butcher the moose. The meat had fed him and Barbara through the winter.

We left Bettles at 6:20 p.m. and flew north to the Dietrich River pipeline camp, which was at an altitude of just over 1,000 feet. Two mountains rose above the camp in the foreground: Snowden, at 5,600 feet, and a triangular mountain, named Sukuk-pak, at 4,200.

It was not the altitude of the Brooks Range peaks that made them so special, but the variety of sizes and shapes, and the fact that they were so far away from the rest of the world, and, most of all, the fact that they seemed to just go on forever in all directions, displaying no traces of the presence of man.

As we flew low, over the haul road, and prepared for landing at the airstrip in the camp, we could see, in fact, stretching out to the horizon on both sides, hundreds of other peaks, most of them nameless, most of them unclimbed, separated by dozens, even hundreds of other valleys, most of which were still unexplored.

Although the haul road marked the eastern edge of the proposed park, it was by no means the edge of the range. The mountains continued to the horizon to the east, and if one had traveled to the farthest point on the horizon and had looked east, to the horizon, once again, the mountains would have continued to that point, too, and beyond. And the same process could be repeated, again and again. And the same would hold true for an even greater distance to the west.

We were met at the camp by a man from the Department of the Interior who drove us fifteen miles up the haul road, to the mouth of Kuyuktuvuk Creek, at the point where it emptied into the Dietrich River. This was where our hike would begin. We would follow the Kuyuktuvuk to its source, at Oolah Pass, two days away. From there, we would descend into the Oolah Valley, and proceed to the larger valley of the Itkillik River. From the Itkillik we planned to hike up a side valley, which had no name, to the base of a 7,600-foot mountain called Cockedhat, because of an unusual rock formation on its top.

Forty years earlier, Robert Marshall, one of the first white men to explore the Brooks Range, had approached Cockedhat Mountain from the west. Marshall had, in fact, given it its name. As far as John Kauffmann or Ray Bane knew, however, no one—at least not since the time of the ancient Eskimos—had hiked up the valley that led to Cockedhat Mountain from the east.

18   The Brooks Range

At 8:15 p.m. we waded across the Dietrich River. The water was low, and we were able to splash across on wet gravel, without having the water come over the tops of our boots. The sun had gone behind the mountains, but there still was strong light in the sky. At this latitude—more than a hundred miles above the Arctic Circle—at this time in August, there would not be full darkness, but we would experience a sort of dusk for a few hours, just after midnight.

We walked, single file, through the brush along the north bank of Kuyuktuvuk Creek. The water in the creek was high and murky, apparently from heavy rains a week ago. Ray Bane pointed out mud stains on the brush that indicated the stream had been at least four feet higher only a few days before. To start a hike at this point would not have been quite so simple then.

There was a game trail through the brush that grew near the edge of the creek. The growth was mostly spruce and willow, and only once, along a steep side hill, for about two hundred fifty yards, did we have to grapple with dense alder growth.

There were many animal droppings on the trail. Moose, Ray Bane would say as we walked past. Or, less often: wolf. We passed scattered bones and skulls that he said were the remains of long-dead caribou. Then he noticed what I had known he would eventually see, but what I had hoped he would have the good taste not to mention: signs of bear. Not droppings, in this case, but tracks. Grizzly bear tracks. Or, rather, one grizzly bear print.

Ray studied it for a few moments and then said it had been made by a bear which probably was three years old, and it had been made, probably, in early afternoon. The track was about a foot long and set maybe two inches deep into the mud of the trail. The imprint of each long, curving, non-retractable claw was clearly delineated. In a three-year-old grizzly, the claws extend several inches beyond the end of the paw. This was a fact which I would have been quite content to encounter in a book, while sipping red wine, perhaps, with my feet up, in front of an open fire. To learn it firsthand, toward late evening, in a wooded area in a wilderness mountain range a hundred miles north of the Arctic Circle, when I would soon have to lie down and go to sleep in these woods, near the bank of this creek, not far at all from this trail, was certainly as much an emotional as an intellectual experience.

We walked for two miles along the bank of the creek. It coursed through braided gravel channels, tumbling and foaming past heavy rocks. When we reached the point where a creek called Trembley joined the Kuyuktuvuk from the southwest, we waded across the Kuyuktuvuk and set up a camp on a level willow bar at the mouth of Trembley Creek.

Before we would continue on our main journey, up the Kuyuktuvuk, John Kauffmann wanted to spend a day hiking up Trembley Creek. There was a pass which, on the topographic map and from the air, had seemed as if it might offer access to the valley of the Hammond River to the west. In the Brooks Range, however, often the only way to determine whether or not a pass was attainable on the ground was to try to attain it on the ground. Knowing which passes could be traversed, and which could not, and how much time, difficulty, and possible danger was involved in each, enabled one to plan an extended hiking trip much more intelligently.

The Park Service was not envisioning a guidebook and trail markers in the Gates of the Arctic—John Kauffmann, in fact, was working strenuously to prevent such affronts—but it appeared likely that within five years hundreds, if not thousands, of people would be passing through Bettles each summer, wanting to hike in the Brooks Range, and many would be asking Ray Bane, and possibly other park personnel, for advice on possible sections to visit and on viable routes. Part of his job, if the park became a reality, would be to separate and disperse these hiking parties, probably through a system of permits and by controlling access by air, so that three hundred hikers would not descend simultaneously upon a well-known scenic area like the Arrigetch Peaks, thus ensuring that none would have a wilderness experience, and that, in all likelihood, however well intentioned each individual turned out to be, just from the force of their numbers, permanent scars would be left on the terrain. It was for purposes such as this, and not just because he enjoyed it—though he did—that Ray Bane had spent fifty-one nights out of doors through the summer, and was about to spend number fifty-two.

Ogden Williams had brought his own one-man tent and slept alone. John Kauffmann and Boyd Norton shared one tent, and Ray Bane and I slept in another.

Although we had come in two miles, and although the Kuyuktuvuk was flowing fast enough to make noise, we were still able to hear the sounds of diesel trucks grinding up the haul road from the pipeline camp. It was, Ray Bane said, the first time he'd ever heard the sound of a truck in the Brooks Range. And it made him realize that there was, ultimately, no escape from development, from industrialization, from destruction of beauty and solitude. At some point, having run as far as you could run, you had to turn and fight to save what you believed in. And that, he said, was why he had taken the job with the Park Service, despite the sacrifice of freedom and individuality it might entail.

This was talk at dusk, after 11 p.m., around a fire that we had built of willow branches. In McKinley Park, much more populated by campers, fires were not allowed, which made for cold nights, with much less post-dinner chat. But this was not a park yet, and we were the only people who had camped here this summer, and probably for some summers before, and we would certainly be the last of the year, if not for several years. And, Ray said, in the morning, or the morning after, before we broke camp and moved on, he would show us how to dismantle the fire and rearrange the rocks and dirt and sticks so that no evidence of our presence here would exist.

Ray added that, although we were undoubtedly the first people here for some time, it did not seem likely that we were the first ever. Because the word Kuyuktuvuk, he said, was the Eskimo word for "place where one makes love repeatedly."

In the distance, we heard the whine of another truck. It wasn't just the noise of the trucks that bothered Ray. There was another reason he would be happier when we had moved on. This close to the road, there was a much greater chance that the grizzly bears would already have had some human contact. That a bear might have been fed by pipeline workers; or might have discovered trash along the side of the road, thrown from passing pipeline trucks; or might have discovered the garbage dump at Dietrich Camp, and thus have come to associate human beings with easy food, and thus have come to develop an attraction for humans, which could easily become an aggression.

Ray always slept with his gun in his tent. His gun, however, was a .357 Magnum, which, he said, would be effective against a grizzly only when fired from inside the bear's mouth.

We piled our packs together in the middle of the camp, by the dying fire. All food was carefully wrapped and sealed tightly inside the Ziploc bags, to minimize odor. We balanced the cooking pots on top of the packs, so that if a bear did come to the packs, searching for food, he would knock over the pots and the noise of the falling pots would awaken us. What would happen next remained vague.

I told Ray, lying next to him inside the low and narrow tent, that I would tap him on the shoulder if I heard a bear in the camp. He told me I had better tap him and then duck. On second thought, he said a moment later, I had better duck before I tapped.

I slept poorly that first night, for lots of reasons. I was not yet tired from a full day's hike. I was still not used to sleeping on the ground, inside a sleeping bag, inside a tent. There was not enough darkness. I was thinking about bears. And the noise of the trucks kept me awake.

We woke up at 7 a.m., to the sound of the creek and to the singing of birds. The morning was sunny and breezy and warm. The worst of the mosquito season was past, but the worst of the mosquito season, in northern Alaska, means you keep your entire body covered and wear a net around your face and the net is so quickly covered with mosquitoes the size of nickels and dimes that you can't even see where you are going. And if you live in a village and own dogs, you rub motor oil inside the dogs' noses and inside their ears, so the mosquitoes and gnats will not crawl in and begin to eat the inside of the dogs' heads. Even past the worst of the season, the mosquitoes, like the bears, are never far from the edge of your consciousness; and, unlike the bears, never very far from your skin.

Boyd Norton and I decided to go with John Kauffmann and Ray Bane on their hike to the pass up Trembley Creek. Ogden Williams said he would spend the day around camp, protect it from bears, ho-ho, maybe fish a little bit in the creek. Ogden had brought with him, attached to his backpack, a folding aluminum camp chair. It was the sort of luxury in which one might indulge himself if there were paid Sherpas to carry the packs, but for a fifty-eight-year-old man to tote his own folding chair around the Brooks Range for two weeks seemed unconventional to say the least.

We started walking at 8 a.m. I carried a small day pack that held lunch and a rain poncho. We walked up a mossy ridge that rose a few hundred feet above the creek. Looking back, to the east, we could see the mountains across the haul road. Table Mountain, at 6,400 feet, and, south of it, a 6,000-foot mountain that had no name. Our camp was at about 2,000 feet. Tree line, at this latitude, was only a few hundred feet higher, and soon, after walking through an open alpine forest, we came onto the treeless tundra slopes of the mountain to our west. Boyd, still suffering the effects of jet lag, or a recent flu, said he was not feeling well and turned back. He would photograph wildflowers by the creek near our camp.

As John Kauffmann and Ray and I walked on, climbing steadily, we gained a good view of the Kuyuktuvuk Valley, up which we would start hiking the next day, on our way to Oolah Pass. It seemed to slope gently upward, toward the headwaters of Kuyuktuvuk Creek, with mountains of 4,000 to 6,000 feet rising above it on both sides. The western mountains—the mountains in the direction we were going—looked steeper, more precipitous than did those to the east. The creek itself looked swift and turbulent: more a small river, Ray Bane said, than a creek.

Having climbed high up the north slope of the Trembley Creek valley, we were reluctant to sacrifice the altitude—and the openness and the view—by dropping back down to the creek bed, and so we trekked across steep scree slopes until we came to a deep ravine. Beyond the ravine was the pass. The sun was hot, I had already drunk several pints of water, and, even with only a day pack, I was weary. We dropped down the ravine to eat lunch. Salami, cheese, and crackers, accompanied with icy water from this noisy little side creek that had no name. After lunch, we climbed up the west side of the ravine and continued to a wide, rolling, relatively level section of the mountain slope. This was a mile, maybe a mile and a quarter beyond the ravine. I liked hiking above tree line. Not just for the views of the mountains, but because the chances of a surprise encounter with a grizzly seemed less than they would have been in the willows by the creek. John and Ray, however, said there was no need to worry about bears. In this sparse Arctic environment, each grizzly required a habitat of approximately a hundred square miles, and despite last evening's track, the chances of an encounter with one were remote.

We turned back at a canyon that cut us off from the pass. To reach the pass, one would have had to stay low, along the creek until past this canyon. It was about a hundred fifty feet deep, and maybe ten to fifteen yards wide at the bottom.

On our way back, we passed again through the ravine in which we had eaten our lunch. This time, however, we were lower, near the mouth of the ravine, where it opened into the creek. Here we spotted a large jawbone and, nearby, clumps of tufted hair. Moose hair, Ray Bane said, with some interest. He looked more closely. Interspersed with the tufts of hair were high, rounded piles of animal droppings. Bear scat, Ray Bane said. Grizzly bear.

He picked up what had been the jawbone of the moose. It had been a fully grown moose, he decided. In the spring, with the snow still deep on the slopes, the moose had come down to the creek to drink. The grizzly, just awake after a winter's hibernation —and very hungry—had caught scent of the moose or, just lucky, had happened to be at the right place at the right time. The right place, in this instance, would have been high on the side of the ravine, looking down at the moose by the creek. The bear would have sprung down onto the moose's back. It would have been a fierce struggle, for a fully grown moose, in good health, is not easy prey; not even for a grizzly bear.

Ray began walking in wider and wider circles at the mouth of the ravine, finding still more clumps of hair, and other, scattered, smaller bones. This was the area in which the unseen struggle had been waged. One dead moose, and one very happy bear, when it was over. A grizzly, Ray said, will expend an enormous amount of time and energy just in pursuit of a single ground squirrel. To come upon a moose at the start of the year was a bonanza beyond a grizzly's wildest dreams.

No question, Ray said, that such a bear was a terrifying creature. But if one could step back for a moment and get some perspective, one could see him, in a more objective light, as a beautifully efficient machine. And one could admire also the thoroughness with which nature worked. Once the bear had eaten his fill—and this would have taken more than one meal, more than one day—once the bear had no further use for the remains, and the other, smaller animals and birds had known that it was safe to do so, they had moved in to pick at what was left. In the months that had passed since the kill, the carrion eaters had done a thorough job. And even the ground squirrels, in need of calcium, had nibbled the bones. Leaving, now, just a jawbone and a dozen handfuls of hair. Life in the food chain. There is nourishment in a dead moose for almost every other inhabitant of the Brooks Range, Ray Bane said, except the fish.

To Ray, this was an exciting find: a vivid illustration of the workings of nature in its undisturbed state. To me, it was more than a little alarming. If a bear could do that to a moose, imagine what the same animal could do to a human being. And if he had eaten the moose in the spring, he probably was pretty hungry again by now. On the other hand, he might be a hundred miles away. But then, there had been that fresh track from yesterday, less than two miles from where we were camped. John Kauffmann told me again not to worry. In all the time he had spent hiking in the Brooks Range, he had yet to see a grizzly bear. He'd observed a couple while on river trips, as his canoe had swung silently around a bend, but never had he been confronted with one on the ground.

Being low, at the mouth of the ravine, we were once again below tree line, and had to work our way back to the ridge through thickets of alder and willow. On our way up, Ray paused at a badly gouged tree trunk. There were light brown, almost blond, hairs all over the tree. Grizzly bear hairs. He'd probably had an itchy back, Ray Bane said, and had stopped here to scratch it. Then, for some reason, maybe because he'd thought there might have been a squirrel inside the tree, he'd taken a swipe at the trunk.

I tried very hard to think about other things. But then Ray mentioned that in Bettles he had heard that a female member of a United States Geologic Service surveying team had been mauled by a bear in the western Brooks Range. She had lost one arm already, and might lose the other. And that, Ray said, had been only a black bear.

I was relieved to get back to camp. However false it might turn out to be, the sight of brightly colored tents, the smell of smoke from a wood fire, and the presence of even two other people, offered a sense of security.

We were in our tents by 9 p.m. I was tired from hiking all day and from not having slept the night before, so I fell asleep quickly. At ten minutes past midnight, gray twilight outside, I was awakened by the voice of Ogden Williams. But it was not me whom he had come to wake up.

"Hello, Ray? Ray, old chap?" He was speaking softly, squatting at the entrance to our tent. Ray woke up.

"I say, old fellow, I don't know if I should be bothering you about this, but it did occur to me that perhaps I should mention it, and you seemed like the logical person." Ogden glanced back over his shoulder, in the direction of Kuyuktuvuk Creek.

"Actually, the fact is, old man, that there's a large grizzly bear out here, just on the other side of the creek."

Ray grabbed his gun. Then he was out of his sleeping bag and out of the tent like a fireman responding to an alarm. He went immediately to John Kauffmann's tent, which was about ten feet from ours, and alerted John and Boyd. The five of us gathered quickly around the circle where our campfire had been. We stared across the creek, through the twilight.

The bear was feeding casually. The soft wind was blowing toward us, thus carrying our scent away from him. The sound of the creek had prevented him, thus far, from hearing us.

"Don't know if I did the right thing," Ogden said. "Hate to make a bloody nuisance of myself."

"Don't worry," Ray Bane said in a low voice. "You did the right thing."

We watched the bear in silence for maybe five minutes. He was about fifty yards from us, but if he so desired he could be across the creek and in our midst within seconds. He was rooting slowly and quietly among the willows. Then he looked up and glanced across the creek, in our direction. He stopped feeding. He stood still, on his four legs, his head raised and pointed in our direction. He had spotted us; or had sensed our presence somehow.

"If he starts across," Ray whispered, "bang the cooking pots together. I'll fire a shot in the air. That should stop him. If he keeps coming, climb the nearest tree you can find, and climb it as high as you can."

I looked around quickly. There was only one tree at the campsite which anyone could possibly climb. One tree, one bear, and five of us.

"What about starting the fire?" I asked.

"Okay," Ray said. "Give it a try." What worried him, he added, was that we were so close to the road. This bear might be used to contact with people. Might be intrigued, rather than startled, by the presence of human beings along his creek. Otherwise, why hadn't he left when he'd seen us? Why was he still just standing there?

I began to snap some willow branches to use for the fire. The noise appeared to startle the bear. He bolted about twenty yards up the creek, further from us. So far, he had shown no inclination to cross.

"Okay," Ray said. "That's the direction we want him to move in. Let's keep making noise." And he began to shout, and then we all did—it was, as well as a bear deterrent, a splendid release from the minutes of tense, dry silence we'd just been through—and then we began to bang the pots and pans together and the bear whirled again and disappeared up the hill, away from the creek.

Ray scanned the area carefully with binoculars, through the twilight, for several minutes. No sign of the bear. Our fire was smoking again and we decided to let it smoke. We returned to the tents, and got back inside our sleeping bags.

"Guess what?" Ray said. "You've just had a wilderness experience."

In the morning, of course, we talked of nothing but the bear. It was another warm day, with a light south wind and scattered clouds.

The .357 Magnum, Ray said, was a very poor compromise between having sufficient protection against a bear and having none. A shotgun would have been the ideal thing to carry, one barrel containing rifled slugs and the other filled with double-ought buckshot. However, in all of his time in the Brooks Range, Ray had never brought a shotgun on a hiking trip. Because, he said, with ammunition, the gun would weigh at least six pounds, and below tree line it would snag in branches, and because 99.9 percent of the time a grizzly bear would not attack a hiker.

I said I didn't see why a hungry bear should be any more reluctant to attack a hiker than a moose. Yesterday's evidence of the predatory nature and the overwhelming power of the grizzly had made a strong impression, and this skin of verbal protection within which we were trying to encase ourselves seemed pretty thin. Especially with the memory of the bear in the night still so vivid. Even if he had, eventually, run away. That had not been a paw print; that had not been just blond hair in a tree; that had not been simply evidence of a kill from months before. That had been a live grizzly bear. Weighing four hundred, maybe five hundred pounds. Standing only fifty yards from us and staring at us. It was going to take more than probability theory to make me feel comfortable.

Well, Ray said, upon further consideration, a grizzly would be reluctant to charge a group of hikers. One person, or two, might be different. The trouble was, no one really knew for sure. The evidence, such as it was, was based only on input from survivors. People like ourselves, who had witnessed a bear behaving in a non-aggressive manner. The people toward whom a bear behaved aggressively generally did not get to deliver their reports.

Ray, however, continued to be optimistic. As long as you allowed a bear to save face, he said, the bear would ordinarily retreat. As long as you didn't surprise him, come upon him suddenly in close quarters. Giving him, in his mind, no recourse but to attack.

"Like yesterday," Ray said. "Remember when I stopped a couple of times coming down the ridge? That was because I thought I smelled bear. I don't like walking through brush. You can't see them if they're feeding. And you might even stumble upon a mother with her cubs, and that, friends, is the most dangerous situation of all."

We agreed that none of us liked walking through brush. And we finished our breakfast as quickly as possible and rolled up our tents, and assembled our packs, and prepared to move on, up the Kuyuktuvuk, where soon, within two days, we would pass beyond the upper limit of the tree line, where, even in the valleys, there would be very little brush.

As he showed me how to fold a tent so it would fit inside its carrying sack, Ray Bane continued to talk about bears. Nothing like a grizzly, he said, to remind you that you were only a visitor here. And despite the nervousness, even fear, there was a certain value to that. The grizzly was as much a part of a true wilderness experience as was the sight of magnificent mountains. And only here, he said, within the Brooks Range, could such an experience be had on such a scale. There were grizzlies in McKinley Park, and grizzlies in southeastern Alaska, and even a few grizzlies left in the Lower Forty-eight; but only here, in the Brooks Range, was their habitat so undisturbed. Only here, in the Brooks Range, was it still possible to experience North America the way it had been when the first European settlers had arrived. That was why, he said, he was so opposed to the opening of the haul road to the public, as had been proposed. He did not want people driving into the Brooks Range to see bears.

"To be able to drive into a park," he said, "is the equivalent of going to a zoo." If just one person could have an experience of unspoiled intensity, such as the one we'd had the night before— such as this hike, in its entirety, seemed sure to provide—then that was more valuable to society, that made a greater contribution to the life force, than if this area received a thousand casual visitors. "And if we screw it up here," he said, hoisting his pack upon his back, "then we won't have any place left to screw it up. Then we can all stop arguing, because there won't be anything left to argue about."

At this point, Boyd Norton interrupted. "Hey, Ray," he called. "Come over here. Look at this." Ray walked over to the soft gray mud of the willow bar, just behind where we had pitched our tents.

Fresh bear tracks. Even fresher—much more distinct—than the ones we had seen as we hiked in from the road. A three-year-old bear, Ray said, judging from the size of the track. Which meant it had definitely not been the bear which we had seen the night before. That had been a larger, older bear. Which meant—we realized—that there had been two bears last night. The one we had seen, fifty yards away from us across the creek, and this one, which had passed, apparently, within fifty *feet* of our tent as we slept.

The tracks were very fresh, Ray said, only a few hours old. The detail of the paw mark was like a fingerprint under magnification. We could see sworls. The morning dew would soon blur this detail. Ray began to walk up and down the willow bar, and soon discovered additional tracks, and he was able to trace the bear's progress. Yes, he had come down this way, from Trembley Creek; from where we had hiked the day before. And look, he had paused here—see these two pads so close together? He must have smelled us, or smelled something that had caused him to stop. He had probably been figuring on working his way over to that game trail on the other side of the Kuyuktuvuk. Then, when he'd got our scent, he'd changed his mind.

Ray walked further down the mud, in the other direction. He pointed to wolf tracks, at least three or four days old. Then more bear tracks, at least a day older than the ones that Boyd had seen. Hard to say if they were from the same bear.

I was beginning to get the feeling that I was in a zoo after all. That I was, in fact, inside the bear cage.

What about that one-hundred-square-mile habitat that each grizzly bear was supposed to need? I asked John Kauffmann. Well, he said slowly, in sort of a drawl, while sucking contemplatively on his pipe, we must have accidentally set up our camp right on an intersection: where three or four habitats coincided. He would make a note of that, he said. Have a sign put up, once this became a national park: DANGER—BEAR CROSSING.

It was 10:30 by the time we got moving. We walked up the west side of Kuyuktuvuk Creek, either on the low gravel bars or, when bluffs cut off this route, on top of the banks, along game trails. We were still in forest and bears remained much on our minds. Mosquitoes, too, however, soon began to compete for attention. The sun was hot; the air almost muggy. At one point we came upon a very young hawk which apparently had fallen from its nest. There was nothing for us to do in its behalf. It seemed doomed. It was not yet able to fly, and a predator of one kind or another would soon devour it.

We walked for three and a half miles, moving slowly through the forest, still getting used to the weight of our packs. Then we reached the first tributary of the Kuyuktuvuk to flow into it above Trembley Creek. We stopped here for lunch. The tributary, which had no name, was just slightly too deep and quick-flowing for us to hop across from rock to rock. We had to change into old running shoes or sneakers for the crossing. This was something of an inconvenience, but the alternative would have been wet boots for the rest of the day. With all the creeks that lay ahead, Ray Bane said, it would mean wet boots for the entire trip. Sneakers for stream crossings were an essential part of Brooks Range hiking equipment.

Beyond the tributary, the footing looked better on the east bank of the Kuyuktuvuk, and so, still in our stream-crossing shoes, with our boots, tied together, either dangling from packs or hanging around our necks, we cautiously waded across the creek.

The pull of the water was strong; the bottom slippery. We unfastened the waistbands of our packs, so that if one of us did fall he would be able to slip out of the pack and not have his arms immobilized underwater, and not be dragged beneath the surface by the weight of the pack.

Once across, we dried our feet in the warm afternoon sun and continued north, up the east bank. After another mile we moved beyond tree line and the country opened out all around us and the hiking began to feel more like what I had imagined the Brooks Range to be.

It had always seemed to me that to get above tree line—to the openness and the freedom and the limitless space—was the main point of hiking in mountains. This was, however, the first time that I had passed beyond tree line simply by heading north, instead of up. The hillsides on either side of the creek were broad and open. Rising toward bare-rocked mountaintops in the 5,000–6,000-foot range. Our own elevation was now approximately 2,500 feet. The mountains were close enough to us so that, even without great height, they seemed significant.

It was not, of course, like standing on the Kahiltna Glacier, gazing up at Foraker and at Mount Hunter. In a way, however, though less spectacular, this was more satisfying. This was land in which man, however much a visitor he must remain, could function pretty much on his own. It was land that contained life, and thus surprises. With boots and some food and a sleeping bag, it could be lived in and explored.

The walls of the valley began to narrow as we continued to the north. Just beyond a second tributary, which, again, we had to put on sneakers to get across, the Kuyuktuvuk flowed through a low canyon. We rock-hopped across to the west bank again, and were forced to climb to higher ground. To the tundra which covered the hillside.

But this turned out to be not the dry tundra that made for good walking. This was wet, boggy tundra, with mushroom-shaped tussocks rising a few inches, in wobbly fashion, above the muck. The hiking through here was slow and very irritating. There was no good way to do it. Between the tussocks, the wet earth sucked at one's boots, but it was impossible to walk only on the tops of the tussocks because, when one put one's weight down, the tussock would tilt to one side or the other, sending one back again to the muck.

Ogden Williams, who had wanted to stay down on the creek, despite the numerous crossings and thus the numerous changes into and out of sneakers this would have entailed, now wondered loudly whose decision this had been. And what the hell kind of bloody fool would choose to walk on this kind of terrain when a creek bed ran parallel just below it? Eventually, we had to give up and drop back down to the creek bed, by which time it was already 6:30 p.m. and no one had the heart to continue.

We set up camp just off a game trail on the narrow west bank, with the steep canyon wall rising above us on both sides. There were a few scraggly willow bushes along the trail and we assembled some dead branches for a fire. Although we were beyond tree line, there was brush growing up the canyon walls on both sides.

Ray walked up and down the game trail in both directions and reported no signs of recent use. He said he did not expect any problems with bears. Although the boggy tundra above us was a poor surface for a human to walk on, it would not bother a bear in the least, and the grizzly who lived in this hundred-mile quadrant would probably keep mostly to the high ground.

The Kuyuktuvuk, flowing down a steeper grade and through a narrower canyon, was considerably more noisy and turbulent than it had been at our first campsite. Our tents were only fifteen yards from it, and we could almost feel the spray. Being down so low in the canyon, we were in shadow before long, and without the sun the temperature dropped sharply, and, still in clothes wet from a hiking day's sweat, I put on my down jacket, for the first time, to cut the chill.

We had covered only six and a half miles. In order to accomplish what John Kauffmann had intended for this trip, we would have to do better than that. But each day should find our condition improving, and the footing, as we worked our way north, and particularly on the far side of Oolah Pass, beyond the Arctic Divide, should get considerably easier. Thus far, it had been an interesting, but by no means a spectacular hike, and bears, rather than mountains, had been the dominating force.

A good sleep. More used to the tent now. Also more tired after a full day with full pack. The morning again was sunny and warm. But Ray Bane warned that the Brooks Range could turn suddenly rainy in mid-August and stay that way for a month, until the rain, in mid-September, turned to snow.

Breakfast was coffee, some sort of gruel which John Kauffmann, extended to his full length on his sleeping pad, prepared with the loving attention of the head chef at a three-star Parisian restaurant, and dried, compressed bacon bars, which were salty but good.

We packed our gear after breakfast. John Kauffmann went down the creek a bit, to where Ogden Williams had set up his tent. They were about thirty yards below Ray and me. Boyd walked toward us, carrying his pack, and then stopped, and put it on the ground, in order to more securely fasten his sleeping bag to it. Ray and I were squatting over our tent, which we had flattened on the ground. Ray said he would take it from there, and I stood to get my sleeping bag, which I had left hanging on a willow branch, to dry it and air it in the morning sun. The creek was making a lot of noise and the wind was blowing freshly from the north. Thus, no sound or scent of us had traveled upstream, which probably helped explain how the grizzly sow and her two cubs had come so close without noticing us.

The bear saw me as soon as I stood. In the same instant in which I saw her. She stopped. I stopped. Her two cubs stopped. They were just above me, on the opposite side of the creek.

"Ray! Bear! Right here!"

He reached for his gun and then he stood, and then Boyd Norton, who'd heard me yell, even above the noise of the creek, stood, too, and the three of us, motionless now, stared at the grizzly and at her cubs, and they, motionless, too, for this frozen, interminable moment, stared back at us, twenty yards away, across the creek.

This was closer, much closer, than the bear had been at our first camp. This was right on top of us. And this—a sow grizzly who had cubs at her side—was the most dangerous of all bear encounters.

As it happened, however, the cubs may have saved us. This might have been—probably was—the sow's first encounter with human beings, but it was certainly a first contact for the cubs, and they reacted the way the laws of bear probability said they should. Startled by the suddenness with which not just one, but three of these strange two-legged creatures had appeared, the cubs turned and bolted up the opposite creek bank into the brush. Had she been alone, the startled sow, at such close quarters, might have charged. There would have been no other way to save face. We were so close, and my standing up had been so sudden, that it would have seemed a direct confrontation; an aggressive action on my part. The sow's first instinct, however, was to stay with her cubs, and they, God bless them, had dashed not toward us, but away.

First the cubs, then the mother scrambled up through the brush, and then reappeared on the top of the opposite bank. They were looking down at us now from a distance probably three times what it had been when I'd first seen them.

I remained still. Ray ran past me, up the hillside on our side of the creek, in order to keep them in better view. Boyd Norton moved quickly after him. Boyd had a camera body in one hand and a telephoto lens in the other, but his hands were shaking so hard that he was unable to fit them together.

As for me, I had undiluted adrenaline rushing from my toes to the tear ducts of my eyes. *Jesus Christ!*

The bear was looking down at us from the bluff. The morning sun, shining toward us from behind her, lit up her nearly blond fur, and produced an almost haloed effect. She paused there only for a moment. Then, as her cubs ran on, still fleeing us, she turned again and ran to join them, disappearing over the rim of the bluff. The whole incident had lasted less than a minute. It was so sudden, and so silent—except for my initial cry—that John Kauffmann and Ogden Williams, just thirty yards downstream, had not even realized it was occurring. The bear had been closer to us than we were to John and Ogden. I began to understand how John Kauffmann had managed never to have seen a grizzly bear on a Brooks Range hiking trip. He just didn't look up. He studied his maps, and cooked the food, and kept his pipe lit, and let his companions be driven half mad with fear.

We began shouting and ran down the creek toward John and Ogden. This had been, even for Ray Bane, the closest encounter ever with a grizzly. He began muttering about how an extra six pounds in the pack might not really be so bad after all. And in the Brooks Range, where so much of the terrain was beyond tree line, the shotgun really wouldn't be in the way.

It had happened so fast. Less than a minute. Under a cloudless sky on a hot late-summer morning in the Arctic. One moment: folding a tent. The next: staring at three bears who were only twenty yards away. It had been the suddenness and proximity that had made this encounter particularly dangerous and unpredictable. Then, as it happened, we'd been lucky. This time. As we'd been lucky the last time. But what about next time? And when would next time be? A hundred square miles for each grizzly? It seemed to me that the Park Service had better run that one through their computer again.

Ray described to John and Ogden what had happened. Then, naturally, we spent half an hour discussing the situation, reviewing it, trying to come to some understanding; when really there was nothing to understand. The bears had been working their way down the creek, in our direction. Had I stood up ten seconds later, they might have been directly opposite us, only ten yards away instead of twenty. Would that have made a difference? No one knew. Because, in the recorded history of mankind, such a situation had not occurred often enough for any meaningful data to have been compiled.

But one thing was certain: it would not have improved matters any. And even twenty yards was a lot closer than any of us ever wanted to be to a grizzly again.

In some ways, of course, it doesn't matter how far you are from the bear. He—or she—sees you, and, particularly when you don't have a reliable weapon in your hands, the initiative, most emphatically, is with the bear. Some years before, Robert Marshall had seen grizzly bears in the Brooks Range and put the matter in proper perspective. "About a hundred and fifty feet ahead," he had written, "were three grizzlies. This may seem like a long distance to a catcher trying to throw a man out stealing second, but not to a man faced by three bears, eleven miles from the closest gun, one hundred and six from the first potential stretcher bearer, and three hundred miles from the nearest hospital."

We had to cross the creek twice during the first mile of hiking, changing into our sneakers each time. Somehow it was not as irritating as it had been the day before. There is nothing like an encounter with a grizzly at close quarters to put things in a different perspective, at least for a while.

After the second crossing, the valley began to widen, and the Kuyuktuvuk curved gradually westward. We were still at only 3,000 feet, and Oolah Pass, which we hoped to reach by the end of the day, was at an elevation of nearly 5,000, so we knew that at some point we would have to do some walking uphill.

With the valley wider, the creek had more room to spread out, and it became braided, and quieter, and easier to cross. We stayed low, on the creek bed, with open tundra rising gently on both sides, and willows growing along the course of the creek. Ray spotted tracks of moose, bear, and wolf, but, after the morning's encounter, mere tracks no longer possessed the emotional clout they once did.

We stopped for a late-morning rest. The sun was so strong, the air still so warm, that we took off our shirts to let them dry, and sat, bare-chested, feeling the soft breeze cool our skin. It did not seem possible that we were more than a hundred miles above the Arctic Circle.

"All this is a lie," Ray Bane said. "A beautiful lie. Winter is the truth about Alaska."

I looked up from a handful of gorp and saw a dark shape moving across the tundra on the far side of the creek. This time it turned out to be a moose. Boyd Norton jumped up and grabbed a camera. Here was an animal he would be able to photograph. It was a big moose, too; a big bull moose with wide antlers, which gave me a renewed and chilling sense of the power of the creature that could reduce such an animal to nothing but a jawbone and clumps of hair.

The moose ambled slowly toward the creek, and then dropped down to lie in some willows. Boyd crossed the creek and crawled toward it, to within what he considered good photographic range. Then he began to shout at the moose, to get it to rise from the willows. He was about thirty yards from it. But from only ten yards away, just to Boyd's left, a second bull moose jumped up instead.

The shock almost caused Boyd to drop his camera. When you are expecting a bull moose to be thirty yards from you in one direction, and you are suddenly confronted with one only ten yards away in an unexpected direction, it can be, while by no means as frightening as a similar encounter with a bear, quite star-tling nonetheless.

Once he recovered, Boyd swung around and began to shoot pictures. Then the original moose jumped to its feet and the two of them crashed together up the hillside, away from this noisy creature with the gray fur all over his face.

In early afternoon, by the creek bed, Ray spotted the tracks of a mother grizzly and two cubs, headed in the direction from which we had come. Those were our bears. They had passed this way in early morning, on their way downstream, toward their unexpected encounter.

We continued around the long, slow bend of the creek until we were heading due west. The valley began to narrow again. Soon the climb to the pass would begin. The footing was good here. We could see new mountains in the distance to the north. These seemed more rugged than the ones we'd come through. It was a good feeling. That was where we were going. I began, for the first time, to feel the pull of the mountains, and curiosity about what they would be like, rather than just a fear of bears.

We moved up from the creek bed a bit to higher ground. I could see deep ravines cutting through the mountains to the north and, through binoculars, sheep feeding high up on mountain ledges. Once through Oolah Pass, and up Oolah Valley, and up the Itkillik Valley, we would be hiking on the other side of those mountains, looking north and west once again, to see new mountains. And had we the time, and the supplies, and the energy, and had we been able to find a suitable route, we could have passed beyond those mountains, too, and could, in fact, have worked our way from valley to valley to valley, never sighting another human being; never seeing any signs that man, except for us, even existed. And we could have kept going that way until winter came and finally stopped us with its snow. Wilderness. The only limits were the limits of nature and the limits imposed by one's own imperfections. This was one of the nice things, Ray Bane said, about the Brooks Range. You didn't have to worry about coming to the end of the trail.

We stopped for lunch at 2 p.m. The creek was crashing and boiling white beneath us as it swept down a slope over boulders of a variety of shapes and colors. In all, so far, we had hiked probably not much more than twelve miles up the creek. But the nature of the terrain here was totally different from what it had been down below. No forest, no alder thickets, no murky water. The Kuyuktuvuk here was a clear, high mountain stream, tumbling down its rocky channel from its headwaters at the pass. All around us, as we sat back and rested, were wide and open tundra slopes. Looking west, one could see the approach to Oolah Pass. We ate quickly, feeling some excitement, eager to see what lay ahead.

Through the afternoon, our climb grew steadily steeper. The creek bed widened, and, above us, we could now see its origins: several braided channels, which cut through rough gravel and rocks. I began to quicken my pace despite the steepness. I moved ahead of the others, up the final slope of four hundred feet.

There was a small lake at the crest of the slope, shallow and murky, maybe three hundred yards long and less than a hundred yards wide. The lake was surrounded by a basin, made up of scree, clay, and a very thin and sketchy tundra growth. The basin was ringed by mountains to the north and south and by low ridges to the east and west. The ridge to the east was the one I had just come across.

I hiked along the edge of the lake toward the ridge that rose to the west above it. High on a mountain to the west, beyond the pass, I could see Dall sheep. Looking through a monocular, I counted eleven of them on the mountain, unexpected specks of white against the somber gray rock face. This was my first glimpse of what we would find beyond the pass. It seemed to be a craggier, colder land. The mountain ridges appeared saw-toothed; their faces more striking and austere.

This would be only logical, since Oolah Pass was not just an ordinary pass, but a part of the Continental Divide. Not the divide between east and west: the Arctic Divide. Below this point, water flowed south, emptying eventually into the Pacific. Beyond it, beyond Oolah Pass, the drainage was to the Arctic Ocean.

On some maps, Oolah Pass still appeared as Ulu. It had been so named by the Eskimos because the two mountains that rose from it on either side formed the shape of an ulu—an early Eskimo tool for scraping hides. It was believed to have been through Oolah Pass that the early Arctic Eskimos had crossed the Arctic Divide: moving from the coast and North Slope into the southern Brooks Range.

On one of his last trips through the range, in 1939, Robert Marshall had searched for Oolah Pass but had not been able to find it. Approaching from the southwest, up Blarney Creek, he had turned east too soon and had emerged at the headwaters of one of the western tributaries of the Kuyuktuvuk; still to the south of the pass. He had wanted very much to reach it: to at least look into, if not travel through, the valley of the Itkillik River. To at least see the water which would flow north to the Arctic. Once, on an earlier trip, Marshall had approached the source of the Itkillik from the south side of the Arctic Divide. "It was a sore temptation to follow it northward," he wrote, "among the unexplored mountains stretching as far as we could see." For lack of time, however, he'd had to classify that as only "a fine dream, unattainable as the end of the bright double rainbow in the canyon below . . ."

Now, on a warm and sunny afternoon some forty years later, we had arrived at Oolah Pass and would, the next morning, travel through it, and follow Oolah Creek down to the Itkillik. And it would all look exactly the same as it would have looked to Marshall had he found it. Not a single alteration in forty years, except whatever changes nature had wrought. And these would be few: in the Arctic, both figuratively and literally, nature moved at a glacial pace.

This seemed yet another concept of wilderness: having to do not just with space, but with time. Where else in the world were things just as they had been forty, or four hundred, years before? And would they still be unchanged forty or—given all the recent political and economic pressures—even four years from now?

258

I walked to the far end of the lake, just below the summit of the pass. I had noticed the breeze as I was walking, but now, as soon as I stopped, I felt the full force of its chill. This was not one of the gentle summer breezes I had grown used to. This was an icy Arctic wind. I had been wearing only a fishnet undershirt as I'd pushed up, through the sunshine, to the pass. Now I put a flannel shirt over that. And then a wool shirt. And, a few minutes later, my down jacket. The wind kept coming; I was shivering, even with the bright sun shining down. With my pack off, I began to move around to stay warm. Then I put on my brand-new bright orange Camp Seven wind parka and zipped it up tight and pulled up the hood, and tied the drawstring tight around my waist. And only then, gradually, did the shivering stop. The others arrived, donning clothing as quickly as I had. There was nothing subtle about the Arctic Divide.

We set up camp about fifty yards from the edge of the lake. The summit of the pass was still a quarter mile to our west, and the final slope that led to it afforded us some protection from the wind. To the east, we could see the mountains above the Dietrich River glowing in the early-evening sun. But to the west, through the pass, the saw-toothed ridge on which I had seen the sheep was rapidly being enveloped by low, swirling clouds that were being blown quickly in our direction.

There were no willow branches here with which to build a fire, and the only water was from the murky lake. The campsite had a stark, high mountain feel to it. Exhilarating in one way, but, in another, just plain cold.

The wind blew harder. The clouds were being funneled through the pass above our heads. It was as if someone were blowing thick smoke through a tube. Within half an hour, we were hidden in a heavy, wet mist. The wind whistled and hissed through the pass and filled the basin around the lake with its sound.

I put on some mittens. We all gulped hot chocolate, cooked on John Kauffmann's stove, and listened to the wind slap against our tents. There was no lingering after dinner for any chats about the value of wilderness. We finished the hot chocolate and washed the cooking pots with water from the lake—not washing them in the lake because, in water that still, any food particles might contribute to algae growth—and as soon as these basic chores were done we crawled into our tents and zipped up tight and listened to

the sound of Arctic wind. Ray Bane said it made him feel nostalgic, bringing back memories of his years on the Arctic coast.

By morning, the wind had stopped, after having kept me awake
most of the night. A heavy fog covered everything and visibility
was no more than a few yards. My clothes, as I put them on inside
the tent, were damp and dirty. My boots were wet, my socks soggy
and unclean, and, after four strenuous days without a bath, I felt
myself to be grubby in the extreme.

It was hard getting started in the fog, and without a morning
campfire to brighten the scene. Breakfast was glop again, with
freeze-dried eggs, and instant coffee served in tin cups, and none
of it tasted very good. Then the wind began to blow and the fog
lifted slightly; enough, at least, so we could see the lake, if not the
pass.

It was 11 a.m. before we broke camp and started to hike. The
excitement of crossing the pass and beginning our descent into this
new Arctic valley was muted to some extent by the fact that we
were hardly able to see where we were going.

We could see enough, however, to know that the valley was
narrow and that the mountains on either side were sharper and
craggier than those to the south of the pass. As the fog gradually
lifted we saw numerous sheep high on mountain slopes. The
downgrade was gentle and the footing was good; the air, however,
remained damp and chilly. I wore my wind parka over a woolen
shirt. After the first half hour, you get used to wet boots and then
you just don't think about them any more until the fire is lit at the
end of the day and you try once again to dry them.

We hiked downhill for four miles. Then, with the fog softening
to distant mist, and with a gentle, gauzy light beginning to drift
down from the sky, we came around a bend and looked into the
main valley that would lead to the Itkillik River.

No one said anything: each of us, independently, came to a
halt. No one, in fact, said anything for quite some time. Each of us
was, I think, a little overwhelmed. Even Ray Bane and John
Kauffmann, who had spent so much time in the Brooks Range.

There was no single, breathtaking feature: it was the harmony
and grace of the whole that so impressed us. A broad and gentle
valley lay beneath us, carpeted by tundra that looked velvety and

green. Precipitous mountains rose steeply from either side; jagged and snow-covered near the peaks. A small glacier was nestled just below the summit of one. Below, the creek ran, as Ray Bane said, like quicksilver, down the middle of the valley floor.

It was so sudden; so unexpected; so unlike anything that had come before. Robert Marshall, had he hiked this far, would not have been disappointed.

Low clouds were drifting across the mountains, covering the faces like thin veils. Then, as we sat there in silence, the sun broke partially through the mist, turning sections of the valley floor a brighter green; shining on aspects of the mountains like a spotlight.

Boyd Norton said, "It's like seeing the world in its youth." There was nothing moving, save the clouds and the subtly shifting light. There were no sounds, except our own quiet breathing. Finally, shaking his head, Boyd spoke again, saying, more to himself than to us, "And I thought I knew what wilderness was."

A whole wall of peaks on the western side of the valley rose to heights close to 7,000 feet. Not one of these peaks had a name. "They don't deserve to have names," Ray Bane said. "They're bigger than names." This seemed true enough, and no one was tempted to argue, but, had Robert Marshall made it through the divide, those peaks and many others would be named. For Marshall, who had discovered the adjacent peaks in the south-central Brooks Range which he had termed the Gates of the Arctic, had given a name to almost every geographical feature he had encountered on his hikes.

Almost unwillingly, we put our packs on again, and stood, our muscles already stiffening from the dampness, and we continued down, a few hundred feet, to the valley floor. A strong wet wind blew up the valley to meet us. We were walking northwest now, on the north side of the creek, toward the Itkillik, which was six miles ahead.

The further down the valley we proceeded, the worse the footing became. Gradually, we were getting back into tussocks, tussocks and bogs, which, Boyd said, sounded like the name of a law firm.

Through most of the afternoon, I walked in the company of Ray Bane. Seeing our reactions to this valley seemed to give renewed vigor to his own. People were always talking about the need for resource development, he said. Why couldn't they recognize that *this* was a resource, just as it was. This was a resource that developed *us*.

He spoke about those who wanted to make Alaska comfortable and predictable. If they succeeded, it wouldn't be Alaska any more. "It's like knowing there are grizzlies around. You're not as comfortable as you would be in the Alps, where they don't have any bears, and grizzlies sure as hell are unpredictable, but without them, an essential ingredient of the wilderness experience would be gone."

"Agreed," I said, "but next time let's bring the shotgun."

Then Ray talked about Jack Hebert, whom he knew and liked, and about the notion of building a cabin in the wilderness, which he did not like.

"It's like having your cake and eating it, too. Once you have it—once you've got your cabin there—you've taken something away, just by the existence of the cabin, from what it was that drew you to the land in the first place." He'd seen it happen a number of times. A man began by building a simple cabin in the wilderness. Then he realized how much wood he'd have to cut to stay warm, so he brought in a chain saw. Then he brought in a snow machine to haul the cut wood. Then he began running out of deadwood, and he started banding the trees, to kill them, so he would have enough deadwood to burn. Then bears came around, looking for food, and because they were dangerous, and because he lived there, he had to shoot them. Then the wolves, reacting to his presence, would also leave. All of which would have an impact on adjacent areas. And before long, as with Jack and Beth, other people would say, what a neat idea, building a cabin in the wilderness, let's do it, too. And before long there would be a little cluster of such cabins. And while it might still be a fine piece of the outdoors, it would not be wilderness any more. And, since true wilderness was already nearly extinct, Ray Bane dug in hard against those who would encroach on what was left. However splendid their motives and however unblemished their characters may have been; and however much he might have shared their sense of adventure.

"Wilderness," he said, seemingly unbothered by the soggy marsh through which we were now hiking, "wilderness is to visit, not to live in. People see a lake and say, oh, what a beautiful place to build a cabin. I say, what a beautiful place *not* to build a cabin."

We could see to the end of the valley, to the main valley of the Itkillik. At first, it appeared covered with fog, but as we grew gradually closer we observed that it was not fog at all, but one long, thin cloud that was being blown back and forth, up and down the valley, by shifting winds. "That cloud is flowing through the valley like a river," Ray Bane said, which indicated how different his orientation was from my own. To me the cloud had seemed like a subway: shuttling between Grand Central Station and Times Square.

We were about two miles from the Itkillik at 4 p.m. The clouds above us were lowering, and the long gray subway cloud seemed to be racing back and forth ever faster, now that the rush hour had arrived. The day had never grown warm enough to be comfortable, and as evening neared, the chill seemed to sink even deeper into our bones. A vote was taken and the consensus was to stop for the day. There was a pingo just ahead—a conical mound, rising about forty feet up from the otherwise level surface of the valley. Pingos are caused by water collecting between the surface of the ground and the permafrost below, and then freezing, forcing the ground above it upward as it expands. Not that the origins of the pingo seemed of much importance at the time. What did matter was that this was the only geographical feature in the entire valley that might help to shield a campsite from the wind. We pitched our tents at the base of the pingo and went searching for firewood, of which there was little; just a few dead willow branches near the creek.

A cold drizzle began to fall at dinnertime. We took turns sitting closest to the fire. The pingo blocked our view of the valley ahead, so we looked instead across the creek at the lower slopes of the mountains that rose on the western side. Only the lower slopes were visible beneath the clouds.

"Say, Ray," said Boyd Norton, "what time has the Park Service scheduled tonight's grizzly for?"

"I'm not sure, Boyd, but given our record so far, I'd say there's a fifty-fifty chance of one right on the other side of that hummock above your head."

"Oh, bosh," said Ogden Williams, who had seen only the first bear, and not the second, third, and fourth. "This isn't still grizzly bear country."

"Yes, it is, Ogden," said Ray Bane. "This whole mountain range is grizzly country."

"Oh, of course, of course, theoretically. But you know as well as I do that they're much more likely to frequent the kind of area where we camped the first two nights than they are to inhabit a barren, exposed valley like this."

"I wouldn't be too sure, Ogden. There could be bears around here."

"Oh, could be, could be, yes, of course. As I said, theoretically, I'm sure you're right, but my point—"

"Excuse me, Ogden," said Ray Bane, pointing past Ogden's shoulder toward the lower mountain slope across the creek. "I didn't mean to interrupt, but there goes a theoretical bear right now."

It was true. Another grizzly. The biggest one yet, by far. An enormous, dark-furred bear. Ambling along the lower slope, beyond the creek, eating berries. At least a quarter mile from us; probably, in fact, closer to half a mile. And not even remotely aware of us.

Still, it was unquestionably a grizzly bear. Which meant that conversation ceased immediately and all eyes were directed toward the bear. With maddening slowness, he picked his way among whatever berries or other edibles grew on the slope.

"He's a real big one," Ray Bane said, looking at the bear through binoculars. I was able to see through the monocular with my hand hardly shaking at all. This was a mark of how far I'd come in a few days. As long as I needed a magnifying device to study them, my new premise went, there was no reason to be afraid of bears.

"A big old-timer," Ray said. "And he's fat. He's not worrying about food right now. Just swiping at a ground squirrel, a berry bush, anything he happens to pass. He's obviously been feeding on something. Might have got himself a caribou. Maybe even a moose."

"Hey, Ray?" said Boyd Norton. "Are you sure there are no other hiking parties in this valley?"

Oblivious to us, and to the wind, and to the chilly drizzle which fell intermittently, the bear eventually disappeared behind

the jumbled rocks of a glacial moraine. We waited for some time
for him to re-emerge, preferably on the far side of the moraine,
further from us, but he remained hidden. Then the cold and the
wet and the futility of this sort of vigil drove us inside our tents
and sleeping bags. But not before we stacked our packs together
carefully, and covered them with ponchos against the rain, and
balanced the pots and pans on top.

In the morning, we would hike the remaining two miles to the
Itkillik Valley. From there, if we were not blown too far off course
by the wind, we would hike alongside the Itkillik River to the first
nameless valley that opened into the Itkillik Valley from the west.
And then, at the upper end of that side valley, which we hoped
to reach by the following night, we would find ourselves at the
base—or near the base, anyway—of Cockedhat Mountain, which
was as much of a destination, in the traditional sense, as anything
was on this hike.

No one, to John Kauffmann's knowledge, had yet hiked to
Cockedhat Mountain from the east. Robert Marshall had come at
it twice, from the south and southwest, on separate journeys, but
there had been apparently no way to cross the Arctic Divide from
that direction. The only way to it, other than by hiking in from the
North Slope and up the length of the Itkillik Valley, or up the
Nanushuk Valley, which was the next large valley to the west, was
to walk through Oolah Pass, as we had done.

We awoke to find the air thick with fog, and heavy frost on the
ground. Ogden, the first man up, had built a fire. I sat near it, and
held my boots and socks over it, in a feeble, but morale-boosting
attempt to get them at least temporarily warm, if not dry. "Beastly
day," Ogden said, and no one demurred.

By the time breakfast was over and our soggy sleeping bags
and tents were packed away, and the fire put out and the black-
ened rocks redistributed across the tundra, charred side down, the
frost had turned to chilly dew and the fog grudgingly lifted to
form a low overcast. The temperature hovered near 40. Every so
often, a misty rain—which might have been a snow shower had
we been a thousand feet higher—fell upon us. Nothing was warm
and nothing was dry and there was nothing to be done about it,
and so, with no alternative, we moved on.

We stayed on the north side of the creek, but gradually angled toward it as it approached the Itkillik. Tussocks and marsh underfoot combined with 40-degree temperature and with feet that were already wet and cold, and the intermittent drizzle, and the low misty clouds which obscured the mountains, to make for a perfect morning of hiking. Perfectly awful.

But, no, it couldn't have been perfectly awful, because soon it got worse. After two miles we reached the braided creek just before it joined the Itkillik. When I figured out our next task, as cold and wet as my boots were, it was only through an enormous effort of will that I was able to remove them from my feet. For here we had to change into sneakers and wade across, not only the several braided channels of the creek, but the Itkillik River itself. Somehow, although I had seen this on the map clearly enough, I had managed to suppress my knowledge of it, and it came now as a most unwelcome surprise.

I don't know the lowest temperature at which river water can still flow but, after wading across in sneakers, I do know the Itkillik could not have been more than two or three degrees above it. Even Ray Bane, who had taken a dog sled through the Brooks Range in the winter, who had slept outdoors at temperatures of 70 below, who was one of the ranking Alaskan sourdoughs of the modern era, agreed that the pain was intense. "But look at the bright side," he said. "The colder it is, the quicker you're numb."

The Itkillik was not a deep river but its valley was wide, by Brooks Range standards. The clouds were high enough now so that we had a good view, if not of mountain peaks, at least of the valley and lower slopes. This again was new country, with a different feeling all its own, and the excitement of having come into it sent a spark of warmth through me, though by no means did the warmth extend to my toes.

We could see about twelve miles down the valley. Substantial mountains rose on both sides. According to the topographical map, the peaks would reach 7,000 feet. Though we were not able to see the peaks, we could imagine, from the sharpness and unevenness and bareness of the slopes, how craggy the upper reaches must be. We noted also the mouths of three side valleys that branched off from the Itkillik, and in the distance, down the main valley, we observed several small lakes.

Even with weather conditions so poor, even so tired and dirty and wet and cold, my first thought was: What a shame we don't have more time. We're only going to get to hike up one of the side valleys; we'll never know what the others are like.

Ray pointed to fresh caribou tracks on the gravel bars of the Itkillik. He said a small group had passed through no more than three days ago. We hiked over three small ridges, trying to stay on the higher, drier, less tussocky ground whenever possible. We were angling south now, temporarily, away from the river, cutting the southeastern corner of the side valley which was our goal. Once across the corner—it was four hours now since the day's hiking had begun—we descended a marshy slope to a dry gravel bar in the creek that had its origins in the snows and glacial ice of Cockedhat Mountain.

The mountain itself, which, according to the map and to John Kauffmann's aerial observations, was surrounded by an imposing cluster of lower peaks, was still about fifteen miles from us to the west; not yet in view. If this weather continued, Cockedhat Mountain might never be in view.

There were, however, other extraordinary sights. Looking west, about two and a half miles up the side valley, in the direction in which we'd soon be walking, we could see where the creek flowed out of a low canyon onto a widely braided gravel bed. Mountains rose on both sides of the valley. But they did not, in all cases, rise straight up. The valley wall to our right, in fact, was composed of steeply tilted layers of rock strata which leaned northward, away from us, away from the valley, as if repelled by the more symmetrical mountains which formed the valley's southern wall. It was as if something had not worked quite right when the valley was being formed, and the whole northern wall had been thrown out of kilter. Neither John Kauffmann nor Ray Bane had seen anything like it in other parts of the Brooks Range. In his notebook, Ray wrote that these mountains seemed to him "great rocky scales on the spiny back of a partially buried, prehistoric reptile."

As we continued to gaze up the valley, the clouds lifted slightly, enabling us to glimpse some of the peaks at the valley's upper end. These were the steepest, most rugged mountains we'd seen yet. The furthest from us, which appeared to be particularly jagged, might even have been the eastern ramparts of the Cockedhat Mountain massif.

Impatient now, we hurried through lunch and resumed hiking. Already, having just turned the corner and entered this valley, we'd received one surprise—the tilted, scaly northern wall—and each of us was eager to discover if there would be any others.

We walked along the south bank of the creek until we reached the canyon we'd seen earlier. We climbed a tundra bluff that rose above the canyon and walked across it until we came to the first tributary stream that flowed from the mountains to our left. Here, we found a small, sheltered ravine, and even though we were still at least three miles from the end of the central portion of the valley, we made camp. The site, with its water and its abundance of dead willow branches for firewood, and the wind shelter offered by the ravine wall, was too good to pass up. Besides, as overcast descended again, our view of the mountains was cut off. Mist swirled around us. Occasionally, it would part, giving us a quick, teasing glimpse, as if the mountains were exotic dancers, using their veils to entice.

"I have an idea," said John Kauffmann, who had seen the Cockedhat Mountain cluster from the air, "that when these clouds finally do disappear, you'll see some things that will knock your eyes out." Then he sucked slowly on his pipe, and stuck a long spoon in the pot to stir the rice. His calmness and confidence—if not necessarily his rice—were proving extremely good for morale.

We stayed up late after dinner, sitting by the fire until 11 p.m., still hoping for a sudden clearing. But it was not to be. Clouds lowered, in fact, and fog again rose from the ground. I gave up and crawled into the tent, scribbling only this in my notebook: "Camp near Cockedhat—can't see thru fog—temp. in 40s—wet feet."

The morning was foggy and still. A solid low overcast blocked all view of anything more than fifty feet above the ground. We stayed in our tents much later than usual. There seemed nothing to get up for. Nothing to see; nothing to do. And we suffered from the extreme frustration of knowing that we had such a limited amount of time remaining to us. We could spend one more night here; possibly two. Then we would have to move on, further up the Itkillik Valley. Or down the valley. Up the map, anyway. Further north. Because there were other areas which John Kauffmann wanted to reach on this trip.

So it seemed possible that, having come all this distance, we would never even see Cockedhat Mountain. Not that the trip would then have been deemed a failure. We had moved, not only beyond tree line, but beyond the standard definitions of concepts such as failure and success. Here, there would be a failure only if someone fell off a mountain or got mauled by a bear. Otherwise, just being here was a success. Still, to spend the remainder of the trip wandering along creek beds in heavy mist would have been, at the least, a disappointment.

I lay in the tent, reading the one book I had brought with me, the Viking portable edition of Faulkner. I had never enjoyed Faulkner very much, but I thought that now, possibly, I would find myself in the mood for his novella *The Bear*.

Ray Bane lay next to me, filling page after page in a notebook. "I don't think a wilderness experience is complete," he said, "until it's been written about."

I wandered outside for a while and tossed a willow branch or two in the fire. I was getting into a mood as gloomy as the day. What a shame that we had, apparently, used up our quota of good weather on what had been, in terms of scenery and terrain, the least dramatic portion of the trip. And what an amazing contrast between one side of Oolah Pass and the other. That bright hot sun the first three days. And now three days of Arctic mist. Here we were, more than halfway up a valley which, quite possibly, no one in modern times had viewed before, except by air. And now we weren't able to see it either. Well, only the bottom fifty feet. Even without John Kauffmann to tell us how dramatic Cockedhat Mountain looked, we could have guessed, just from studying the topographical maps, that something splendid and unusual lay at the valley's upper end. Just from the way all the little brown contour lines wriggled around. We had reached a point, however, where maps did not satisfy. We were hungry for the real thing. But we had absolutely no control over whether or not we would ever be able to see it, and absolutely no way of predicting what direction the weather pattern might take. Sometimes, Ray Bane said, weather like this blew off in a couple of days. Sometimes it settled in for weeks. The general rule, however, was that as August progressed, weather in the Arctic turned damp, as well as colder. We were right at the midline. Two weeks earlier, Ray said, he could have predicted with confidence that the sun would be shining within a couple of days. Two weeks later, he would have advised us to pack our things and move on. Right now, he could not guess. So we sat around the fire and tried to convince ourselves that the overcast was rising, or brightening, just a bit. But then new drizzle started and we all returned to our tents.

"Okay," Ray said. "I've had enough. Drastic measures are called for." He put down his notebook and unzipped the netting at the front of our tent. He stepped outside into the mist. I lay down my Faulkner and followed.

He began shouting, in an angry, guttural voice, at the sky. He was shouting something in Eskimo, repeating the same phrases several times.

"There," he said, "that ought to do it."

"What did you say?"

"I'm not sure I really ought to translate," he said. "It's pretty vulgar." But by then everyone else had come out of their tents, too, hearing the noise, and Ray had no choice. It was, he said, an old Eskimo chant, used to anger the sun; to provoke it into coming out from its hiding place behind the clouds. In translation it was: "Sun, Sun, your vagina smells horrible." Sometimes, Ray said, crude methods prove to be the most effective.

The weather did not improve, but by midday restlessness overcame our depression. We decided to split up and take day hikes in different directions. John Kauffmann and Boyd would go up the ravine in which we were camped. Ray said he would venture further up the main valley so that, if the weather did improve the next day, he would have an idea of the best route to Cockedhat. Ogden said his feet were bothering him and that he really rather welcomed a day off. He would spend the afternoon in camp.

I looked at the mountain just above us. Its lower slope began across the tributary stream, just on the other side of the ravine. The slope was composed mostly of scree and talus: loose rock debris. The upper, craggy, rocky section disappeared into the mist. On the map, the summit, which would be almost directly above our camp, across the ravine, seemed to be about 5,500 feet. I decided I would hike up the lower slope, until it became too difficult to go higher.

It was 1 p.m. when I began. I crossed the tributary and hiked up the east side of the ravine for about a mile. Then I began to cut diagonally up the slope, back in the direction from which I'd come. The higher I went, the steeper the side of the slope became, and when I looked down, after about forty-five minutes, I was surprised both by how far up I had come and by how sharply the slope dropped off beneath my feet. I was also surprised at the looseness of the scree. Every time I stopped, for even a moment, I could feel the slope begin to give way beneath my boots, and start to slide. Therefore, I had to keep moving.

There was a rock ledge above me. I couldn't be sure how far, maybe another two hundred feet. I started toward it, thinking that, once there, I would at least be able to sit and rest. I began scrambling diagonally, on all fours, across the scree, which got looser the higher I went, and seemed ever more prone to start sliding. I was already so high by this time, and the mountainside below me so steep, that I decided I'd be better off continuing up. From that ledge above me, I could probably find an easier and safer route down. Now, if I could only reach the ledge before the whole damn mountain started to slide.

The scree was turning to powder now, and more and more was giving way beneath me with every step. I would start to slide downward, then claw my way back, always trying to move diagonally upward toward the ledge. Once a real slide started, it might not stop, and with nothing solid to cling to below the ledge, I might become part of the slide.

I was badly out of breath now, and getting worried, but I continued to scuttle, as best I could, gradually higher. The ledge appeared to be only fifty feet above me, but those fifty feet suddenly took on a new and more alarming degree of steepness. There was now almost a sheer wall of scree, and I scrambled up frantically, grabbing at any rock that looked larger than my hand. I could find nothing—neither handhold nor foothold—that would support me for more than seconds, until I reached the base of the ledge.

I wedged a boot into a crevice between two loose rocks, tested it with weight, and it held. I grabbed quickly at rocks that jutted out overhead, and found a couple of cracks into which I was able to squeeze my fingers. I clung to the side of the ledge, panting for breath. Then I made the mistake of looking down.

From below, it had seemed I could just continue to scramble up the scree all the way. I had not realized until too late that the last fifty feet were not a scree slope at all, but that they were, in fact, the side of a cliff.

I was stuck. I was hanging on to the cliff now, precariously, and there was no orderly, safe way to climb down. All I could have done was to let go, which, I realized, would have meant an unbroken fall of at least thirty feet to looser rocks below, and then probably an uncontrollable slide down the scree. A process which seemed quite certain to result in, if not loss of life, then loss of consciousness and, more than likely, broken bones. Not a cheery prospect deep in the Brooks Range.

Up was the only way to go. And I had to move fast, because this temporary hold I had was giving way. This was most definitely rock climbing now; not by any stretch of definition was it hiking. What was worse, it was climbing on extremely unsuitable rock, alone, with no equipment, no training, and absolutely no aptitude for the techniques.

I moved quickly. From both fatigue and fear. My legs, when I would find a jutting rock on which to support them, were trembling so hard I was afraid that that motion alone would dislodge the rock. My calf and thigh muscles had not been expecting this; nor had the muscles of my arms. I wasn't even wearing gloves, in fact—this was supposed to have been just a little walk on the lower slope—and my fingers were now scraped and bleeding.

I paused once more, looking up. I still could not see how far I had to go to reach the ledge. What if it had not really been a ledge? What if I had judged it incorrectly from below? I was going higher and higher now, up the crumbling rock face of a mountain, and with every new frantic scramble, the consequences, were I to fall, grew more severe.

Once more I reached above me for something to cling to as I tried to push myself upward with my legs. I could feel rocks all around me giving way. This was an old decayed mountain. The whole face seemed about to collapse. Another handhold, and then another, and then—thank God!—I hoisted myself up over the ledge, onto a small plateau that was covered by a thin layer of tundra. I lay there, panting, in my no longer brand-new Camp Seven wind parka. I kissed the tundra. How magnificent it felt; how splendid it looked; how fine it was to feel living earth again.

The ledge was the size of about three or four double beds pushed together. Once my breath and composure had returned, I began to look around, trying to decide what to do next. I felt like a cat up a tree, but I was a long way from the nearest fire department.

Descending the way I had come up was out of the question. But in what other direction could I go? I had approached this ledge from the southwest, originally, cutting back toward the main valley after my hike of a mile or so up the ravine. The ledge was on the western, or ravine, side of the mountain. Just east of it, there was a long, sharp drop, and then the main mountain wall rose even higher. Looking up in that direction, I could see an old, dirty glacier about a hundred yards away. It was just a rim of ice, really; flanked by moraine. There was a ridge leading out from the rock wall to the left of this glacier, a long ridge which leveled out quickly and then proceeded in a northerly direction, rising, as it did, toward what I considered the front of the mountain—the aspect which overlooked the valley. It seemed that if I started out along the ridge that led north from the ledge I was on, I might at some point be able to cut across the scree side of a basin between the ridges and reach the second, longer ridge. From there, I might proceed to the northern face of the mountain, and, I hoped, find a way back down to the valley floor.

I was reluctant to leave the hard-won security of my little ledge, but a cold mist was now swirling around me, and a steady drizzle was starting to fall. It was already 4 p.m., and if I were not back in camp by dinnertime the others would worry, and eventually come looking for me. To cause them that inconvenience would have been a serious breach of hiking etiquette. Besides, my instinct for self-preservation had made me extremely eager to get back to the valley floor.

Amazing, how relative it all was: a week earlier, a campsite halfway up a nameless side valley that led from the Itkillik River to Cockedhat Mountain in the central Brooks Range, north of the Arctic Divide, would have seemed the ultimate in wildness and remoteness. It was still not exactly an urban ambience, but from 2,000 feet higher—from a tundra-covered perch two-thirds of the way up a nameless and unstable mountain—that camp seemed the essence of security and comfort.

Within a quarter mile, the ridge that my ledge opened onto began a steep climb to a rock wall of which I wanted no part. I dropped down from the ridge and tried to work my way around the scree rim of the basin, to the ridge that led down from the glacier. It was the same syndrome as before: scurrying along on all fours with the slope sliding away beneath my feet. By now, though, I was familiar enough with the sensation to be merely worried, and not panic-stricken, and I already was sufficiently experienced in the technique to know enough not to stop.

I made it to the new ridge, which was longer, wider, and more substantial than the one I had left. I was able to walk along it comfortably, heading north, toward what would be the front of the mountain. This ridge, too, sloped upward, at first gradually, then sharply, but here, instead of a sheer, unclimbable rock wall, there was a sharp slope of loose talus and patches of tundra, up which I was able to pick my way. I was once again on hands and knees—climbing, not hiking—and the larger rocks and boulders of the talus seemed scarcely more stable than the scree, but there were little veins of tundra threaded among them, and, by choosing my route carefully, I was able to work my way to the top without mishap.

I climbed over a final row of boulders, onto a ledge, looked around, and only then realized that I had, quite by accident, ascended to the summit of the mountain. To the front summit, at least. Whether or not it was the true summit depended on where one considered that one mountain ended and another began, for a mile or so further back, above the glacier, this ridge, and the rock wall it led to, climbed to an even higher point. But where I was now standing was what had appeared as the summit of this mountain from below, from our camp, and without having had the slightest intention of doing so, I had reached it.

Across the ravine, there was a 6,800-foot peak about a mile and half back to the southwest. It was a craggy, barren mountain, as was the one I was on, and its summit was enshrouded by fog. My own altitude seemed to be about 5,500 feet.

Looking due west, I could see to the upper end of the valley, to where the front walls of the Cockedhat Mountain mass began to rise. They appeared made of dark gray, almost slate-colored stone, but it was hard to tell much about them because even the lower slopes were quickly hidden by drifting mist.

To the east, I could look all the way down the valley, to the Itkillik Valley and, where clouds permitted, to the Oolah Mountain sector that lay beyond.

But it was the view directly across the side valley, the view of the weird, unearthly, jumbled, tilted, platelike, scaly, multi-layered valley wall, that held my eye.

We had experienced some sense of it yesterday, from the head of the valley, but from here, looking straight across, from this higher altitude, the scene was much more astonishing.

I had no idea what sort of geologic activity had formed these mountains, or why they were—in angle, shape, and texture—so unlike any other mountains I'd ever seen, but looking at them through the mist, from my hard-won mini-summit, was like being given a unique glimpse into prehistoric times.

It was as if a giant had been sleeping in this valley and had rolled to one side, pressing back the northern valley wall. Then another image came to mind: the angle at which those mountain walls sloped back from the valley floor seemed the same as that angle at which human figures in certain Renaissance paintings recoiled from the image of the newly risen Christ.

I stepped forward to the front of the ledge and looked down, through the mist, to the bottom of the valley. A rainbow arched toward the lower end. Looking just below me, and slightly to the left, across the ravine, I could also see, very faintly, through my monocular, and through the mist, the specks of bright color that were our tents.

Foolishly, and in a hurry, I decided to work my way straight down the front of the ledge, instead of descending to the east, on a more gradual slope that led back down the valley, away from the camp. I had to come down chimney fashion, my back wedged against one side of a little rock chute, my feet against the other, with rocks and boulders, loosened by my passage, beginning to tumble down behind me. I clung to the sides, fighting for hand-holds and footholds, just as I had done coming up, but here, with the rocks even bigger, though just as loose, the situation was, in a way, even more precarious. Several times the rolling rocks, and the smaller stones and loose scree that fell behind them, almost carried me away, and at this angle it would not have been a slide that resulted in only cuts and bruises, it would have meant, once again, a fall, of undetermined distance, the consequences of which I much preferred not to imagine.

Tired and trembling, both from exhaustion and from the aftermath of fear, I slid back into camp at 6 p.m. The others were already there. Ogden, in fact, had spotted me, through binoculars, about halfway down, and had followed my progress the rest of the way.

"Jolly good show," he remarked. "Thought you might have been in for a bit of a tumble."

Freeze-dried stew and freeze-dried rice in the damp and chilly fog and it was the best meal of the trip. I kept looking up at where I had been; not really sure I had done it, and wondering whether I had intended to all along. It was, actually, an ordinary-looking mountain, and the front summit, I determined from the map, was not much more than 1,500 feet above our camp. But I knew how deceiving appearances were. I had been up there. And it was very different from down here.

John Kauffmann and Boyd had continued up the canyon about three miles, to the pass where the tributary stream originated. From that vantage point—lower than mine, and further south— they had seen, in the direction of Cockedhat, high, jagged peaks, wrapped in clouds. They'd seen just enough to whet their appetites even further, as had I.

Ray Bane had gotten considerably closer. He had walked two and a half miles up the valley, to a point where the main valley swung left and the three streams which formed the central valley creek came together.

The northernmost of these streams flowed out of a small fork of the main valley to the north. The southern branch could be traced through the main valley, first south, then west again, as the valley wound around the southeastern base of the Cockedhat massif and rose gently for another five miles to a point just behind—from the perspective of our camp—the summit of Cockedhat itself.

Most interesting to Ray had been what lay directly ahead of him, across a shallow basin at the upper end of the central valley. The middle branch of the main creek came from here. As he followed its course, visually, he found himself looking at two vast, sheer mountain walls, rising straight up from the basin and quickly disappearing into the clouds. These were the ramparts of Cockedhat itself. They were separated by a steep, rocky ridge, about two hundred feet above the valley floor. The mist had obscured his view, but Ray's instinct, combined with his skill in interpreting a topographical map, had led him to believe that behind this ridge lay some sort of hidden plateau. Judging from the map, it might extend back a mile or more, between the rampart mountains whose front walls Ray had seen. There was no way to know what was there, and no way to know if what was there would be accessible to us, or whether the ridge, as appeared likely, made the ramparts inaccessible. Ray's description of the possibilities, however, caused us to vote unanimously that the next day, no matter what the weather, our exploration should take that direction.

In late evening, the cloud cover slowly started to lift, revealing more of the mountains to the west. The peaks were still hidden, but in the pale, late Arctic light, we had our clearest look in the direction in which we would proceed, and we went to sleep feeling heightened anticipation.

Seven a.m. Ray rolled right out of the tent and I followed. It was to be our last full day at this location. What we didn't see today, we would not see. Fog would have been a crushing blow. Instead, we found ourselves blinking in a bright light to which we had grown unaccustomed. There were only high, broken clouds in the sky. We scrambled to the top of the little ravine in which we were camped and looked west. For the first time we could clearly see the distant peaks, though from our side of the valley Cockedhat itself was not in view.

Breakfast was quick. We were all in a hurry to get started. This would be a hike with only day packs. Although Ray had said there were good camping sites further up the valley, no one wanted to take the time and trouble to break camp, just to set it up again three miles away.

The sun was shining, but the air was much cooler than it had been on the south side of Oolah Pass. We began walking at 9:30, wading the creek to the north side of the valley, then climbing to the top of a low bluff. The surface was mostly dry tundra and the walking was easy. As we turned westward and started up two miles of gentle slope, we could see clearly the two mountains whose lower slopes Ray had spotted the day before.

The southern mountain, to the left, was the more precipitous of the two: thrusting upward to a series of needlepoint spires. The northern one, to the right, was the more massive. It swept upward at the same odd angle as did the components of the northern valley wall. Toward the top, at about 6,000 feet, its tilted strata ended in a sharp and jagged ridge.

Thick clouds, which were probably formed by the mountain itself, continued to block our view of Cockedhat's upper reaches, but beyond the ridge which separated the two mountains in the foreground, we could clearly see the spires and vertical walls that rose around it. Even from this distance—still several miles—they seemed unearthly. Not even remotely comparable to any other mountain formation which I, or any of our group, had ever seen. These mountains were even more bizarre than the tilted, jumbled northern valley wall.

We walked down a tundra slope and across a broad grassy plain, heading toward the base of the ridge, which was about a mile in front of us. We could see a waterfall tumbling out of the ridge, forming the middle branch of the creek. We walked toward it, across a wide, velvety basin. At the far end, we waded the middle branch into which the waterfall was pouring, and then entered a narrow corridor between the bases of the two rampart mountains, and walked a quarter mile further to the base of the ridge itself. From here, we looked up.

The waterfall was just above us, to our left, at a height of about two hundred feet. It fell almost from the top of the ridge. From this angle, the mountain that rose from the left side appeared to rocket straight up, as if it were being launched into space. Conical-shaped, with deep vertical striations, which emphasized the rocketlike thrust, it soared straight to a needlelike spire more than 2,000 feet above its base.

The broader mountain to our right, just above us, tilted north, away from us. The gigantic rock slabs which formed its near wall seemed to have been stacked haphazardly upon one another and one could almost imagine them sliding down. It was as if a child had tried to build a mountain out of tiles.

The waterfall roared and crashed down the steep talus slope. We could feel the spray on our faces as we gazed up. The ridge was far too steep and sheer to climb directly, so we tried ascending a talus slope to the right, beyond the north end of the ridge. For once, something turned out to be easier than it had looked.

There were large rocks, some covered with moss and tundra,

forming almost a staircase up the slope. The staircase, however, seemed to end in a blank wall where the ridge ran into the solid base of the massive mountain to the north.

But just as we had climbed as far as it appeared we would be able to, Ray discovered an opening in the solid rock. A notch, six feet deep, through which we were able to clamber. This led to a steep-sided, narrow passageway; a corridor through the rock; almost a tunnel, with the blocking ridge forming one side and the northern mountain wall forming the other. We walked quickly through this and around a bend with the high rock walls on both sides, and then, descending slightly, we traveled another fifty yards. The rock walls parted and suddenly we found ourselves standing at one end of a broad and grassy meadow. A sudden, astonishing, hidden meadow. With the high spires soaring above us on all sides, to form an amphitheater.

"My first reaction to the scene that confronted us," Ray Bane wrote later, "was awe. It was like entering a massive religious cathedral, empty of people. The air is heavy with silence and holiness. Before us, almost completely enclosed in light gray rock walls, was an enchanted meadow, absolutely level. A tiny lake, like a liquid mirror, was nestled in the soft tundra, reflecting the towering grandeur. A small creek meandered lazily through the meadow, passing into and then out of the still lake. Approximately one mile to the west, the lush green gave way to gray scree and finally the west end was closed by a rising tundra slope and then by a massive, sheer-faced rock wall. The south wall of the basin is formed by rock strata rising vertically towards a climax of thin stiletto-like spires and peaks—some 2,000 feet or more above the meadow. The north wall is formed by massive rock slabs rising less sharply—but still steeply—leaning away from the vertical mountain as though each slab were trying to cover over the one below in a frozen effort to escape the threatening spears of the opposite mountain."

Shangri-la. The meadow so pristine, so silent, so still. Its lushness even more incongruous against the starkness of the spires which rose so bizarrely above it, with lingering mist brushing lightly against the tips.

We were not sure whether we had entered a cathedral or whether we had stumbled across the gateway to a lost, forbidden land. Even now the last survivors of an unknown, undiscovered civilization might be watching us, in silence, or darting quickly, high above us, from rock to rock.

But, no. All was still. There was nothing here. There never had been. And given its location—hidden behind a ridge at the far end of a dead-end valley in an obscure section of the continent's most remote mountain range—both John Kauffmann and Ray Bane said there was every reason to believe that we were the first human beings ever to see it; ever to set foot upon the meadow grass; ever to look up and see those sweeping rock walls curving like waves high above us.

We remained hushed and still. It seemed almost sacrilegious to venture further. It was awe, rather than exhilaration, that we felt, with the sky now gray again above us, and the gray mountain walls muting the green of meadow grass, and with the shallow lake so perfectly still and mirror-clear.

Slowly, savoring each step, and almost reluctant to put a foot down where, in all likelihood, no human foot had ever been before, we proceeded through the meadow to the far end. It was about a mile from one end to the other, with the meadow at no point more than a quarter mile wide.

At the western end, we reached the base of a rock shoulder and then began a steep and steady climb up a slope that led to the base of the sheer-faced western wall. There we sat, beneath clouds that were lowering once again, and stared, for many minutes, in silence, at this astonishing display which had seemed to give each of us a deep and sudden and private flash of insight into the very process of the creation of the earth.

Ray Bane, who had seen so much, over so many years, was locked in an almost physical struggle to describe it.

"The great swirls of rock strata, splendid spires, and ponderous slabs." Perhaps, he wrote, it was "a symphony in rock," in which "one can almost hear the sonorous chords described by the heavy leaning strata, the soaring crescendoes of the peaking spires and the unifying, sometimes hidden melody of the meadow."

He paused, looked around slowly, and after more thought, tried again. "Considering the opposing angles of strata, jagged peaks and ridges and stark shades of gray, one might liken the scene as to being in the midst of a petrified thunderstorm. One can almost feel the violent turbulence of conflicting forces, explosive thunder, and wild expenditure of energy."

This crashing thunder of the petrified storm as counterpoint to the holy silence and stillness of the cathedral.

We sat there, mostly in silence, through much of the long afternoon. The wall above us did not rise straight, but, almost as if it were an optical illusion, actually bent back in upon us, like a giant frozen wave about to crest. No one had anticipated that we would ever come upon such a place. No one had suspected its existence. This had begun as a wilderness trip; as a hike in a remote mountain range. But, as of now, it had transcended even that, and had carried each of us to a new and unexpected level of experience. We had been allowed to discover, and to enter, and to remain, for a few hours, in such a place, and it seemed we had been given a rare gift of immeasurable value. None of us was quite sure how to respond. The fact that, in all likelihood, we were the only human beings who had walked through this secret meadow, who had sat high on this western barrier and looked back at this remnant of paradise, was more than I, at least, knew how to respond to.

The day was ending, and we had to leave. We walked back through the meadow slowly, lost in thought. Or still, perhaps, adrift in a space beyond thought. At the end of the meadow, I turned for one final look. Then, feeling an intense and confusing mixture of joy and sorrow and awe, I turned away again and headed quickly through the rock-walled corridor toward the notch at the end of the ridge that would lead back to the outside world.

The next day, we hiked through marsh and tussocks back to the main Itkillik Valley. The same low cloud that had been there four days earlier was once again whooshing back and forth. With the sun still shining on our backs from the direction of Cockedhat Mountain, we hiked into this mist and turned left and proceeded another four miles, setting up camp at the edge of the Itkillik River, about a quarter mile from a lake. It was very cold, very windy, and very foggy overnight. We seemed to be deep inside the cloud.

By midmorning, however, the fog had lifted—or the cloud had dispersed—and the airplane that John Kauffmann had chartered arrived. He needed to do some aerial surveying, as well as hiking, on this trip, and had arranged for the plane to ferry us twenty-five miles north, down the main Itkillik Valley, to Itkillik Lake at the northern edge of the Brooks Range. He would then keep the plane for the afternoon and check out the things he needed to check out by air. We would resume the hike the next morning, looping around the northern edge of the range, from Itkillik Lake to the Itikmalak River, and up a tributary, through a pass, and down to the Galbraith Lake pipeline camp, where the trip would come to its end.

There was a group of archaeologists at Itkillik Lake. They had been there all summer, living in big canvas tents, excavating for evidence of ancient Eskimo culture, with some success. They had, in fact, found artifacts which dated back at least to 5,000 B.C. Having been there for the entire summer, they were well supplied. They had beer and they had Scotch and they were eager to share both, as well as to talk of their experiences and to listen to us talk about ours.

We told them a lot about bears. And about the early portion of the hike. But when we got to the part where we had begun walking toward the ridge with the waterfall and the two ramparts of Cockedhat rising up on either side, we trailed off. What we had seen and felt beyond that ridge was something too special and private. We were not yet ready to share it.

I had a hard time, actually, conversing about anything. The past twenty-four hours had been too much of a sudden uprooting, too rude an awakening from a beautiful dream. It had taken us five days of hiking, and five grizzly bears of various sizes, to reach our camp in the valley that led to Cockedhat Mountain. Then we had waited through another two days of bad weather. And then had been rewarded with a mystical experience. Now, within one day, we'd been exposed to an airplane, the northern limit of the Brooks Range—which proved that the mountains, and our experience of them, were not endless after all—and these cheerful, friendly, noisy archaeologists. We just were not ready for it. At least I wasn't. I slipped into a silent and gloomy frame of mind, almost a depression. Which lasted until I was introduced to the brother of one of the archaeologists, a doctor from Vermont. He was, in fact, a doctor from Burlington. He was, in fact, a professor of medicine at the University of Vermont medical school.

I said, "Oh, do you know Joanna Shaw?"

He said, "Yes, of course. We're very good friends."

And then I suddenly snapped back from my depression. Realizing that all that was happening was that the circle was finally completing itself.

A year and a half earlier, it had been my friend Peter Herford who kept me up late talking about mountains, and then about this amazing place called Alaska, in which he had spent time as a young man. And now, at the conclusion of what had been not just my ultimate Alaskan experience, but, in many ways, the most intense experience of my life—now, within twenty-four hours of that—I was in conversation, on the damp and chilly shore of Itkillik Lake, in the Arctic, with a physician from Burlington, Vermont, who was a very good friend of Joanna Shaw, a physician from Burlington, Vermont, and the woman whom Peter Herford was about to marry.

A strong south wind began to blow overnight, warming the air but bringing hard rain by early morning. Then the wind shifted abruptly to the opposite direction, and began to blow equally hard from the north. The air turned suddenly clear and it felt to me like mid-November.

The archaeologists gave us a motorboat ride to the north end of the lake, about four miles away. As we cruised along the eastern shore, looking at the northernmost mountains of the Brooks Range, which were to our east, and then at the lower foothills to the west, and then at the utter flatness which stretched to the northern horizon—a jarring sight—we spotted a sow grizzly bear and two yearling cubs, much larger than the other cubs we had seen, romping along the lakeshore.

"Goddamn," said Boyd Norton. "I never thought the day would come when the sight of a grizzly bear would make me nostalgic."

We hiked around the northernmost mountains, heading east. Walking the border between the Brooks Range and the North Slope.

We turned south, to follow the Itikmalak upriver. Under the circumstances, a hike such as this for a day and a half could have been an exotic adventure. In this instance, however, it seemed to be merely a mopping up.

There was bright sun and the north wind kept the air Novemberish even at midday. We ate our last lunch of sardines, cheese, and crackers, packed up the remains, and walked on. At some point we would have to wade across the frigid Itikmalak, a deeper and faster-flowing river than the Itkillik. But thoughts of that foot-numbing were temporarily dispelled by the sudden noise of a helicopter overhead.

It began to circle behind us, coming low, buzzing in first one direction and then another. We kept walking. This was a helicopter from the Galbraith Lake pipeline camp, on its way to resupply the archaeologists. As a public relations gesture, the pipeline company was funding such projects.

What we couldn't figure out was why the helicopter kept buzzing around about a quarter of a mile behind us. And, at that point, we didn't much care. Then it flew over us, circled once again, and landed on a level gravel bar by the river. There were two men inside. The pilot stayed at the controls, keeping the big rotor flapping, while the other man jumped out, crouched low, and ran toward us.

"Just thought I ought to let you know," he shouted over the chopping noise of the blades. "There was a grizzly on your trail, stalking you. We spotted him about a quarter mile back, but I think we've spooked him, at least for now. But I figured you ought to be aware."

We thanked him, felt the by now familiar spurt of adrenaline, and hiked on, a little faster, with frequent glances over our shoulders.

In late afternoon, we climbed the ravine that led to the pass that would, the next day, take us out to Galbraith Lake. And after a long day, which had involved twelve miles of hiking—almost double what we had been capable of at the start of the trip—we found a fine site for our last camp, high in the ravine. To the south, eight miles distant, we could see a glacier that was three miles wide. Clinging to the face of a mountain 7,500 feet high. Neither, of course, had a name.

I stayed awake, staring at the glacier, until true darkness finally arrived. In the morning, under sunny skies, and with the temperature rising into the 60s, we walked for two hours, descending from the pass to the Galbraith Lake pipeline camp, where a cigar-smoking man with a flannel shirt hanging over his belly asked where we had come from and then said, when we told him, "Goddamn. You guys must be nuts. Don't you know there's bears out there?" We said yes, we knew that, but there were other things out there as well.

Back in Anchorage, the Glacier Pilots' season was over. High school football teams were practicing in Mulcahy Park. It had started to get dark again at night. Soon the first faint traces of snow would be visible atop the mountains to the east. Termination dust, it was called. Time for seasonal employees to collect their final paychecks and go home.

BICYCLE TOURS OF ITALY

by Gay and Kathlyn Hendricks

Savor the rich sights, sounds, and flavors of Italy while enjoying America's fastest growing new sport—bicycle touring. Thousands of adventurous Americans have already traded in the rigors of high-stress, high-cost travel for the fun of biking it to the world's greatest getaways. And now you can do it, too. With this extraordinary guide, you'll learn everything you need to know to put your vacation plans in gear.

There's an epidemic with 27 million victims. And no visible symptoms.

It's an epidemic of people who can't read.

Believe it or not, 27 million Americans are functionally illiterate, about one adult in five.

The solution to this problem is you... when you join the fight against illiteracy. So call the Coalition for Literacy at toll-free **1-800-228-8813** and volunteer.

Volunteer Against Illiteracy. The only degree you need is a degree of caring.